AMERICAN LAW AND PROCEDURE

VOLUME XII

Constitutional Law

CONTENTS

CONSTITUTIONAL LAW.

PART I.

GENERAL CONCEPTIONS.

CHAPTER I.

Preliminary Topics.

SECTION 1.

Nature of American Constitutional Law.

SECTION 2.

Making and Changing American Constitutions.

SECTION 3.

Separation of Departments of Government.

i

CHAPTER II.

Function of Judiciary in Enforcing Constitutions.

SECTION 1.

Power to Declare Laws Unconstitutional.

SECTION 2.

Limitations Upon Exercise of Power.

SECTION 3.

Effect of an Unconstitutional Act.

CHAPTER V.

Personal and Religious Liberty.

CHAPTER VI.

Protection to Persons Accused of Crime.

SECTION 1.

Bills of Attainder and Ex Post Facto Laws.

SECTION 2.

Self-Incrimination.

SECTION 3.

Unreasonable Searches and Seizures.

CHAPTER VII.

Due Process and Equal Protection of Law: Procedure.

SECTION 1.
Due Process of Law.

SECTION 2.
Equal Protection of the Laws.

CHAPTER VIII.

Due Process and Equal Protection of Law: Powers of Regulation—Police Power.

SECTION 1.
General Conceptions.

SECTION 2.
Regulation of Social Interests.

SECTION 3.
Economic Interests.

SECTION 4.
Administrative Regulations.

CHAPTER IX.

Due Process and Equal Protection of Law: Taxation.

CHAPTER X.

Due Process and Equal Protection of Law: Eminent Domain.

CHAPTER XI.

Laws Impairing Obligations of Contracts.

PART III.

THE FEDERAL GOVERNMENT.

CHAPTER XII.

Federal Powers and Their Exercise.

CHAPTER XIII.

Territories, Dependencies, and New States.

CHAPTER XVII.

Intergovernmental Relations.

SECTION 1.

Interstate Privileges and Immunities of Citizens.

SECTION 2.

Other Interstate Relations.

SECTION 3.

Relations between the United States and the States.

CHAPTER XVIII.

Jurisdiction of the Federal Courts.

SECTION 1.

In General.

SECTION 2.

Suits Against States.—Eleventh Amendment.

CONSTITUTIONAL LAW*

PART I.

GENERAL CONCEPTIONS.

CHAPTER I.

PRELIMINARY TOPICS.

SECTION 1. NATURE OF AMERICAN CONSTITUTIONAL LAW.

§ 1. **Modern constitutional government.** The subject of American Constitutional Law deals with certain large principles intimately connected with modern theories of political self-government. The protection of the individual in his personal, property, and political rights, at the same time that order is maintained and the welfare

---

* The United States Constitution is printed as Appendix A in this volume.

1

of the state conserved, is the aim of modern constitutional government. We are so accustomed to the acceptance of these doctrines that it is difficult to realize how new they are as actual working principles efficiently controlling governmental action. It is only a little over three hundred years ago that Philip II of Spain condemned to death without trial all of the inhabitants of the Netherlands. It is only two hundred years ago that the court of king's bench in England solemnly affirmed the right of the king at his pleasure to dispense with any penal statute passed by Parliament. In legal theory, at least, the property and persons of the vast majority of the governed were to a considerable extent at the disposal of the governing majority. As a matter of fact, rulers did not usually deal with their subjects with an outrageous disregard of justice, but this was due to the wisdom, the kindness, or the fear of the rulers and not to their obedience to any word of law superior to their wills. The divine right of kings was the dogma at the basis of political theories of the state, tempered though it might be by admissions of moral obligations upon rulers to govern justly. In the brief space of a few hundred years all this has changed. With very few exceptions, every government that now makes any pretension to modern civilization exercises its powers in conformity with the precepts of a body of unwritten custom or written law designed to secure the individual from oppression at the hands of those who are actually.in governing positions, or even from the oppression of a majority of his peers. Indeed, the function that brings American constitutions most frequently before the courts is that of protecting the rights of individuals against the acts of popular legislatures.

§ 2. **What is a constitution?** When we think of a constitution in America we naturally conceive a written instrument formally setting forth a frame of government and containing a variety of checks upon governmental action, chiefly upon the legislature. It may seem a little strange to think of constitutions existing in an unwritten as well as a written state. Though it is more or less a matter of definition, the simplest conception of a constitution for the government of a state is the body of existing precepts, written or unwritten, designed to control governmental action until modified in some authorized manner.

§ 3. **The English constitution and Parliament.** The best example of a country with an unwritten constitution is England. Large volumes have been written about the English constitution, but so far as that constitution is applicable to legislative action it is entirely unwritten. The English Parliament does not confiscate private property, or condemn men to death without trial, or even impair the obligation of existing contracts. Writers on English law say that to do these things would be unconstitutional, meaning thereby contrary to the great body of past legislative custom and usage, which forms the standard by which the present is judged. Yet if the English Parliament were to do any of these things they would not be illegal, though they might be unconstitutional. Parliament is absolutely supreme in legal theory, and whatever it chooses to enact is legal, is a law, and will be enforced as such by the English courts.

Really, Parliament has a double function. It is both the law-making and the constitution-making power of Great Britain. Thus, at present we say it is unconstitutional for Parliament to impair the obligation of contracts in individual instances—not speaking now of bankruptcy laws. If Parliament chose to do this in two or three instances only, we should still say such action was unconstitutional but that there was no way of enforcing the constitution against the will of Parliament. If such parliamentary action became common, we should then have to say that the English constitution had been altered and that to impair the obligations of private contracts was no longer unconstitutional in England. That is, the English constitution, so far as it affects legislative action, is purely one of customary obligation, and when adherence to any part of it is no longer customary, the constitution has simply been altered by the authorized English method, acts of Parliament approved by the crown.

Where the English constitution touches executive action, it is partly written. Magna Charta is an instance of this. The English Bill of Rights of 1689, placing certain restrictions on the acts of the sovereign, is another. So is the Act of Settlement of 1701, regulating the succession to the crown and the tenure of judges. So are all the various acts of Parliament somewhat permanently regulating the exercise of executive power throughout the British Empire.

§ 4. **Differences between written and unwritten con-**

stitutions. The English unwritten constitution is really just as much a constitution as our written ones. The great difference is in the organ by which constitutional changes may authorizedly be made. In England this organ is Parliament. In the American states it is usually a constitutional convention whose proceedings must generally be ratified by popular vote. For the United States Constitution it is the joint action of three-quarters of the states acting through legislatures or conventions (1). On the continent of Europe it is often the legislative bodies of the state acting together by a two-thirds or three-quarters vote, and perhaps also requiring the assent of the executive or the people.

The legal effect of the various modes of amending American constitutions we shall consider later. Two important consequences have grown out of the differences between English and American constitutions. One is that the American legislature is much less free than the English one. The other is that the American judiciary has been made the guardian of the constitution. The English courts cannot declare an act of Parliament unconstitutional. An American court does this constantly with the acts of American legislatures. It is this latter consequence that gives the greatest practical importance to the study of American constitutional law.

§ 5. **Written constitutions in America.** In all American states certain fundamental personal, property, and political rights are secured by written constitutions. These constitutions have several distinct functions:

---

(1) Const., Art. V.

First, they are constructive. They provide a form of government, divide the various powers into convenient groups, and prescribe the proper mode of their exercise. This is the oldest and commonest function of a constitution.

Second, they are prohibitive. They place a number of restrictions upon legislative and executive powers and even upon the power of the individual to make certain contracts or use his property in certain ways. The most important of these prohibitions are designed to protect the individual citizen from governmental oppression, and it is the existence of these prohibitions in modern constitutions that most sharply distinguishes them from the governmental instruments of antiquity. As compared with the total bulk of constitutions, these supremely important provisions are but a small part. In the constitution of New York they form less than one-twentieth, and of South Dakota less than one-thirtieth. They secure personal and religious liberty, freedom of speech and of the press, rights of assemblage and petition, equal protection of the laws, compensation for property taken for public use, protection to persons accused of crime, immunity from unreasonable searches or seizures, and due process of law for all attempts to deprive persons of life, liberty, or property.

Third, in the case of the Federal Constitution, it also divides the powers of government between the states and the United States, and provides for the orderly administration of our Federal system.

§ 6. **Outline of American constitutional history before**

1789. A brief summary of the principal facts of our constitutional history, before the present Constitution, may conveniently be inserted here. The English colonies in America were settled or acquired by Great Britain between 1607 (Virginia) and 1732 (Georgia). Most of them had governors, appointed by the crown or colonial proprietors, and popular assemblies convened under the authority of crown or proprietors. In Rhode Island and Connecticut, governor and legislature were chosen by the people. The part taken by the colonists in the French and Indian war (1754-63) that wrested Canada from France gave a considerable impetus toward colonial unity, which was much increased by the unwise and irritating attempts of Parliament to tax the colonies and hamper their foreign trade. The Stamp Act congress of 1765 was attended by representatives from most of the colonies to petition against this legislation and make a declaration of colonial rights. The stamp act was repealed and an import duty levied on goods entering the colonies. A feature of the resistance to this was the "Boston tea-party" at which some cargoes of imported tea were forcibly thrown into the harbor. Parliament replied by an act closing the port of Boston and changing the charter of Massachusetts. In 1774 the first Continental Congress met and adopted resolutions and addresses declaratory of American rights. The battle of Lexington and Concord followed in 1775, and the Revolution began. The second Continental Congress met shortly after and assumed the conduct of the war. Under its recommendations (§ 7, below) the early state governments were formed, and it continued to act as a central governing body of dubious authority in all but military and diplomatic matters, until the adoption of the Articles of Confederation in 1781, which for the first time created a formal organic union between the states. The Declaration of Independence, adopted by this Congress in 1776, was its principal political act, and marks the legal date of the beginning of our existence as an independent nation. Perhaps the most important events of the Confederation were the cession to the United States of the lands claimed by various states west of the Alleghanies (§ 256, below), and the adoption, by the Congress of the Confederation, of the Ordinance of 1787 for the government of the Northwest territory thus ceded, with a provision excluding slavery from it. The failure of the Confederation and the adoption of the Constitution are related in §§ 9-10, below.

SECTION 2. MAKING AND CHANGING AMERICAN CONSTITUTIONS.

§ 7. **Earliest American state constitutions.** Under the American system of government written constitutions play so important a part that a brief consideration of the methods by which they may be adopted and changed is desirable.

During the first eighteen months of the Revolutionary war the governments of most of the revolting colonies were conducted by provincial conventions or congresses in each colony, made up of delegates chosen in various irregular ways; and their acts and recommendations, under stress of war, were very generally respected and obeyed by the Revolutionary party. Connecticut and Rhode Island, under their colonial charters, had popular anti-British assemblies that continued to administer their governments. As the expectation of an early peace with England diminished, the Continental Congress, in response to several requests, advised the informal governing bodies in each colony to call a full representation of the people, in order to form a more permanent frame of government during the continuance of the war. Beginning with New Hampshire in 1776, brief constitutions were promulgated by the provincial congresses, or by conventions called for this purpose, without any submission of them to the people, in all of the colonies except Connecticut, Rhode Island, and Massachusetts. Connecticut and Rhode Island continued under their colonial charters, but events in Massachusetts took a different course.

§ 8. **Constitution of Massachusetts.** In June, 1775, acting upon the advice of the Continental Congress, the provincial convention of Massachusetts wrote letters to the towns in the colony requesting them to choose representatives to form an assembly. The assembly when elected chose a council and the two of these together constituted the Massachusetts general court or legislature. In 1778 this body prepared a constitution that was submitted to the people and rejected. The year following, the people voted that a new constitution should be drafted by a convention especially called for this purpose. The legislature made provision for the election of delegates to such a convention by the votes of all resident freemen, twenty-one years old. The convention met in September,

1779, and in March, 1780, the new constitution was laid before the people, to be approved by two-thirds of the male inhabitants of the age of twenty-one, voting. Over two-thirds approved, and the convention, having re-assembled, declared the constitution established and re-solved that it should take effect the October following. It is notable that although this constitution contained a provision limiting the suffrage under it to persons having a specified property qualification, yet all freemen over the age of twenty-one were empowered to vote upon its adoption. It was the first American constitution adopted by popular vote.

Of all the constitutions originally formed by the first American states that of Massachusetts alone is in force today. It has been frequently amended, but all attempts to substitute a new constitution for it have failed. All other states, except those most recently admitted to the Union, have had more than one constitution. Texas has had seven altogether, and Kansas had three in three years.

§ 9. **The Articles of Confederation.** The Articles of Confederation, framed by the second Continental Congress, were presented to the legislatures of the various states in 1778, and were ratified by the last of them in March, 1781. Article VIII provided: "The articles of this Confederation shall be inviolably observed by every state, and the Union shall be perpetual; nor shall any alterations at any time hereafter be made in any of them, unless such alteration be agreed to in a Congress of the United States and be afterwards confirmed by the legis-latures of every state."

The government of the Confederation speedily failed for want of coercive authority to execute its powers. It could neither tax, regulate trade, carry out its international obligations, nor keep internal peace, but was obliged to rely upon recommendations to the states for carrying out these measures. The urgency of war once removed, natural differences of opinion among the states rendered united action impossible, and the central government fell to pieces with unchecked rapidity. Various efforts to amend the Articles of Confederation so as to give the Congress at least some powers of taxation were defeated by the requirement of unanimity among the states.

§ 10. **Adoption of the United States Constitution.** In 1786 Virginia called a meeting of commissioners from all of the states to consider the adoption of such an act as would enable Congress to provide for a uniform system in their commercial relations. Commissioners from five states met at Annapolis in September, 1786, in conse-quence of this call. They recommended a convention to meet at Philadelphia the next May to devise provisions to render the Constitution of the Federal government ade-quate to the Union, and their report was sent to Congress and to the states. In February, 1787, Congress passed a resolution recommending such a convention " for the sole and express purpose of revising the Articles of Confed-eration and reporting to Congress and the several legis-latures such alterations and provisions therein as shall, when agreed to in Congress and confirmed by the states, render the Federal Constitution adequate to the exigencies of government and the preservation of the Union.''

Representatives of all of the states except Rhode Island attended the convention, and on September 17, 1787, adopted the Constitution. The convention directed the Constitution to be laid before Congress, and recommended that it should be afterward submitted to a convention of delegates chosen in each state by the people under the recommendation of its legislature. Article VII of the proposed Constitution provided that the ratification of the conventions of nine of the states should be sufficient for the establishment of the Constitution between the states ratifying. The convention recommended to Congress that, as soon as nine of the states had ratified, Congress should fix a time for the appointment of electors, a time when they should vote for president, and a time and place for commencing proceedings under the Constitution.

It will be noticed that the new Constitution provided that it should become effective as soon as ratified by nine states, while the Articles of Confederation provided that they should not be changed except by unanimous consent of the states. Eleven states at first ratified the Constitution, and the new government went into effect between them March 4, 1789. North Carolina ratified in November of that year, and Rhode Island in May, 1790.

§ 11. Modes of amending constitutions. The constitutions of our states are amended or wholly remade with great frequency, and upon fourteen different occasions the Federal Constitution has been amended. Questions frequently have arisen respecting the proper mode of amending constitutions and these may conveniently be discussed under several heads: 1. The previous constitution may contain no provisions regarding its amendment. 2. A mode of amendment may be provided, but may not be made expressly exclusive of other modes. 3. An exclusive mode of amendment may be expressly provided.

§ 12. Same: **Where constitution contains no express provision.** The first constitutions of most of the thirteen original states contained no express provisions at all concerning their amendment. That of Massachusetts provided that in 1795 the people should vote upon the expediency of revising the constitution, and that if two-thirds voted in favor of this a new convention should be called. Nothing was done in 1795, but 1820 the legislature secured an affirmative vote of the people in favor of a convention for revising the constitution. The convention was held and various amendments proposed by it were adopted, among them an amendment providing an orderly method for future amendments. This early incident is typical of the usual American practice. Where a constitution contains no express provision for its amendment, the legislature may call a convention of delegates chosen by the people, the call being made directly by the legislature, or in consequence of a previous vote of the people authorizing the legislature to do so. The convention so called may propose changes in the constitution and submit them to the people, and when ratified by the vote of the latter the constitution is changed accordingly.

§ 13. **Same: Where constitution provides a non-exclusive mode of amendment.** Where a state constitution expressly provides that it shall be amended by calling a convention and submitting amendments to the people, doubtless there is no implied power to amend in any other way. This method, however, though well adapted for a general revision of a constitution, is expensive and cumbersome for dealing with isolated specific amendments. Most of our constitutions, therefore, provide for their amendment by the submission to the people of proposals first passed by the legislature, or by two successive legislatures. It is generally held that this permission to amend in the legislative mode does not impliedly deny authority to amend by the agency of a convention called as set forth in § 12, above. This original and typical method may always be employed unless expressly forbidden.

§ 14. **Same: Exclusive mode of amendment expressly provided.** If a constitution expressly provides that it shall be amended by a certain method or methods, only, there can be no legal warrant for employing a different mode, and acts done under the latter do not acquire the force of law except as the fruit of an accomplished revolution against the prior form of government.

§ 15. **Peaceful revolutions.** In a few instances the procedure mentioned as illegal in § 14, above, has been pursued, and a new constitution or constitutional amendments have been adopted thereunder and acquiesced in by the people and departments of government. This must be regarded in the light of a peaceful revolution. akin to that by which the Old Confederation was displaced, in direct denial of its provisions, by the new Constitution in 1788.

§ 16. Amendment of Federal Constitution. The United States Constitution contains in Article V an express provision for proposing amendments by a two-thirds vote of each house of Congress, or by a convention called by Congress upon the application of the legislatures of two-thirds of the states. The former method has been uniformly pursued heretofore. Perhaps Congress could not call a convention upon its own motion, in the ordinary American method (§ 12, above), even though this is not expressly forbidden (§ 13, above); for Congress has only the powers delegated to it by the Constitution, not the general residuary powers of a state legislature (§§ 24-27, 249-51, below), and it would be difficult to show that such a power was fairly implied from the character of the national government. Amendments proposed by either method must be ratified by three-fourths of the states acting either through their legislatures or through conventions called for that purpose. The principal practical question that has arisen over this is whether a state may withdraw a ratification once given, if it does so before the amendment has been adopted by the requisite number of states to make it part of the Constitution. This occurred with respect to both the Fourteenth and Fifteenth Amendments, and Congress by resolution declared the attempted withdrawal ineffective (1a).

_____

(1a) The topics of §§ 11-16, above, are fully discussed in Jameson on Constitutional Conventions (4th ed.), secs. 563-85.

SECTION 3. SEPARATION OF DEPARTMENTS OF GOVERN-
MENT.

§ 17. General American doctrine. The prevalent
American doctrine is that the legislative, executive, and
judicial departments of government should be separated
so far as is practicable, and that their respective powers
should be exercised by different men or groups of men.
The Federal Constitution does not require this of the
state governments (§ 138), but all state constitutions require it to varying extents. A few illustrations will make
clear how this works in practice.

**§ 18. Judicial powers cannot be exercised by legis-
lative and administrative bodies.** In an early New Hampshire case (2) a law suit had been decided against one
Merrill, and the court had refused his motion for a new
trial and rendered judgment against him. The legislature
on Merrill's petition passed an act granting him a new
trial in the case. The New Hampshire court decided this
act to be unconstitutional and void, as an attempted exercise of judicial power by the legislature, saying: "No
particular definition of judicial powers is given in the
constitution; and considering the general nature of the instrument none was to be expected but 'powers judicial,'
'judiciary powers,' and 'judicatories' are all phrases
used in the constitution, and though not particularly defined are still so used to designate with clearness that department of the government which it was intended should
interpret and administer the laws. On general principles, therefore, those inquiries, deliberations, orders,

---

(2)   Merrill v. Sherburne, 1 N. H. 199.

and decrees, which are peculiar to such a department must in their nature be judicial acts. Nor can they be both judicial and legislative, because a marked difference exists between the employment of judicial and legislative tribunals.

"The former decide upon the legality of claims and conduct; the latter make rules upon which, in connection with the Constitution, these decisions should be founded. It is the province of the judges to determine what is the law upon existing cases. In fine the law is applied by the one and made by the other."

§ 19. **Same: Further illustrations.** In Kansas the legislature created a so-called court of visitation which was given power to regulate public service companies, to determine the reasonableness of the regulations thus made, and then to enforce them. The Federal circuit court held that this combination of judicial with legislative and administrative powers was forbidden by the constitution of Kansas, which provided for separate executive, legislative, and judicial departments, though it did not expressly forbid the powers of one to be exercised by the others. The court said: "That, in a broad sense, powers of one of these departments shall not be conferred upon either of the others is not only within the true spirit of these provisions, but also substantially within the letter thereof; and the addition thereto of an express prohibitory declaration, such as is contained in the constitutions of some of the states, that the powers of one department shall not be exercised by another, would add very little to their effect, so far as concerns the question under consideration. The universal doctrine of American liberty under written constitutions requires the distribution of all the powers of government among three departments—legislative, judicial, and executive—and that each, within its appropriate sphere, be supreme, coordinate with, and independent of both the others." (3).

Nor can an administrative body like the Interstate Commerce Commission or the National Labor Relations Board be given power to compel obedience to its orders by a judgment of fine or imprisonment. Such obedience, under the Constitution of the United States, can be compelled only by a competent judicial tribunal having jurisdiction of the case (4).

§ 20. **Non-judicial powers cannot be conferred on courts.** Courts cannot be required to exercise non-judicial powers. A statute provided that any street railway company might apply to the superior court to approve and adopt a location for its tracks with such regulations regarding streets, cars, construction, and motive power as the court might prescribe. The supreme court of Connecticut held this not to be the exercise of judicial power, and that it could not be conferred upon a court. Instead, it was a proper matter for legislative and administrative action (5). But if the question left to the court is whether certain definite circumstances exist or

---

(3)   Western Union Tel. Co. v. Myatt, 98 Fed. 335. Re Opinion of the Justices, 87 N. H. 492, 110 A.L.R. 819.

(4)   Interstate Commerce Commission v. Brimson, 154 U. S. 447. N.L.R.B. v. Jones & Laughlin Steel Corporation, 301 U. S. 1, 108 A.L.R. 1352.

(5)   Norwalk Street Railroad's Appeal, 69 Conn. 576.

conditions have been fulfilled upon which a license may be granted or a town incorporated, it is generally held a proper matter for judicial determination (6).

The courts cannot be required to decide questions or decisions which will later be subject to revision or review by other departments of the government. The final finding of a court, when not appealable to another court, is not a judicial determination unless it is enforceable by some process or is made by statute the final or indisputable basis of action by other departments of government (7).

Of the latter nature are actions against itself permitted by the state or the United States, where it is made the duty of the government sued to pay any judgment that may be rendered against it.

§ 21. Inherent powers of departments of government. As a corollary to the doctrine of the separation of powers in American governments, each department has certain inherent powers of which it cannot be deprived by the action of the other departments, even though the latter do not attempt to exercise them. Roughly speaking they are such powers as are necessary to maintain the effective independence of the departments in the discharge of their appropriate duties. For instance, a Virginia statute attempted to deprive the courts created by the Virginia con-

---

(6)   McCrea v. Roberts, 89 Md. 238; Forsythe v. Hammond, 142 Ind. 505.

(7)   In re Sanborn, 148 U. S. 222.

stitution of their power to punish contempts summarily, and to substitute a jury trial for the action of the court itself. This was held unconstitutional, and the court stated its conclusions: ''That in the courts created by the constitution, there is an inherent power of self-defense and self-preservation; that this power can be regulated but cannot be destroyed, or so far diminished as to be rendered ineffectual by legislative enactment; that it is a power necessarily resident in and to be exercised by the court itself, and that the vice of an act which seeks to deprive the court of this inherent power is not cured by providing for its exercise by jury; that while the legislature has the power to regulate the jurisdiction of the courts, it cannot destroy, while it may confine within reasonable bounds, the authority necessary to the exercise of the jurisdiction conferred'' (8).

Similarly the United States Supreme Court has said: ''In order that the court may compel obedience to its orders it must have the right to inquire whether there has been any disobedience thereof. To submit the question of disobedience to another tribunal, be it jury or another court, would be to deprive the proceeding of one-half its efficiency'' (9).

There are conflicting views as to whether the independence of the courts requires them to control admissions to the bar. In many states including Illinois, Massachusetts, Nebraska and Pennsylvania a legislature may not compel the admission to the bar of persons who have not complied

---

(8) Carter's Case, 96 Va. 791, 816.
(9) In re Debs, 158 U. S. 564, 595.

with the requirements demanded by the courts (10). New York and North Carolina hold contra (11).

§ 21a. **Same: Of the President of the United States.** The doctrine of separation of powers limits the powers of the executive department as it does the legislative and judicial. There are certain specific grants of power to the president of the United States. These are found in Article II of the Constitution.

Note particularly the provision that "the executive power shall be vested in a president" that "he shall take care that the laws be faithfully executed," and that "he shall be Commander-in-Chief of the Army and Navy." He is given no legislative power except the veto power and the power to make recommendations. The Constitution specifically provides that "all legislative powers herein granted shall be vested in a Congress of the United States." This, by implication, is a denial of such powers to the president.

In Youngstown Sheet and Tube Co. v. Sawyer (11a) the inherent powers of the President and the extent to which they are limited by the doctrine of the separation of powers came before the court. On April 4, 1952, after a long standing dispute between union employes and the steel companies, the union gave notice of a nation-wide strike to begin on April 9. The president, believing that this would cause such curtailment of steel production that it would mean disaster on the war fronts in Korea, on April 8, issued an executive order directing the Secretary of Commerce to take immediate possession of the steel

(10)   State ex. rel. Ralston v. Turner, 141 Neb. 556 and not in 144 A. L. R. 150 where the cases are collected.

(11)   Re Cooper, 22 N. Y. 67; Re Applicants for License, 143 N. C. 1.

(11a)   343 U.S. 579, 26 A.L.R. 2nd, 1378, decided in 1952.

plants and operate them for the government. The steel companies obtained an injunction restraining enforcement of the executive order. The court upheld the injunction.

Justice Black speaking for the majority of the court said that if the president had authority to issue such an order it must be found in some provision of the Constitution or in an act of Congress, that there was no statute expressly authorizing the president to take possession of property in this manner, and that no act of Congress had been called to the court's attention from which such a power could be fairly implied. That the power could not be sustained as an exercise of the President's military power as Commander-in-Chief of the Armed forces; nor could the seizure order be sustained because of the several constitutional provisions that grant executive power to the president. The president's power to see the laws are faithfully executed refutes the idea that he is a law maker.

The opinion concluded: "The Founders of this nation entrusted the law making power to Congress alone in both good and bad times. It would do no good to recall the historical events, the fears of power and the hopes for freedom that lay behind their choice. Such a review would but confirm our holding that this seizure order cannot stand."

Justices Frankfurter and Douglas, in the course of concurring opinions, refer to the possible delays and apparent inefficiency which may at times result from the separation of powers, but quote, with approval, the following from Mr. Justice Brandeis: "The doctrine of the separation of powers was adopted by the convention of 1787, not to promote efficiency but to preclude the exercise of arbitrary power. The purpose was, not to avoid friction but by means of the inevitable friction incident to the distribution of the governmental powers among three departments, to save the people from autocracy'' (11b).

§ 22. **Limitations of general doctrine.** The doctrine of the separation of powers is not susceptible of rigorous application. Each department, as a matter of convenience and necessity, or to protect its own independence, must in a certain measure exercise powers that strictly belong to other departments. The legislature must often make investigations to ascertain the facts preliminary to legislation, and for this purpose must summon witnesses, examine them, and punish their refusal to answer. These proceedings, though judicial, are necessary to a proper exercise of legislative power, and so may be conducted by a legislature (12). Both the executive and courts may make rules concerning their procedure, which are legislative in character, but yet properly incidental to executive and judicial duties. Congress cannot delegate its legislative powers. But in declaring the National Industrial Recovery Act invalid, the Supreme Court held that if Congress lays down policies and fixes standards, it may then leave to the executive or others the making of subordinate rules within the prescribed limits (12a).

§ 23. **Same: Appointment of officers. Taxation.** Some functions, like the appointment of officers, are of such a nature that they may be conferred on any department (13). The Federal Constitution, however, expressly

---

(11b)   Myers v. United States, 272 U. S. 52.
(12)   People v. Keeler, 99 N. Y. 463.
(12a) Schechter v. U. S., 295 U. S. 495, Panama Ref. Co. v, Ryan, 293 U. S. 388.
(13)   Fox v. McDonald, 101 Ala. 51.

provides that Congress may by law vest the appointment of such inferior officers, as they think proper, in the President alone, in the courts of law or in the heads of departments (14). In a number of the states an early practice of giving inferior courts the power of levying local taxes and assessing property therefor has been continued (15). It has been said: "The ascertainment of values of property is strictly judicial, and in governments perfectly separated into the three distinct departments of legislative, executive, and judicial would of necessity belong to the judicial. It has, however, been considered a necessary adjunct of the strictly legislative power of levying taxes." This power, then, in connection with an assessment, may properly be conferred upon the judiciary (16). Some states, however, wholly deny the validity of such practices (17).

SECTION 4. THE STATES AND THE UNITED STATES

§ **24. General theory of state powers.** When the British colonies in America freed themselves from the British government by the successful Revolution of 1774-81, the newly created American states succeeded to the powers of the British government; and to their legislatures descended the powers of the British Parliament.

"The accepted theory upon this subject appears to be

---

(14)　Const. Art. 2, sec. 2, § 2.

(15)　State v. Gazley, 5 Ohio, 14; Ballard v. Thomas, 19 Gratt. (Va.) 14.

(16)　Wheeling Property Co. v. Paul, 39 W. Va 142.

(17)　Munday v. Rahway, 43 N. J. L. 338; Auditor v. Railroad, 6 Kan. 500.

this: In every sovereign state there resides an absolute and uncontrolled power of legislation. In Great Britain this complete power rests in the Parliament; in the American states it resides in the people themselves as an organized body politic. But the people, by creating the Constitution of the United States, have delegated this power as to certain subjects, and under certain restrictions, to the Congress of the Union; and that portion they cannot resume, except as it may be done through amendment of the national Constitution. For the exercise of legislative power, subject to this limitation, they create, by their state constitution, a legislative department upon which they confer it; and granting it in general terms, they must be understood to grant the whole legislative power which they possess, except so far as at the same time they saw fit to impose restrictions. While, therefore, the Parliament of Britain possesses completely the absolute and uncontrolled power of legislation, the legislative bodies of the American states possess the same power, except, first, as it may have been limited by the Constitution of the United States; and, second, as it may have been limited by the constitution of the state. A legislative act, cannot, therefore, be declared void, unless its conflict with one of these two instruments can be pointed out" (18).

§ 25. **Powers of state governments before 1789. The Confederation.** After the Declaration of Independence in 1776 all of the American states, except Connecticut and Rhode Island, adopted constitutions providing a frame

---

(18) Cooley, Const. Lim. 241 (7 ed.).

of government, distributing its powers, and enjoining certain limitations upon their use. Connecticut and Rhode Island continued under their colonial charters, Connecticut expressly retaining its charter as a constitution with a few brief additional prohibitions, and Rhode Island going on without any express readoption of its charter. Connecticut did not adopt another constitution until 1818, nor Rhode Island until 1842.

These early American constitutions contained bills of rights that in general prohibited to the political departments of the state the exercise of powers already found by English experience and by their present quarrel with Great Britain to be fraught with danger to individual rights. The principal ones of these are enumerated in § 5, above. Subject to these or similar restrictions and to the few restrictions upon the powers of the state contained in the Articles of Confederation, adopted in 1781, the early state governments kept the entire remaining field of legislation. The prohibitions upon the power of the states in the Articles of Confederation chiefly limited their power to enter into political relations either with foreign countries or with each other, save with the consent of Congress; and secured to the people of each state rights of intercourse with other states without discrimination. Provision was made for the interstate extradition of criminals, the interstate recognition of judicial proceedings, and the settlement of interstate boundary disputes; and Congress was given control of interstate post offices, Indian affairs, the alloy and value of coin, and the standards of weights and measures.

The Confederation was virtually a league between the states, and the powers given to it were in the main dependent for their enforcement upon the law of the states themselves. It could not effectively act upon individuals in the states.

§ 26. **Division of powers between state and nation effected by Federal Constitution.** The failure of the Confederation and the adoption of the Constitution created an entirely new political situation. The theory of the division of powers between the new national government and the older state governments has been judicially stated with accuracy as follows:

"In 1789, the Constitution of the United States, having been adopted by the required number of states . . . went into operation, and became the law of the land. This system was founded upon an entirely different principle from that of the Confederation. Instead of a league among sovereign states, it was a government formed by the people, and, to the extent of the enumerated subjects, the jurisdiction of which was confided to and vested in the general government, acting directly upon the people. 'We the people,' are the authors and constituents; and 'in order to form a more perfect union' was the declared purpose of the constitution of a general government.

"It was a bold, wise, and successful attempt to place the people under two distinct governments, each sovereign and independent within its own sphere of action, and dividing the jurisdiction between them, not by territorial limits and not by the relation of superior and subordinate, but classifying the subjects of government and designating

those over which each has entire and independent jurisdiction. This object the Constitution of the United States
proposed to accomplish by a specific enumeration of those
subjects of general concern, in which all have a general
interest, and to the defense and protection of which the
undivided force of all the states could be brought
promptly and directly to bear.

"Some of these were our relations with foreign powers
—war and peace, treaties, foreign commerce and commerce amongst the several states, with others specifically
enumerated; leaving to the several states their full jurisdiction over rights of person and property, and, in fact,
over all other subjects of legislation, not thus vested in
the general government. All powers of government,
therefore, legislative, executive, and judicial, necessary
to the full and entire administration of government over
these enumerated subjects, and all powers necessarily
incident thereto, are vested in the general government;
and all other powers, expressly as well as by implication,
are reserved to the states" (19).

§ 27. **Nature of the Federal Government: Of limited
powers.** From the nature of the Constitution of the
United States, there result two great constitutional principles. The first one is that the United States is strictly
a government of limited powers. The rule for construing
its powers is exactly the opposite of that for construing
the powers of the states. The state governments have unlimited powers, except where prohibited by the United

---

(19)   Opinion of Justices, 14 Gray, 615-16.

States Constitution or by their own constitutions. The United States, on the other hand, can exercise no powers whatever except those found granted to it in the Constitution. Of course all of these Federal powers need not be expressly granted, but may fairly be implied from those that are expressly granted. For instance, the United States is given express power to establish post offices and post roads. As incidental to this power and implied from it, the United States may carry the mail, regulate the character of mailable matter, and provide penalties for any interference with these rules. But unless a power can be found granted to the United States by the Constitution, either expressly or by fair implication, Congress cannot constitutionally exercise it.

§ 28. **Same: Supreme in its sphere.** The second great principle is that although the United States is a government of limited powers, its control over such powers as are granted to it is full and absolute, and that its laws passed in the exercise of the granted powers are superior to all state laws conflicting therewith. For instance, Congress having been given control of the post office may, if it sees fit, control entirely everything reasonably connected with the postoffice, even to the extent of making it a government monopoly. The supremacy of its laws over those of the states is probably secured by implication from the nature of the government it creates, but is also expressly provided for in Article VI of the Constitution: "This Constitution, and the laws of the United States which shall be made in pursuance thereof; and all treaties made, or which shall be made, under the authority of the United States, shall be the supreme law of the land; and the judges in every state shall be bound thereby, any thing in the constitution or laws of any state to the contrary notwithstanding.''

The principles stated in this and the preceding subsection are further discussed in §§ 249-55, below.

CHAPTER II.

FUNCTION OF JUDICIARY IN ENFORCING CONSTITUTIONS.

SECTION 1. POWER TO DECLARE LAWS UNCONSTITU-
TIONAL.

§ 29. Departments of government. Modern political analysis divides the powers of government into three great departments, the legislative, executive, and judicial; and modern constitutional government has decreed a considerable separation of these departments to prevent abuses. Of course an absolute separation is impracticable because the departments are but different aspects of one government and are closely connected at many points. American constitutional doctrines as to the separation of governmental powers have been discussed in §§ 17-23, above.

§ 30. Power to declare laws unconstitutional. Where does it reside? Now, having a written constitution attempting in a general way to divide the powers of government between the three departments and to prohibit the exercise of certain powers altogether, the very interesting question presents itself: Who, and under what circumstances, is to determine when any given department oversteps its proper sphere, or attempts to exercise a forbidden power?

§ 31. Same: European doctrine. As a matter of pure

theory, there is of course no more reason why one of three departments of government, admitted to be of equal and coordinate powers, should have the right to declare acts of the others unconstitutional than that any of the others should have the same power. Each department might be left to judge for itself what was constitutional within its own sphere, and when there was a conflict they could compromise or get along otherwise as best they could. This is the view adopted on the continent of Europe. No European court acting under a written constitution can declare invalid an act of its coordinate legislative body. The legislators take an oath to obey the constitution, but within the legislative sphere they are the judges of what is constitutional, and the duty of the courts is to enforce the laws actually passed. The determination of what laws are constitutional is the function of the legislature. In like manner the executive decides for himself what are the constitutional duties he is sworn to perform, and, except where there are provisions for impeaching him, this decision is not subject to review by any other department of government. The same can be said of the acts of the judiciary. Each judge swears to obey the constitution, but the court is its own judge of what this requires within its sphere.

The result is that a written constitution in Continental countries is a rule binding the political morality and common sense of each of the departments of government, but its provisions are not enforceable by one coordinate branch of the government against another, except where some express provision to this effect is inserted in the constitution.

§ 32. Same: English doctrine. As the result of a series of constitutional struggles in England between the crown and the people the legislative power of Parliament had established itself as supreme over the executive power of the crown, and the judiciary also had become independent of the crown by a life tenure of office. The attempts of Parliament to coerce America by passing acts of taxation that were felt to be tyrannous, gave rise to speculation as to the extent of this power of Parliament. Was it supreme, no matter to what extent it might go, or were there limits to its power based on natural justice and common right, and if so could the courts enforce these limitations by declaring acts of Parliament that overstepped them to be void?

In spite of a few dicta of English judges to the effect that acts of Parliament repugnant to reason and common right were void, there can be no doubt that an act of Parliament when clearly expressed is supreme and binding on the English courts, no matter how unjust or unwise its provisions (1). Opinions to the contrary, however, based chiefly on political grounds and the intense opposition of the colonists to taxation by England without representation, were quite widespread among American statesmen before the Revolution, and no doubt had some influence in determining the course of American practice in controlling acts of the legislature.

(1) Webb v. Outrim (1907), A. C. 81, 89.

§ **33. Colonial practice. Its influence.** The American
colonies for a long time prior to the Revolution were governed under colonial charters, written instruments
granted by the monarchs of England. They had legislatures whose laws had to conform to the provisions of
these charters. If they did not, they were void, and could
be so declared by the colonial courts, or, on appeal, by the
privy council of England. There was nothing strange
about this. Neither the legislature nor the colonial courts
were independent departments of government, each supreme in its sphere. Both were subject entirely to the
laws of Parliament and the English king.

Now when the colonies became free, and there was no
longer any governmental authority superior to the courts
and legislature of the late colonies, this reason for the
courts disregarding the acts of the legislature disappeared. Both were now coordinate departments of government, supreme in their own spheres, and responsible
only to the people at the end of their terms of office. Both
were subject to the state constitution, but there was no
provision of that constitution which expressly authorized
the court to refuse to enforce unconstitutional laws, any
more than the legislature was given authority to refuse
to appropriate money for the judges' salaries if the legislature thought the court had acted unconstitutionally.
The executive, for example, has no right to refuse to enforce a law passed over his veto, which he considers unconstitutional. If he does so, he may be impeached. But
the colonies had been in the habit of seeing colonial laws
occasionally declared void by the courts. To the con-

servative classes of the community, which at that time had a strong controlling influence, this seemed a wise and sensible means of enforcing constitutional guarantees of security of property against the possible excesses of a legislature chosen by popular suffrage. So, on the adoption of the state constitutions, the courts tacitly assumed the function of interpreting the constitution for the legislature, and this was generally acquiesced in, though not without some opposition (1a).

§ 34. **Early American decisions.** The earliest American decision that judges might disregard legislative acts forbidden by the constitution appears to have been given in New Jersey in 1780, in the case of Holmes v. Walton (2). It was followed by a case in New York in 1784, Rutgers v. Waddington (3), in which the court so construed an act of the New York legislature as to avoid a violation of the treaty of peace with Great Britain. The decision excited considerable popular discontent, and the New York assembly passed a resolution denying the right of the court to dispense with an act of the legislature. A little later the judges in Rhode Island likewise declared void an act of the legislature in violation of the constitution, in the case of Trevett v. Weeden (4). The Rhode Island legislature summoned the judges before it to explain their reasons for this. After an explanation by the judges the legislature voted its dissatisfaction with

---

(1a)   James B. Thayer in 7 Harv. Law Rev. 130-34.
(2)   4 American Historical Review, 456.
(3)   Pamphlet, edited in 1866; 1 Thayer, Cas. C. L., 63.
(4)   2 Chandler's Crim. Trials, 269; 1 Thayer, Cas C. L., 73.

their reasons, and a motion was made to dismiss the judges from office, but this attempt was finally abandoned. There were also several other judicial expressions of opinion by colonial courts to the same effect before the adoption of the United States Constitution.

§ 35. Decision under Federal Constitution: Marbury v. Madison. When the Philadelphia convention met in 1787 to frame the Constitution of the United States, its legal members, of whom there were a number of much prominence, must have known of these decisions, and it is likely that the convention expected the courts to exercise the power of disregarding unconstitutional acts of Congress. In the Federalist papers, No. 78, it was argued by Hamilton that the courts would have this power under the Constitution of the United States. In 1803 the question finally came before the Supreme Court of the United States in the great case of Marbury v. Madison (5). The Constitution expressly limited the original jurisdiction of that court to certain cases, but an act of Congress attempted to give it jurisdiction in another case. The opinion of the court, given by Chief Justice Marshall, held the act unconstitutional and laid down the principle that it was the duty of the court to disregard such acts. The judges had sworn to support the Constitution, which they could not do if they gave effect to a law inconsistent with it. The act of Congress was inferior to the Constitution and when the two were inconsistent the judges were bound by their oath to disregard the inferior law.

---

(5) 1 Cranch (U. S.) 137

§ 36. Reasons for the doctrine. It may be doubted whether this reasoning is really so forcible as it at first seems. The President has also sworn to support the Constitution of the United States. Is he, therefore, at liberty to refuse to enforce an act of Congress that he deems unconstitutional? Is it any part of his duty under the Constitution to decide this question? The generally accepted doctrine is that the executive is not charged with this function; nor are the courts necessarily charged with such a duty, merely because they have sworn to support the Constitution. The true reasons for the American practice in this regard, which is now universally recognized in this country, are political. It is desirable that such a power be lodged outside of the departments upon whose action our constitutions have placed restrictions in the interests of the rights and liberties of the individual. The departments upon which these checks have been placed are chiefly the executive and the legislative. For them to measure their own powers in a popular government in times of public excitement is to make a constitution inoperative in the very emergencies for which these prohibitions were inserted. The judiciary is the weakest of the three departments of government. It controls neither the purse nor the sword, and unassisted it can do little that is injurious to political or civil liberty. Its members are likely to be more conservative, and to be less influenced by momentary passion than are the members of the legislature. Giving the judiciary a certain negative control over the acts of the other departments is likely to result in the provisions of a constitution being more faithfully observed than would otherwise be the case.

This construction, political rather than logical, has been amply vindicated in American experience, and the doctrine that our judiciary may declare laws unconstitutional is perhaps the most important single American contribution to the science of governmental administration.

SECTION 2. LIMITATIONS UPON EXERCISE OF POWER.

§ 37. Power is strictly judicial in character. What is the nature of this power of the courts to declare laws unconstitutional, and what are the proper occasions for its exercise? It is not a power that is exercised as a matter of course by the courts as each statute of doubtful validity comes from the legislature. The power is strictly a judicial one, to be exercised by the courts only in the course of litigation in which the question of the constitutionality of a legislative act necessarily arises. It may not be for the interest of an individual to raise the question, and so an unconstitutional law may be enforced upon the statute books for years before it is actually brought into question before a court. When a national bank was first chartered by the United States in 1791 grave doubts were expressed of its constitutionality, and those doubts continued for years, yet it was twenty-eight years before a suit actually came before the courts requiring a decision on this question.

§ 38. Unconstitutionality should be clear. Sometimes the question of the constitutionality of a legislative act is a very close one, depending upon the interpretation of

complex social and economic facts, where reasonable men
may disagree widely in their conclusions. The legislature
is charged in the first instance with the duty of interpreting the constitution, of deciding what it permits, and
what, within the limits of permissible action, is politically
expedient. The legislature is chosen so as to represent a
wide constituency and many shades of political and social
opinion. When it has decided upon a course of action
and embodied it in a statute, perhaps of doubtful constitutionality, what should be the attitude of the courts?
Suppose for instance that the legislature has passed an
act making eight hours a day's labor in a mine, or has
forbidden the payment of wages to employees by store
orders. On the one hand the legislature is forbidden to
deprive a man arbitrarily of his right to work and contract as he thinks best, but on the other hand it is the
duty of the legislature to guard the welfare of the community even against the improvident acts and contracts
of individuals. It may well be that a large number of
thinking persons in the community feel that eight hours
work underground daily is all that average human health
can stand, and that there are abuses connected with the
payment of wages in store orders that can only be rem-
edied by the abolition of the practice. An equal number
of competent persons may perhaps disagree with either
of these positions, on equally reasonable grounds. If
the constitutionality of the act is to be decided according
to the individual social or economic views of the judges,
then inevitably their opinions rather than those of the
legislature will be enforced; and if the question is one of

any importance the same political influences that created
the legislative majority in favor of the statute will seek
to create a judicial majority in the court in favor of it,
and judges will be chosen on account of their social and
economic views, rather than on account of their legal
ability. These undesirable results can only be avoided
by the courts taking the position that legislative acts are
valid if they may reasonably be thought to be constitutional, even though there is a rational difference of
opinion, and even if the judges as individuals may hold
opinions contrary to the legislature. A settlement of
such reasonable differences of opinion is exactly what a
legislature is for, and it is no part of the judicial function
to enforce one reasonable view rather than another reasonable one that conflicts with it.

§ 39. Same: Judicial declarations to this effect. It is
commonly deemed by courts, therefore, that they are not
to declare laws unconstitutional unless the matter is clear.
In Pennsylvania, for instance, it has been said: "For
weighty reasons it has been assumed as a principle in
constitutional construction by the Supreme Court of the
United States, by this court, and every other court of
reputation and influence, that an act of the legislature is
not to be declared void unless the violation of the constitution is so manifest as to leave no room for reasonable
doubt" (6).

The United States Supreme Court has said: "This
declaration should never be made except in clear cases.

---

(6)   Commonwealth v. Smith, 4 Binn. (Pa.) 117.

Every possible presumption is in favor of the validity of the statute and this continues until the contrary is shown beyond all rational doubt. One branch of government cannot encroach on the domain of another without danger. The safety of our institutions depends in no small degree on a strict observance of this salutary rule'' (7).

Judicial statements to this effect are very common (8).

§ 40. **Exercised only in actual litigation.** Besides the qualification just discussed, that a statute should be declared unconstitutional only in a very clear case, there are several other limitations upon the power.

1. As suggested above, it can be exercised only in the course of actual litigation. Courts will not judicially declare laws unconstitutional in moot cases, nor pass upon their validity at the request of the other departments of government outside of ordinary litigious procedure. An apparent exception to this in the case of so called ''advisory opinions'' is discussed in § 47, below. If no one cares to question an act of the legislature, or if the existing statutes regulating the jurisdiction and procedure of the courts do not permit a proper remedy, it may be impossible to secure a judicial declaration of the invalidity of a statute really unconstitutional. For instance, Congress has apparently not provided any effective procedure for the enforcement in the Federal courts of the right of suffrage in a state, even when improperly denied by the state through the requirement of an unconstitu-

---

(7)   Sinking Fund Cases, 99 U. S. 700, 718.

(8)   People v. Rice, 135 N. Y. 473 at 483-4, Dendy v. Wilson, 142 Tex. 460, 151 A. L. R. 1217.

tional system of registration as preliminary to voting (9).

§ **41. Power not applicable to political acts.** 2. The courts have no power to declare invalid acts of the legislature touching political matters, unless expressly given these by the constitution. As to such matters the executive and legislature are the sole judges of the constitutionality of their own acts, just as the courts are the sole judges of the extent of their own judicial powers. For instance, the United States Constitution (10) provides that the United States shall guarantee every state in the Union a republican form of government. In 1841-2 a condition of civil disorder existed in the state of Rhode Island and two separate organizations each claimed to be the legal government of the state. Violent encounters took place between the partisans of the rival governments and when suits arising therefrom came into the United States courts it was questioned which was the lawful government of the state. In Luther v. Borden (11) the Supreme Court said:

"The Constitution of the United States ... has treated the subject as political in its nature and placed the power in the hands of that department. It rests with Congress to decide what government is the established one in a state. For as the United States guarantee to each state a republican government, Congress must necessarily decide what government is established in a state before it can determine whether it is republican or not. And when

---

(9)   Giles v. Harris, 189 U. S. 475.

(10)   Const. Art. IV, sec. 4.

(11)   Luther v. Borden, 7 How. 1.

the senators and representatives of a state are admitted into the councils of the Union, the authority of the government under which they are appointed, as well as its republican character, is recognized by the proper constitutional authority. And its decision is binding on the other departments of government, and could not be questioned in a judicial tribunal." . . .

Similarly, after the Civil war, the state of Georgia sued the Secretary of War to prevent the execution of certain provisions of the Reconstruction Acts on the ground that the state was unconstitutionally deprived of its political rights. The court denied the relief, saying:

"That these matters, both as stated in the body of the bill, and the prayers for relief, call for the judgment of the court upon political questions, and, upon rights, not of persons or property, but of a political character, will hardly be denied. For the rights for the protection of which our authority is invoked, are the rights of sovereignty, of political jurisdiction, of government, of corporate existence as a state, with all its constitutional powers and privileges" (12).

At one time it was held that, even though a state constitution prescribes how the state shall be divided into legislative districts, the division is a political function and an improper one cannot be invalidated by the courts, in the absence of express constitutional authority (13). However, in a recent decision, the Supreme Court did take jurisdiction, saying that the issue of redistricting is not a nonjusticiable political question, that it was a

---

(12) Georgia v. Stanton, 6 Wall. 50.
(13) People v. Rice, 135 N. Y. 473.

complaint arising under the Constitution of the United States and that its citizens have standing to sue (13a).

For the same reason the Supreme Court refused to determine whether a proposed amendment to the Constitution had been ratified by a state within a reasonable time—what is a reasonable time? being a political question (13b).

§ **42.   When other departments cannot be compelled to act.** 3. Generally the courts cannot compel the legislature or the chief executive to act, nor even a subordinate officer to act where he is entrusted with a discretion. In Mississippi v. Johnson (14) in a case arising under the Reconstruction acts the court said:

"The single point which requires consideration is this: Can the President be restrained by injunction from carrying into effect an act of Congress alleged to be unconstitutional? . . .

"A ministerial duty, the performance of which may, in proper cases, be required of the head of a department, by judicial process, is one in respect to which nothing is left to discretion. It is a simple, definite duty, arising under conditions admitted or proved to exist, and imposed by law. . . . Very different is the duty of the President in the exercise of the power to see that the laws are faithfully executed, and among these laws the acts named in the bill. By the first of these acts he is required to assign generals to command in the several military districts, and to detail sufficient military force to enable such officers to discharge their duties under the law. By the supplementary act, other duties are imposed on the several commanding generals, and these duties must

(13a) Baker v. Carr, 7 1. ed 663.
(13b) Coleman v. Miller, 307 U. S. 433, Decided in 1939.

necessarily be performed under the supervision of the President as commander-in-chief. The duty thus imposed on the President is in no just sense ministerial. It is purely executive and political. . . .

"The Congress is the legislative department of the government; the President is the executive department. Neither can be restrained in its action by the judicial department; though the acts of both, when performed, are, in proper cases, subject to its cognizance."

However, the courts may compel a public officer to act where he has a duty to act or where refusal to act amounts to an abuse of discretion (See Sec. 4, P. 210, Extraordinary Remedies).

It is generally held that the governor of a state cannot be compelled by the state courts to perform any act whatever, even though involving no discretion, because he represents the supreme executive authority of the state (15) although some states hold the contrary view as to purely ministerial acts (16).

Another illustration of the inability of the courts to compel the political departments of government to discharge their functions, even when the latter unconstitutionally neglect them, is that afforded by the unhonored section of the Fourteenth Amendment to the United States Constitution which prescribes that when the right of suffrage is denied to any male citizen of a state over twenty-one years old, except for crime, such state's representation in Congress shall be proportionately reduced No power except that of Congress can enforce this section

(15)   People v. Morton, 156 N. Y. 136.
(16)   State v. Nash, 66 Ohio 612.

of the constitution, and the latter has never chosen to act thereunder.

§ 43. Laws not invalid merely because unwise. 4. The courts cannot declare a law unconstitutional merely because it is unwise, or oppressive, or contrary to the spirit of our institutions. As regards this the courts have said:

"If a particular act of legislation does not conflict with any of the limitations or restraints [in the constitution] which have been referred to, it is not in the power of the courts to suggest its unconstitutionality, however unwise its provisions may be, or whatever the motive may have been which led to its enactment" (17).

"The theory that laws may be declared void when deemed to be opposed to natural justice and equity, although they do not violate any constitutional provisions, has some support in the dicta of learned judges, but has not been approved so far as we know by any authoritative adjudication, and is repudiated by numerous authorities. . . . Admitting as we do the soundness of this view and fully approving it, we come back to the proposition that no law can be pronounced invalid, for the reason simply that it violates our notions of justice, is oppressive and unfair in its operation, or because . . . it is not justified by public necessity or designed to promote the public welfare. If it violates no constitutional provision it is valid and must be obeyed." (18) "The judiciary can only arrest the execution of a statute when it conflicts with the constitution. It cannot run a race of opin-

---

(17) People v. Draper, 15 N. Y. 532.
(18) Bertholf v. O'Reilly, 74 N. Y. 509.

ion upon a point of right, reason, and expediency with the law-making power'' (18a).

§ 44. Administrative regulations of the power. 5. In addition to the more important restraints upon the power of the judiciary to declare laws unconstitutional that have been discussed above, there are certain administrative rules usually regarded by courts in dealing with the matter. Among these are requirements that the question must be raised by a party really interested, that the litigation must be genuine and not merely collusive, that ordinarily laws should not be pronounced unconstitutional save by the highest state or Federal courts and with a full bench of judges; and that the decision of the constitutional point must really be necessary to the disposition of the case.

The only one of these rules that perhaps requires any explanation is the one against collusive litigation. This is to prevent the necessity of deciding constitutional questions without adequate argument in a friendly suit between two parties who really wish the same decision. It does not forbid the consideration of constitutional questions in any suit merely because both the plaintiff and the defendant desire the same decision, provided that the government or other parties adversely interested are given a full opportunity to be heard. In the great Income Tax case of 1895, for instance, a stockholder of a New York trust company brought suit to enjoin the trust company from paying the income tax to the Federal government. He was interested in not having his dividends

(18a)   Cooley, Const. Lim. 236-7 (7 ed.). See also U. S. v. Butler, 297 U. S. 1.

reduced, and of course all the officials of the trust company sympathized with this and would scarcely have made
an active defense. At the very beginning of the suit,
however, the attorney-general of the United States inter-
vened with able counsel and the government's side of the
case was fully presented at every stage. The litigation
was therefore real, even though both the nominal parties
desired the same result (19).

SECTION 3. EFFECT OF AN UNCONSTITUTIONAL ACT.

§ 45. In general. Incidental effect. Generally speaking, when a statute is declared unconstitutional private
rights are left unaffected by it, just as they would have
been had it never been passed. The unconstitutional
statute, indeed, may afford protection to an officer from
prosecution for a crime requiring a particular state of
mind, which, owing to his reliance upon the unconstitutional statute, he may not have had. He could not, for
instance, be convicted of larceny for taking the property
which he thought himself authorized to do under a statute really unconstitutional. His reliance upon the statute
has prevented his having the state of mind necessary to
make him a thief. Moreover, acts done upon the faith of
an unconstitutional statute may raise moral obligations
that the government is justified in discharging, when, but
for such a statute no such obligations would have been
incurred. For instance, the United States passed an act
giving a pecuniary bounty to sugar producers, which was
shortly afterwards repealed. Congress then passed an
act making certain reimbursements to persons who had
expended money upon the faith of the previous bounty

(19)   Pollock v. Farmers' Loan & Trust Co., 157 U. S. 429.

act. Regarding the validity of this latter provision, the court decided that, even though the original bounty act were unconstitutional, there was still sufficient doubt about it to make it proper for the government, in discharge of a moral obligation, to reimburse those who had spent money upon the faith of the act (20). In so far as an officer, even though acting in good faith, invades rights of private property and personal immunity under an unconstitutional statute, he is liable civilly to injured persons, just as though the act had not been passed (21). On the other hand, if a public officer honestly thinks the act unconstitutional and therefore declines to obey it, he is liable for refusal if the law is later upheld by the courts (22).

§ 46. **Effect of partial unconstitutionality.** More difficult questions arise where an act is unconstitutional in part only. Does the entire act fail in this case, or do only the unconstitutional parts of it? This question was discussed in the Income Tax case of 1895. Congress had attempted to levy a tax upon incomes in excess of $4,000, from whatever sources derived. A majority of the court held that the income from real estate and invested personal property was a direct tax, and hence forbidden to Congress unless it were apportioned according to population, which had not been done. Of course there remained a large number of taxable incomes from the professions, trades, and other employments, but the income from $65,000,000,000 of real and personal property would

---

(20)   United States v. Realty Co., 163 U. S. 427.

(21)   Campbell v. Sherman, 35 Wis. 103.

(22)   Clark v. Miller, 54 N. Y. 528.

be excluded, leaving the entire burden to fall on other incomes. The court said:

"It is undoubtedly true that there may be cases where one part of a statute may be enforced as constitutional, and another declared inoperative and void, because unconstitutional; but these are cases where the parts are so distinctly separable that each can stand alone, and where the court is able to see and declare that the intention of the legislature was that the part pronounced valid would be held enforceable, even though the other part should fail. To hold otherwise would be to substitute for the law intended by the legislature one they may never have been willing by itself to enact."

Measured by this test a majority thought Congress could not have intended to tax incomes at all, if the income from real and personal property was to be excluded (23).

SECTION 4.   ADVISORY OPINIONS AND DECLARATORY
JUDGMENTS.

§ 47. Nature and effect of advisory opinions. As previously explained in this chapter, it is usually held unconstitutional to require the courts to give opinions to the other departments of the government for their convenience in advance of actual litigation, as such opinions have not a judicial character. The constitutions of a few states, however, expressly require the rendition of such opinions by the highest court of the state at the request of the governor or legislature. Even in these cases such opinions do not acquire a judicial character and bind the

(23)   Pollock v. Farmers' Loan & Trust Co., 158 U. S. 601.

court as precedents. Being ordinarily rendered without the arguments of counsel, the court is far less likely to consider all phases of the question; and so, even though it may have given an opinion in favor of the validity of the proposed law to the executive or legislature, it holds itself free to reconsider the question entirely on its merits, if it afterwards comes before the court in actual litigation (24).

Opinions thus given to assist other departments of government in the discharge of duties are called "advisory opinions," and the better usage of government in this country tends to discourage the practice of giving them It is thought, with reason, likely to draw the judges into the heat of partisan controversies and to impair public confidence in their impartiality, without any corresponding advantage.

§ 48. **Declaratory Judgments.** The usual and customary practice of the courts has been to confine their judgments and decisions to cases in which there exists a real cause of action—a situation where actual injury has already occurred or is threatened. Perhaps, in the absence of statute, no court would take jurisdiction of a case merely for the purpose of declaring in advance the rights, duties, and obligations of the parties in the absence of an actual controversy.

Statutes have been enacted in many states giving courts jurisdiction to render declaratory judgments. A uniform

(24)   Green v. Common'wealth, 12 Allen, 155.

declaratory judgment act has been adopted and recommended by the National Conference of Commissioners on
uniform state laws, and it has been enacted in a number of
states. In 1934, Congress conferred upon the Federal
Courts power "to declare rights and other legal relations
of any interested party petitioning for such declaration
whether or not further relief is or could be prayed" in
cases of actual controversy, and provided that such declarations should have the force and effect of a final judgment or decree. Many of the earlier declaratory judgment
statutes were held unconstitutional on the ground that
they undertook to impose upon the courts the duty of per-
forming non-judicial functions (25). The judicial power
is defined to be the right to determine actual controversies arising between litigants, duly instituted in courts of
proper jurisdiction. Another ground of unconstitutionality sometimes advanced was that the parties are thereby
deprived of a trial by jury. These objections have been
met in the later statutes by requiring an actual controversy and by providing for jury trials where the controversy is such as to require it.

The United States Supreme Court has held the Federal
Declaratory Judgment Act of 1934 within the power of
Congress to enact, "so far as it authorizes relief which is
consonant with the exercise of the judicial function in the
determination of controversies to which, under the Constitution, the judicial power extends." The following, quoted
from the Court's opinion in Aetna Life Insurance Com-

---

(25)   Muskrat v. U. S., 219 U. S. 346; Anway v. Grand Rapids R. Co.,
211 Mich. 592, 12 A.L.R. 26.

pany v. Haworth (26), is very enlightening as to the limits of the power of the courts.

"A 'controversy' in this sense must be one that is appropriate for judicial determination. A justiciable controversy is thus distinguished from a difference or dispute of a hypothetical or abstract character; from one that is academic or moot. The controversy must be definite and concrete, touching the legal relations of parties having adverse legal interests. It must be a real and substantial controversy admitting of specific relief through a decree of a conclusive character as distinguished from an opinion advising what the law would be upon a hypothetical state of facts. Where there is such a concrete case admitting of immediate and definitive determination of the legal rights of the parties in an advisory proceeding upon the facts alleged, the judicial function may be appropriately exercised although the adjudication of rights of the litigants may not require the award of process or the payment of damages (27)."

----

(26)   300 U. S. 227, 108 A.L.R. 1000.

(27)   § 48 added by publisher's editorial staff.

NOTE.—There is no omission of material here. The next subsections begin with number 62. Owing to a mistake in the plates, there are no subsections numbered from 49 to 61.

PART II.

FUNDAMENTAL RIGHTS.

CHAPTER III.

HISTORY AND SCOPE OF FUNDAMENTAL CONSTITUTIONAL RIGHTS.

SECTION 1. CLASSIFICATION OF CONSTITUTIONAL PROVISIONS.

§ 62 (1) **Provisions establishing the frame of government.** Broadly speaking, the provisions of American constitutions, state and national, fall into four great classes:

1. Provisions dealing with the frame of government itself. Of this character are those clauses of our constitutions that divide the government into departments, provide for officials, regulate their qualifications, duties, and the modes of choosing them, distribute the powers of government between the various departments, and provide for the manner of their exercise. These provisions are mainly political in their nature, and the careful discussion of them belongs rather to the subject of political science than to the law of private rights. They will therefore receive little attention in this article.

§ 63. **Provisions guaranteeing fundamental private rights.** 2. Provisions securing certain fundamental political, religious, and civil rights to citizens or other per-

(1) See note on page 49b.   50

sons within the jurisdiction, mainly by prohibiting the exercise of governmental powers to the prejudice of these rights. These are the parts of our constitutions supremely important to the individual, and these are the ones treated at greatest length in this article.

Both the United States and the states are forbidden to infringe these fundamental rights. The prohibitions upon the United States are of course contained in the United States constitution. Those upon the states are partly in the United States constitution and partly in the separate state constitutions. For convenience, similar prohibitions, whether upon the United States or the states, will be treated together, although the illustrations used will be drawn so far as possible from the decisions of the United States Supreme Court. For instance, the Fifth amendment of the Constitution forbids the United States to deprive anyone of liberty without due process of law. The Fourteenth amendment of the Constitution forbids any state to deprive a person of liberty without due process of law. All of the state constitutions likewise forbid their governments to deprive anyone of liberty without due process of law. It may be alleged, therefore, that the United States has violated the Fifth amendment; or that a state has violated either the Fourteenth amendment or its own state constitution, and upon similar states of fact it is very likely that similar decisions will be given in regard to each of these three separate allegations. Similar prohibitions, no matter in what constitution found, may thus with propriety and convenience be considered together.

§ 64. **Provisions regulating intergovernmental relations under our Federal system.** 3. Provisions regulating
the relations of the states to each other, to the United
States, and to foreign states. They define the governmental spheres of the states and the United States and
provide for the interrelations that exist in our peculiar
Federal system. These provisions of our constitutions
are considered at some length in this article, as a knowledge of them is necessary not only to a comprehension of
our political system, but in many cases to an understanding of the substance of individual rights themselves.

§ 65. **Provisions regulating government in detail.** 4.
Provisions regulating in detail the exercise of power, both
as to substance and procedure by the various departments
of government. The early American constitutions contained relatively few of these provisions, being satisfied
to secure fundamental rights from governmental aggression and to leave the state governments a free hand in
other respects. The later state constitutions have im-
mensely increased the scope and detail of such regulations. In very recent state constitutions the greater part
of a lengthy instrument of government is taken up by
such provisions, which not only deprive the principal governmental departments of a large proportion of their discretionary powers, but make it increasingly difficult to
enact any important legislation whatever that shall not
violate some one of a multitude of petty restrictions. Not
a little of the superior efficiency of the Federal government is due to the fact that the United States Constitution was adopted before such a minute regulation of the

powers of government became customary. This article will not deal at all with constitutional provisions of this character.

SECTION 2. STATE AND FEDERAL CONSTITUTIONAL GUARANTIES BEFORE 1865.

§ 66. **Early state constitutions and original Federal Constitution.** When the United States Constitution was adopted in 1788, each of the thirteen original states had a constitution of its own, containing a number of fundamental guaranties of liberty and property, in the form of prohibitions upon the various departments of its state government. These prohibitions were commonly collected in one place in each constitution and collectively were called "Bills of Rights." The national government created by the Constitution was given extensive powers, and then several prohibitions were placed upon particular methods of exercising these powers. In the original Constitution these prohibitions are mainly to be found in Article I, section 9. Most of these prohibitions were not to secure fundamental personal rights, but had certain political, administrative, economic, or social purposes. Two prohibitions in section 9, however, secured fundamental rights from aggression by the Federal government. These forbid the suspension of the writ of habeas corpus, except in case of rebellion or invasion, and prohibit bills of attainder and ex post facto laws.

§ 67. **Federal bill of rights. Amendments I to X.** One of the principal objections urged against the adoption of the Constitution by the states was its failure to

provide a more extensive bill of rights, and its opponents
pointed out that there was nothing to prevent the proposed national government, while acting within the scope
of its extensive national powers, from confiscating property, or abolishing jury trials, or forbidding free speech,
or even from putting men to death by executive order
without a trial. In several states the opposition to the
new Constitution was so strong that its adoption was only
secured by the assurance of its advocates that amendments to it should be speedily adopted incorporating an
adequate bill of rights. Accordingly, one of the early acts
of the new government was the submission to the states of
a number of amendments for this purpose, and ten of
these were ratified by the necessary number of states so
that they became a part of the Constitution in 1791. These
were amendments one to ten (see Appendix A). They
secured to the people of all of the states as against the
United States government the principal fundamental
rights which the people in their own state constitutions
had secured against their state governments. It has been
repeatedly decided that the prohibitions of the first ten
amendments apply only to the Federal government, not
to the states (1a).

§ 68. **Federal prohibitions upon the states before 1865.**
The original Constitution contained a few express prohibitions upon the action of the state governments. The
objects sought by these were mainly political, commercial, or connected with interstate comity. See Article I,

---

(1a)   Barron v. Baltimore, 7 Pet. 243.

section 10, and Article IV, sections 1 and 2. Of a political character, for instance, were the prohibitions in Article I, section 10, forbidding the states to enter into any treaties or agreements with other states or foreign powers, or to keep troops or ships of war in times of peace, or to engage in war unless in actual peril of invasion. Of a commercial character were the prohibitions in the same section against coining money, emitting bills of credit, making anything but gold and silver coin a legal tender, taxing imports or exports, or levying tonnage duties. Designed to secure interstate comity were the prohibitions in Article IV, sections 1 and 2, that each state should give full faith and credit to the public acts, records, and judicial proceedings of every other state; that the citizens of each state should be entitled to all privileges and immunities of citizens in the several states; and that fugitives from justice and escaping slaves from any state should be delivered up in the other states. But the only prohibitions in the original Constitution designed to protect state citizens in their fundamental rights against the aggressions of their own state governments were the prohibitions in Article I, section 10, against a state's passing bills of attainder, ex post facto laws, or laws impairing the obligation of contracts. Even the last of these was introduced chiefly on account of commercial considerations, for there may be many laws impairing the obligation of contracts, like bankruptcy laws, for instance, that do not deprive men of fundamental rights. The framers of the Constitution had abundant faith that the inhabitants of each state might be trusted to protect themselves in their

own state constitutions against their own state governments, and that it was not necessary for the nation to
protect individual rights against local tyranny. The prohibitions against bills of attainder and ex post facto laws
were doubtless largely designed to protect resident loyal-
ists who had adhered to Great Britain during the Revolution, and so were evoked by the demands of a passing
political situation rather than by a conviction that the
state governments could not ordinarily be trusted in these
respects as regards their own citizens. The Eleventh
Amendment, adopted in 1798, enlarged the immunity of
the states by protecting them from the suits of individuals, except with their consent; and the Twelfth Amendment, adopted in 1804, merely regulated the details of
presidential elections.

SECTION 3.   SCOPE OF LATER AMENDMENTS TO FEDERAL
CONSTITUTION.

§ 69.   **Thirteenth Amendment.**   It was not until three
generations after the adoption of the Constitution and
in the heat of passion engendered by a great civil war
that the power of the states was further restricted by constitutional amendment. The existence of slavery caused
the Civil war, and it was inevitable that the institution
should not survive the victory of the north. Lee surrendered in April, 1865, and on December 18th of the same
year the Thirteenth Amendment, duly ratified by three-
quarters of the states, was proclaimed to be in force as
a part of the United States Constitution. The amendment reads:

"Section 1. Neither slavery nor involuntary servitude, except as a punishment for crime whereof the party shall have been duly convicted, shall exist within the United States, or any place subject to their jurisdiction.

"Section 2. Congress shall have power to enforce this article by appropriate legislation."

This amendment, as has been frequently said, is self-executing so far as its terms are applicable to any existing state of circumstances. By its own phrases it abolished slavery and established freedom, and the power of Congress to enforce it authorizes the direct punishment by the Federal government of all persons who enslave or attempt to enslave others. It operates directly upon all individuals within the jurisdiction of the United States (2). State legislation authorizing slavery, and all acts of individuals tending to establish it, whether authorized by state law or not, are void and illegal, and all individual acts in pursuance thereof may be punished by the United States. See §§ 101-4, below.

§ 70. **Adoption of Fourteenth Amendment.** A brief experience sufficed to show that while the Thirteenth Amendment had freed the slaves it would not protect them against a multitude of oppressive and discriminating laws, which were likely to be enacted with reference to the late bondmen as soon as the dominant elements of the white population in the southern states regained control of their state governments. To prevent this, among other purposes, the Fourteenth Amendment was proposed

---

(2) Clyatt v. U. S., 197 U. S. 207, 216-7, quoting from Civil Rights Cases, 109 U. S. 3.

and was proclaimed to be in force in July, 1868. Sections 1 and 5 of this are of permanent and increasing importance. They read as follows:

"Section 1. All persons born or naturalized in the United States, and subject to the jurisdiction thereof, are citizens of the United States and of the state wherein they reside. No state shall make or enforce any law which shall abridge the privileges or immunities of citizens of the United States; nor shall any state deprive any person of life, liberty, or property, without due process of law; nor deny to any person within its jurisdiction the equal protection of the laws.

"Section 5. The Congress shall have power to enforce, by appropriate legislation, the provisions of this article."

§ 71. Analysis of Fourteenth Amendment. The citizenship clause in the Fourteenth Amendment is discussed in Chapter IV, §§ 76-85, below. The remaining clauses in section 1 contain three sweeping prohibitions upon state governmental action; (1) no state shall make or enforce any law which shall abridge the privileges or immunities of citizens of the United States; (2) no state shall deprive any person of life, liberty, or property, without due process of law; (3) no state shall deny to any person within its jurisdiction the equal protection of the laws. The due process clause is copied from the Fifth Amendment, where it is a prohibition upon the United States government. The other two clauses impose limitations upon the state governments that are not expressly imposed upon the United States government in any other part of the Constitution. Each of these clauses will be made the subject of a separate discussion in other parts of this article and the last two clauses are of such immense importance that they will form the subject of several chapters. Just here we shall inquire against whom these provisions are enforceable by Congressional legislation.

§ 72. **Fourteenth Amendment forbids state action only.** In 1875 Congress passed a law known as the Civil Rights act. It provided that all persons in the United States should be entitled to equal privileges in inns, public conveyances, and public places of amusement, without discrimination on account of race, color, or previous condition of servitude. Any person who denied such equal privileges to others was made guilty of an offence against the United States and liable in damages to the person aggrieved. Various persons were indicted under this statute for denying to negroes equal privileges in hotels, theatres, and upon railroad trains. Their cases were carried to the United States Supreme Court and the statute was held unconstitutional. The court said, in discussing the character of the provisions in the Fourteenth Amendment:

"It is state action of a particular character that is prohibited. Individual invasion of individual rights is not the subject-matter of the amendment. It has a deeper and broader scope. It nullifies and makes void all state legislation, and state action of every kind, which impairs the privileges and immunities of citizens of the United States, or which injures them in life, liberty or property without due process of law, or which denies to any of them the equal protection of the laws. It not only does this,

but, in order that the national will, thus declared, may not
be a mere brutum fulmen, the last section of the amendment invests Congress with power to enforce it by appropriate legislation for correcting the effects óf such prohibited state laws and state acts, and thus to render them
effectually null, void, and innocuous. This is the legislative power conferred upon Congress, and this is the whole
of it. . . . And so in the present case, until some
state law has been passed, or some state action through
its officers or agents has been taken, adverse to the rights
of citizens sought to be protected by the Fourteenth
Amendment, no legislation of the United States under said
amendment, nor any proceeding under such legislation,
can be called into activity; for the prohibitions of the
amendment are against state laws and acts done under
state authority. . . . An inspection of the law shows
that it makes no reference whatever to any supposed or
apprehended violation of the Fourteenth Amendment on
the part of the states. . . . It steps into the domain
of local jurisprudence and lays down rules for the conduct of individuals in society towards each other, and
imposes sanctions for the enforcement of those rules,
without referring in any manner to any supposed action
of the state or its authorities. . . .

"In this connection it is proper to state that civil rights,
such as are guaranteed by the Constitution against state
aggression, cannot be impaired by the wrongful acts of
individuals, unsupported by state authority in the shape
of laws, customs, or judicial or executive proceedings.
The wrongful act of an individual, unsupported by any

such authority, is simply a private wrong, or a crime of that individual; an invasion of the rights of the injured party, it is true, whether they affect his person, his property, or his reputation; but if not sanctioned in some way by the state, or not done under state authority, his rights remain in full force, and may presumably be vindicated by resort to the laws of the state for redress." (3)

§ 73. **What amounts to state action.** It being well settled that the prohibitions in the Fourteenth Amendment, section 1, apply to the states rather than to individuals, it remains to be considered what kind of action is treated as that of a state for the purpose of the amendment. A United States statute forbade any officer charged with the duty of summoning jurors to exclude any citizen on account of race, color, or previous condition of servitude. A Virginia county judge, although not authorized thereto by Virginia law, excluded all colored men from the juries selected by him. In holding that the action of the county judge was state action and therefore prohibited by this statute, the court said: "A state acts by its legislative, its executive or its judicial authorities. It can act in no other way. . . . Whoever, by virtue of public position under a state government, deprives another of property, life, or liberty without due process of law, or denies or takes away the equal protection of the laws, violates the constitutional inhibition; and as he acts in the name of the state and is clothed with the state's power, his act is that of the state" (4).

---

(3)   Civil Rights Cases, 109 U. S. 3, 11 ff.
(4)   Ex parte Virginia, 100 U. S. 339.

A further illustration of what is state action is found in Shelley v. Kraemer (4a). Where the court held that enforcement by the state courts of a restrictive agreement between private persons providing that certain property should not be used or occupied either as owner or tenant by any person not of the caucasian race was state action, that by doing this, the state had denied the petitioners the equal protection of the laws.

The Fourteenth Amendment therefore enables Congress to act against individuals only in so far as the latter are acting in an official capacity as representatives of a state. Acts of a state in violation of the Fourteenth Amendment are void and may be disregarded with impunity by persons affected by them, but Congressional action can go no farther than indicated.

§ 74. **What are privileges and immunities of citizens of United States?**   The second sentence of the Fourteenth Amendment, section 1, provides, "No state shall make or enforce any law which shall abridge the privileges or immunities of citizens of the United States." With the other clauses in the section this one was adopted primarily to protect the newly freed slaves from oppression at the hands of the state governments in the south. It is, perhaps, doubtful just what privileges or immunities were meant to be protected from abridgment by those who proposed the amendment. The Congressional debates of the time leave the matter in doubt, and perhaps most of

---

(4a)   334 U. S. 1, 3 A.L.R. 2nd, 441 (1948).

those who voted for the amendment had no clear conception of the exact scope of this clause.

The first case under the Fourteenth Amendment brought before the Supreme Court involved the meaning of this clause. Louisiana passed a law forbidding individuals to maintain slaughter houses in New Orleans and its vicinity, and conferred upon a single corporation the exclusive right for twenty-five years to maintain in this territory places for killing animals for meat. Various individual butchers alleged that this law deprived them of the privileges and immunities guaranteed by this clause of the Fourteenth Amendment. The Supreme Court said:

"It is quite clear that there is a citizenship of the United States, and a citizenship of the state, which are distinct from each other. . . . The paragraph mainly relied upon by the plaintiffs speaks only of privileges and immunities of citizens of the United States, and does not speak of those of citizens of the several states. . . . It is only the former which are placed by this section under the protection of the Federal Constitution, and the latter, whatever they may be, are not intended to have any additional protection by this paragraph of the amendment. . . . The first occurrence of the words 'privileges and immunities' in our constitutional history is to be found in the Fourth Article of the old Confederation. . . . In the Constitution of the United States, the corresponding provision is found in section 2 of the Fourth Article in the following words: 'The citizens of each state shall be entitled to all of the privileges and immunities of citi-

zens of the several states.' . . . Up to the adoption of
the recent amendments, no claim or pretense was set up
that those rights depended on the Federal government for
their existence or protection, beyond the very few express
limitations which the Federal Constitution imposed upon
the states—such, for instance, as the prohibition against
ex post facto laws, bills of attainder, and laws impairing
the obligation of contracts. . . . Was it the purpose
of the Fourteenth Amendment, by the simple declaration
that no state should make or enforce any law which shall
abridge the privileges and immunities of citizens of the
United States, to transfer the security and protection of
all the civil rights which we have mentioned, from the
states to the Federal government? And where it is declared that Congress shall have the power to enforce that
article, was it intended to bring within the power of Congress the entire domain of civil rights heretofore belonging exclusively to the states?

"All this and more must follow, if the proposition of
the plaintiffs in error be sound. For not only are these
rights subject to the control of Congress whenever in its
discretion any of them are supposed to be abridged by
state legislation, but that body may also pass laws in advance, limiting and restricting the exercise of legislative
power by the states, in their most ordinary and usual
functions, as in its judgment it may think proper on all
such subjects. . . . The argument, we admit, is not
always the most conclusive which is drawn from the consequences urged against the adoption of a particular construction of an instrument. But when, as in the case be-

fore us, these consequences are so serious, so far reaching and pervading, so great a departure from the structure and spirit of our institutions; when the effect is to fetter and degrade the state governments by subjecting them to the control of Congress in the exercise of powers heretofore universally conceded to them of the most ordinary and fundamental character; when, in fact, it radically changes the whole theory of the relations of the state and Federal governments to each other and of both these governments to the people; the argument has a force that is irresistible, in the absence of language which expresses such a purpose too clearly to admit of doubt'' (5).

Privileges and immunities of citizens of the United States are those derived from the Federal government, Constitution, and laws, like the right to use the navigable waters of the country, to engage in interstate commerce, to demand Federal protection when out of the country, to become a citizen according to the Fourteenth Amendment, and the other rights secured by the Thirteenth, Fourteenth, and Fifteenth Amendments.

One of the important rights which every citizen has is the right to move freely from state to state. This is clearly shown in the concurring opinions in Edwards v. People (5a). Edwards was convicted of violating a statute of the state of California which made it a misdemeanor knowingly to bring into the state any indigent person who was not a resident of the state. The case

---

(5)   Slaughter House Cases, 16 Wall. 36.
(5a)   — U. S. —, decided in 1941.

was carried to the Supreme Court of the United States which held the statute invalid because it imposed an unconstitutional burden on interstate commerce, one that could not be justified as an exercise of the state's police power. Having so held, the court deemed it unnecessary to consider other provisions of the Constitution.

Some members of the court, however, were not willing to base the right of citizens to travel from state to state solely on the commerce clause. They therefore rendered opinions concurring in the results of the court's opinion, but pointing out what they considered more substantial grounds for upholding this important right.

Mr. Justice Jackson said: "The migrations of a human being, of whom it is charged that he possesses nothing that can be sold and has no wherewithal to buy, do not fit easily into my notions as to what is commerce. To hold that the measure of his rights is the commerce clause is likely to result eventually either in distorting the commercial law or in denaturing human rights. I turn, therefore, away from principles by which commerce is regulated to that clause of the Constitution by virtue of which Duncan (the indigent person whom Edwards was convicted of bringing into the state of California) is a citizen of the United States and which forbids any state to abridge his privileges or immunities as such.

"This clause was adopted to make United States citizenship the dominant and paramount allegiance among us. The return which the law had long associated with allegiance was protection.

"This court should hold squarely that it is a privilege of citizenship of the United States, protected from state abridgement, to enter any state of the Union either for temporary sojourn or for the establishment of permanent residence therein and for gaining resultant citizenship thereof.

"Does indigence as defined by the application of the California statute constitute a basis for restricting the freedom of a citizen, as crime or contagion warrants its restriction? We should say now, and in no uncertain terms, that a man's mere property status, without more, cannot be used by a state to test, qualify, or limit his rights as a citizen of the United States. 'Indigence' in itself is neither a source of rights nor a basis for denying them. The mere state of being without funds is a neutral fact—constitutionally an irrelevance, like race, creed, or color. I agree with what I understand to be the holding of the court that cases which may indicate the contrary are overruled."

Mr. Justice Douglas stated that this right to move freely from state to state is an incident of national citizenship protected by the privileges and immunities clause of the Fourteenth Amendment and that it had been recognized as "a right fundamental to the national character of our Federal Government" before the Fourteenth Amendment. These statements are supported by numerous decisions (5b), (5c).

(5b) Crandall v. Nevada, 6 Wall. 35; Twinning v. New Jersey, 211 U. S. 78.

(5c) Section revised by publisher's editorial staff.

§ **75. Fifteenth Amendment.** This amendment to the Constitution contains a prohibition against both the states and the United States. It was adopted in March, 1870, in the following words:

"Section 1. The right of citizens of the United States to vote shall not be denied or abridged by the United States or by any state on account of race, color, or previous condition of servitude.

"Section 2. The Congress shall have power to enforce this article by appropriate legislation."

This, like the Fourteenth Amendment, is in terms a prohibition upon governmental action, not upon the action of individuals who are not acting as official representatives of the state or Federal governments. It has accordingly been held that this amendment gives Congress no power to punish individuals who by bribery or intimidation prevent colored men from voting in a state (6). Congress could, of course, punish individuals for misconduct at Federal elections, because the Constitution (Art I, sec. 4) gives Congress power to regulate these; but the Fifteenth Amendment confers no such power upon Congress as to elections generally.

§ **75a. Amendments not growing out of the Civil War.** The Sixteenth Amendment was adopted in 1913 for the purpose of enabling Congress to impose income taxes without their being apportioned among the several states according to population, and without reference to the source from which the income was derived. Congress already had power to tax incomes, but it was impractical

---

(6)   James v. Bowman, 190 U. S. 127.

to exercise the power because of the restrictions indicated (7). If before the amendment was adopted Congress had no power to impose a tax on a particular class of income, it does not have the power after the adoption of it. But where Congress had power before, it may impose the tax now without reference to apportionment, or whether the tax is direct or indirect, or whether the income is from lands, salaries, or dividends. Thus, before the amendment, Congress could not impose an income tax on the salary of a Federal judge because of provisions of Article III, Sec. 1 of the Constitution which provides that judges shall receive for their services a compensation which shall not be diminished during their continuance in office. After the adoption of the amendment Congress still lacks such a power (8).

The Seventeenth Amendment, ratified May 31, 1913, provides for the election of United States Senators by popular vote. It departs somewhat from the theory upon which the Congress was originally organized and tends to make the Senate more responsive to public opinion.

The Eighteenth Amendment, which went into effect January 16, 1920, prohibited "the manufacture, sale, or transportation of intoxicating liquors within, the importation thereof into, or the exportation thereof from the United States and all territory subject to the jurisdiction thereof for beverage purposes." It was repealed by the Twenty-first Amendment, which was ratified and went into effect on December 5, 1933.

---

(7)   Pollock v. Farmers Loan & Trust Co., 157 U. S. 427.
(8)   Evans v. Gore, 253 U. S. 245.

The Nineteenth Amendment extends the right of suffrage in the United States to women and is limited to that. It does not automatically render women eligible for jury service. But in states where the law previously provided that qualified electors of the state who have the other required qualifications should be competent jurors, it may indirectly have that effect.

The Twentieth Amendment provides that the terms of the President and Vice President shall end at noon on the twentieth day of January and the terms of senators and representatives on the third day of January of the years in which such terms would have otherwise ended. It also provides that Congress shall assemble at least once each year on the third day of January unless they shall by law appoint a different day. Various contingencies in succession to the offices of President and Vice President are provided for.

The Twenty-first Amendment repeals the Eighteenth Amendment and prohibits the transportation or importation of intoxicating liquors into any state or territory in violation of the laws thereof.

The Twenty-second Amendment prohibits the election of any person to the office of the presidency of the United States for more than two terms.

The Twenty-third Amendment gives citizens of the District of Columbia the right to vote in national elections.

CHAPTER IV.

POLITICAL RIGHTS.

Section 1. Citizenship.

§ 76. Federal citizenship before Fourteenth Amendment. The basis of English nationality under the common law was birth within the allegiance of the British crown and subject to its protection. Children of aliens, if born within the British dominions, were natural-born subjects of the crown. When the United States Constitution was adopted it recognized a citizenship of the United States, but made no attempt to define it. Representatives and senators, for instance, were required to have been respectively seven and nine years citizens of the United States, and the President was required to be " a natural born citizen or a citizen of the United States at the time of the adoption of this Constitution." As regards white persons, at least, it has been judicially affirmed that the English rule of nationality by birth was in force in all of the English colonies of America and in the United States afterwards (1). Before the Civil war several states had expressly recognized free negroes as citizens, but in the Dred Scott case three judges were of the opinion that no native born slave or descendant of slave par-

---

(1)   United States v. Wong Kim Ark, 169 U. S. 649, 658.

67

ents could become a citizen of the United States by birth, on account of Article IV, section 2, of the Constitution, which requires each state to give equal privileges to the citizens of other states. It was thought that the slave states could not have intended a contrary doctrine when ratifying the Constitution (2).

§ 77. **Citizenship by birth under Fourteenth Amendment.** After the war a definition of citizenship was made in the Fourteenth Amendment, which provides: "All persons born or naturalized in the United States, and subject to the jurisdiction thereof, are citizens of the United States and of the state wherein they reside." Under the Chinese exclusion acts the question arose whether a child of alien Chinese parents born in California was a citizen of the United States, and therefore not deportable under the exclusion acts. It was held that he was a United States citizen, although his parents could not have been naturalized under the existing laws, and that the Fourteenth Amendment enacted into the Constitution the English rule of nationality by birth within the allegiance (3).

§ 78. **Limitations upon citizenship by birth.** The Fourteenth Amendment, however, by its own terms. falls somewhat short of conferring citizenship upon everyone born within the dominions over which the United States government is sovereign. To come within the Fourteenth Amendment, a person must be born "within the United States" and must also be "subject to the jurisdiction

---

(2)   Dred Scott v. Sandford, 19 How. 393, 404-23.
(3)   United States v. Wong Kim Ark, 169 U. S. 649.

thereof.'' These phrases suggest limitations upon citizenship by birth that now demand consideration.

§ 79. Meaning of "born within the United States.' What do the words "United States" mean in the citizenship clause of the Fourteenth Amendment? Several different meanings might be attributed to them. 1. They might mean only the states that have been admitted to the Union. Taking this view, a person born in Guam would not be considered a citizen by birth by reason of the Fourteenth Amendment, though he might be through some act of Congress. 2. The words may mean the admitted states plus such other territory as may have been made by statute or treaty an integral part of our country, as contrasted with territory that is still held in the condition of a colony. Under this theory the territory of Alaska (prior to statehood), having been incorporated into the body of our country by treaty and acts of Congress, would be a part of the United States. 3. The words might possibly be construed to include all territory over which our government, either permanently or for an indefinite period, exercises sovereign powers. The interpretation, making the words "United States" the name of the entire American Empire, would give citizenship to everyone born in the ceded Spanish colonies since the treaty of 1898.

The Spanish treaty of peace of 1898, however, provided in Article 10: "The civil rights and political status of the native inhabitants of the territories hereby ceded to the United States shall be determined by the Congress." The intention of this article apparently is to leave the question of citizenship to the discretion of Congress rather than to settle it irrevocably under the Fourteenth Amendment.

Since the problem is primarily one for the political departments of government, Congress, in the "Nationality Act of 1940" (3a), and the Immigration and Nationality Act passed in 1952, have probably given the definition which will prevail at least until it is amended by act of Congress. They define the term "United States" when used in a geographical sense for the purposes of these acts, as "the Continental United States, Alaska, Hawaii, Puerto Rico, Guam and the Virgin Islands of the United States." "Outlying Possessions" is defined to mean American Samoa and Swains Island.

§ 80. **Persons excluded as not "subject to the jurisdiction."** What qualification upon citizenship by birth is introduced by the phrase, "and subject to the jurisdiction thereof?" This has been judicially explained to exclude from citizenship five classes of persons who have been actually born within the territorial limits of the United States. The exclusion of four of these classes results from the rules of public international law in view of which the Fourteenth Amendment was adopted and in the light of which it has to be interpreted. The fifth class is one peculiar to our own government, but having an origin and history that as fully entitle it to exclusion as the other four.

§ 81. **(a) Children of diplomatic representatives.** By a fiction of international law each organized government, in the absence of its own express statute to the contrary, regards the more important diplomatic representatives

---

(3a) U. S. Code. Title 8— § § 501-907.

of foreign governments as remaining subject to their own governments only, despite their actual residence in the country to which they are sent. The children of ambassadors and public ministers, therefore, although born within the United States, are not "subject to the jurisdiction thereof" and so are not citizens of the United States. This exemption, however, does not apply to the children of consuls nor to other foreign agents whose duties are not diplomatic. Of course it would apply to the principal executive officers of foreign nations themselves.

82. **(b) Children born on foreign public vessels.** Similarly the public vessels of a foreign country are deemed by international law to remain subject to the jurisdiction of their own flag, even though wholly within the domestic waters of another country. Children born upon such vessels in United States waters, therefore, are not citizens of the United States. The principal class of public vessels is ships of war, though any other vessel representing the sovereignty of a nation is similarly treated. Private vessels are not within the rule.

§ 83. **(c) Children of public enemies in hostile occupation of territory.** The children of enemies born during the hostile occupation of our territory are not born subject to the jurisdiction of the United States. The place of their birth is not at the time actually subject to our governmental control, and the parents, being hostile enemies, owe no allegiance to our government. This situation existed in Castine and other towns of eastern Maine during the war of 1812, when the eastern part of that state was for some time in the actual control of British troops.

§ 84. (d) **Expatriated persons.** Persons who, though born or naturalized in the United States, have renounced their allegiance to our government with its consent, and have thus dissolved their political connection with the country, are no longer citizens. Such renunciation is called expatriation, and is now permitted, subject to certain qualifications, by most civilized governments. It was expressly recognized by Congress in 1868 (4).

§ 85. (e) **Tribal Indians.** The last class of persons, who, though born within the United States, were not citizens, were the tribal Indians. When the Constitution was adopted, large tracts of territory within the United States were occupied by still powerful Indian tribes, the members of which regarded themselves as owing a direct allegiance to the tribe, rather than to the United States government. In an international sense these tribal Indians were subject to the jurisdiction of the United States because they were within our boundaries and did not owe allegiance to any foreign power, yet our state and national governments had always dealt with these tribes upon the footing of their quasi-independence. Treaties were made with them, defining their commercial and territorial rights, and until very recently all of our government's dealings with the Indian tribes were carried on in this anomalous fashion. Historically, therefore, tribal Indians, so long as the tribal relation continued, were not regarded as subject to the jurisdiction of the United

(4) U. S. R. S. § § 1999-2000X, U. S. Code, Title 8, § § 800-810.

States within the meaning of the citizenship clause of the Fourteenth Amendment. A tribal Indian who voluntarily left his tribe and took up his residence among white citizens in a state, and adopted the habits of civilized life, could not thereby become a citizen of the United States without the consent of Congress (5). But in 1887 a United States statute conferred citizenship upon such Indians as thereafter should separate themselves from their tribes and adopted the habits of civilized life, and in 1924, citizenship was conferred on all Indians born within the United States.

§ 86. **Status of native inhabitants of Territory ceded to United States.** Assuming that the native inhabitants of the territory ceded to the United States do not become citizens unless and until made so by act of Congress, it is apparent that they are not aliens, inasmuch as they owe complete allegiance to our government as the sole sovereign of the territory in which they reside. The United States Supreme Court has so held (6). Their relationship is similar to that of British subjects in the colonies of the British Empire. The word "subjects" is the appropriate term according to international usage, for such persons. But the term is distasteful to Americans. The word "Nationals" has been suggested as a substitute and has been adopted by Congress, in the Nationality Act of 1940 (7) and in the Immigration and Nationality Act enacted in 1952 which superseded it.

---

(5) Elk v. Wilkins, 112 U. S. 94.
(6) Gonzales v. Williams, 192 U. S. 1.
(7) U. S. Code. Title 8, § § 501-604.

§ 87. Status of corporations. Corporations are not citizens within the meaning of any clause of the Constitution, except that giving the Federal courts jurisdiction of suits between citizens of different states (8). For the interpretation of this clause, see §363, below.

SECTION 2. NATURALIZATION.

§ 88. Exclusive power of Federal government over national citizenship. Article I, section 8, § 4 of the United States Constitution gives Congress power to establish a uniform rule of naturalization. It was decided in 1817 that this power was of such a nature that it ought to be exercised exclusively by the United States, although the Constitution does not expressly deny it to the states (9). Another section of the Constitution (Article IV, section 2) requires each state to grant to the citizens of other states all privileges in it that it permits to its own citizens, and it was naturally thought that a single state, without the consent of the others, ought not to be allowed to confer full national citizenship upon aliens who might then demand the rights of citizens in any other state in the Union.

The present naturalization laws of the United States fix the eligibility for naturalization as follows: ''The right of a person to become a naturalized citizen of the United States shall not be denied or abridged because of race or sex or because such person is married.'' This provision

(8) Paul v. Virginia, 8 Wall. 168.
(9) Chirac v. Chirac, 2 Wheat, 259.

applies not only to those whose applications for naturalization are filed after the effective date of the Immigration and Naturalization Act—but also to those whose applications were pending at that time (10).

§ 89. **Collective naturalization.** Although statutes commonly require aliens to become naturalized by making individual application to some court or officer and swearing allegiance to the United States government, they may also be naturalized collectively, without any individual proceedings or the requirement of oaths of allegiance. The act of Congress making United States citizens of Indians who abandon their tribes, mentioned above (§ 85), is an illustration of this. Another is occasionally presented by the terms upon which a new state is admitted to the Union, in which aliens resident therein may be collectively recognized as voters and members of the new political community (11).

§ 90. **Power to confer state citizenship.** Before the Fourteenth Amendment it was admitted that a state might confer a local citizenship, valid within that state, upon any person it pleased. It was only the power to make national citizens who might carry their citizenship into other states, that was exclusively for the Federal government (12). The Fourteenth Amendment now provides that persons born or naturalized within the United States shall not only be citizens of the United States, but citizens of the state wherein they reside. It is arguable

---

(10)   § 311 of the act.
(11)   Boyd v. Thayer, 143 U. S. 135.
(12)   Scott v. Sandford, 19 How. 393, 405-6, 579-80, 586.

that this was intended to provide an exclusive method of obtaining state citizenship, as well as United States citizenship, but probably it has not changed the former rule; at any rate it has not limited the power of Congress to naturalize persons, even though the latter be not at the time of naturalization subject to the jurisdiction of the United States. Children born abroad of American parents, for instance, are made American citizens by an act of Congress, subject of course to the consent of the country in which they are born, during the time of their residence there (13).

SECTION 3. SUFFRAGE.

§ 91. **Early qualifications for state suffrage.** When the newly-born American states set up independent governments in the course of the Revolutionary war, the written constitutions which they adopted contained careful definitions of the inhabitants admitted to the suffrage. In the main, suffrage was restricted to white male freemen, above the age of twenty-one years, who could satisfy a substantial property qualification. In Massachusetts, for instance, voters had to have a freehold estate of the annual income of three pounds, or other estate of the total value of sixty pounds.

§ 92. **Original provisions of Federal Constitution.** The United States Constitution did not purport to interfere with the absolute control of each state over the suffrage of those who voted for state officers. Not only was this left unrestrictedly in the hands of the states, but even

---

(13)   United States v. Wong Kim Ark, 169 U. S. 649, 688.

the qualifications of electors who voted for members of Congress were left in the control of each state by the provision: "The electors in each state shall have the qualifications requisite for electors of the most numerous branch of the state legislature." (Article I, section 2.) Article I, section 4 of the Constitution, provides that "the times, places, and manner of holding elections for senators and representatives shall be prescribed in each state by the legislature thereof; but the Congress may at any time, by law, make or alter such regulations, except as to the places of choosing senators." Under this clause the Federal power to regulate congressional elections was fully upheld during the Reconstruction period under the so-called "Force bill" (14).

As regards presidential electors, the Constitution says (Article II, section 1, §§ 2, 4): "Each state shall appoint, in such manner as the legislature thereof may direct, a number of electors, equal to the whole number of senators and representatives to which the state may be entitled in the Congress; but no senator or representative, or person holding an office of trust or profit under the United States, shall be appointed an elector. . . . The Congress may determine the time of choosing the electors and the day on which they shall give their votes; which day shall be the same throughout the United States." The small control that the Constitution gives to the United States over the election of its chief executive is noticeable. The present method of choosing presidential

---

(14)   Ex parte Yarbrough, 110 U. S., 651.

electors in the states by a direct vote of the people happens to be uniform throughout our states, merely because similar democratic tendencies have been at work in each of them. The present practice depends upon no uniform Federal law, nor could Congress constitutionally enact such a law. At first presidential electors were chosen by the state legislatures, and South Carolina did not abandon this practice until after the Civil war. So completely is the control of this matter left with the states that the United States Supreme Court has said concerning presidential electors: "They are no more officers or agents of the United States than are members of the state legislatures when acting as electors of Federal senators, or the people of the states when acting as electors of representatives in Congress" (15).

§ 93. Constitutional changes affecting suffrage before Fifteenth Amendment. Between 1800 and 1850 the suffrage clauses of most of the American states were changed so as to abolish all property qualifications. Only a few states, however, admitted free negroes to the ballot. The vast political and social changes wrought by the Civil war, which in destroying the Confederacy also dragged down the institution of slavery, affected the right of suffrage throughout the nation. Two important clauses were added to the United States Constitution bearing upon this. In the original Constitution three-fifths of the slaves had been counted in determining the basis of a state's representation in Congress. The second section of the Four-

---

(15)   In re Green, 134 U. S. 377, 379.

teenth Amendment provided that representatives should be apportioned among the states according to their total population, excluding Indians not taxed; but that when the right to vote at state or Federal election was denied to any adult male citizen of the state, except for crime, the state's basis of representation should be proportionately reduced. This left any state free to disfranchise any class of persons it saw fit, as before, but penalized such disfranchisement by a loss of representation in Congress. In a short time, however, racial antagonism in the southern states assumed such an aspect that many persons believed that the negro freeman must be given the ballot for his defence, and this was also advocated by many others from motives of political partisanship. As a result, the Fifteenth Amendment to the Constitution was adopted in 1870 in the words: "The right of citizens of the United States to vote shall not be denied or abridged by the United States, or by any state, on account of race, color, or previous condition of servitude."

§ 94. State limitations upon suffrage since Fifteenth Amendment. The Fifteenth Amendment does not directly confer the right of suffrage upon negroes. So far as this amendment alone is concerned the states are free to restrict the suffrage for state officers, for members of Congress, and for presidential electors in any way they see fit, save only that it must not be on account of race, color, or previous condition of servitude. It does not restrict qualifications of sex, age, education, property, or birth. After the adoption of the Fifteenth Amendment, several states adopted qualifications of education and property, payment of a poll tax, and clauses providing that persons may vote not having these qualifications, provided they are descendants of persons who could vote in any state before January 1, 1867. On January 1, 1867, Negroes could not vote in any of the Southern states and in only four or five other states, where Negroes formed a very small percentage of the population. This so-called "grandfather clause" was held unconstitutional in both municipal (16) and state (16a) elections. In effect, it excluded from the suffrage practically all Negroes who did not satisfy the educational and property tests, while admitting to the suffrage most white persons who registered within the required time. Literally interpreted, it did not in terms exclude anyone on account of race, color, or previous condition of servitude, nor did it in actual operation result in the absolute exclusion of all possible Negro voters, for resident descendants of the few Negroes who could vote in this country in 1867 would be admissible to suffrage as well as whites.

Educational qualifications, such as requiring the ability to read and write, understand and explain any article of the state (16b) or Federal Constitution, which may disfranchise a greater percentage of Negroes than whites, are valid in the absence of a showing that in fact the laws had been applied or administered unconstitutionally (16c). Where such laws have been applied in a discriminatory manner, they are unconstitutional (17). Generally speaking, the privilege of membership in a political party

(16)   Myers v. Anderson, 238 U.S. 1915.
(16a) Guinn v. U.S., 238 U.S. 347.
(16b) Lassiter v. Northhampton County Board of Election, 360 U.S. 45.
(16c) Williams v. Mississippi, 170 U.S. 222.
(17)   Davis v. Schell, 81F. Supp. 872.

is no concern of the state. Where parties' primaries have
become a part of the machinery for choosing state and
national officials, the political party may not exclude
Negroes from voting in its primary (17a), nor may a
private association which conducts its own primary for
public offices and whose successful candidates enter and
win in both the Democratic primary and general election,
exclude Negroes from its primaries on racial grounds
(17b). The Fourteenth Amendment bans racial discrimination in any election, whether conducted in community,
state, or nation, in which public officials are elected or
public issues decided. This constitutional right is not to
be nullified by a state's permitting a private organization to duplicate its election processes for the purpose
and with the effect of excluding Negroes from participation.

§ 95. **Suffrage not a necessary incident of citizenship.**
A few years after the adoption of the Fourteenth amendment a case was carried to the United States Supreme
Court from Missouri, based upon that clause of the Fourteenth Amendment which provides: "No state shall make
or enforce any law which shall abridge the privileges or
immunities of citizens of the United States." The plaintiff, a woman, claimed that the right to vote for presidential electors, congressmen, and other officers, was a privilege of citizens of the United States, of whom she was
one, and that the Missouri state constitution unconstitutionally restricted the suffrage to male citizens. The
court decided that, while there was no doubt that women
might be citizens of the United States and of a state,

(17a) Smith v. Allwright, 321 U.S. 649.
(17b) Terry v. Adams, 345 U.S. 461.

either by birth or by naturalization, there was no ground for the claim that the right of suffrage was a privilege necessarily attaching to citizenship. From the time of the adoption of the Constitution qualifications for voting had been prescribed by the states, under the Constitution, and at no place had these qualifications ever been the same as for citizenship. Requirements of age, sex, property, religious belief, and education had always excluded a large majority of citizens from the suffrage in various states (18).

§ 96. **Relation of suffrage limitations to congressional representation.** The Fourteenth Amendment requires Congress to reduce proportionately the representation of states that deny the suffrage to adult male citizens for other reasons than participation in crime. In recent years various suffrage qualifications have much reduced the numbers of electors in several states, but it is argued that the suffrage is not really denied to a person when a qualification is imposed that can be rather easily met. A requirement that a voter register, for instance, or the ability to read and write, or the payment of a small poll tax, or perhaps the requirement of a small property qualification can in the main be so readily met that it does not amount to a denial or abridgement of the suffrage in the sense of the Fourteenth Amendment. There is enough strength in this position to leave the matter in genuine doubt, but this argument could scarcely be applied to such a requirement as discriminating in favor of persons whose ancestors could vote on a certain prior date. Such disability is as permanent as race or color itself.

§ 96a. **The Nineteenth Amendment.** This amendment,

---

(18)   Minor v. Happersett, 21 Wall. 162.

which was adopted in 1920, provided that the right of citizens of the United States to vote shall not be denied or abridged by the United States or by any state on account of sex.

SECTION 4. MISCELLANEOUS POLITICAL RIGHTS.

§ 97. Republican form of government, invasion, and domestic violence. "The United States shall guarantee to every state in this Union a republican form of government, and shall protect each of them against invasion; and on application of the legislature, or of the executive (when the legislature cannot be convened) against domestic violence" (19).

It has been suggested that a republican form of government in this provision is intended to be distinguished from monarchical forms on the one side and those of pure democracy on the other, the government by chosen representatives being the principal distinguishing mark (20). If a state chooses to establish and use the initiative and referendum largely in legislation, would such a government be republican? The affirmative answer can scarcely be doubted (20a). A local referendum upon various questions like liquor selling or the issue of bonds has often been upheld.

Where there are competing governments in the same state it rests with the political departments of the United States to decide which one is legitimate and the courts will not revise this determination (21).

---

(19) Const., Art. IV, sec. 4.
(20) Cooley, Constitutional Law, 213.
(20a) Pacific Sts. Co. v. Oregon, 223 U. S. 118.
(21) Luther v. Borden, 7 How. 1.

§ 98.   **Freedom of speech and press.** ''[Congress shall make no law] abridging the freedom of speech or of the press'' (22).

The freedom of speech and press secured by the First Amendment against abridgment by the Federal government is similarly protected by the due process clause of the Fourteenth Amendment against abridgment by state action (23), including state action in the form of municipal ordinances adopted under state authority (24).

The constitutional right embraces the liberty to discuss publicly and truthfully all matters of public concern without previous restraint (prior to publication) or censorship (25) or fear of subsequent punishment (26). It covers every sort of publication which affords a vehicle of information and opinion, such as newspapers, movies, plays, television, radio broadcasting, periodicals, books, pamphlets and leaflets (27). It covers the publication, and even the distribution (28) and right to receive the matter distributed (29), as both are essential to the freedom of publishing. All ideas having even the slightest social importance whether unorthodox, controversial or even ideas hateful to the prevailing climate of opinion have the full

(22)   Const., Amend. 1.
(23)   Hughes v. Superior Court of Calif., 339 U.S. 460.
(24)   Staub v. Baxley, 335 U.S. 312.
(25)   Patterson v. Colorado, 205 U.S. 454.
(26)   Thornhill v. Alabama, 310 U.S. 88.
(27)   Lovell v. Griffin, 303 U.S. 444.
(28)   303 U.S. 444.
(29)   Martin v. Struthers, 319 U.S. 141.

protection of the constitutional guaranties unless excludable because they infringe on more important interests (30). The right extends to freedom of association (31) and the right to picket. It is designed to secure freedom of public and private discussion, especially in regard to political matters, as may be necessary for the proper formation of public opinion.

The right of free speech and press is not absolute and unlimited at all times and under all circumstances, even as to prior restraints (32). This constitutional provision "does not permit the publication of libels, blasphemous or indecent articles, or other publications injurious to public morals or private reputations (33). The constitutional guaranties will not protect a man who falsely shouts "Fire" in a theater and causes a panic (34), nor would it prevent the expulsion of hecklers from assemblies or permit religious worship to be disturbed by those desirous of preaching atheism (35). The state in the exercise of its police power may limit the exercise of this right, just as it regulates and limits other rights of person and property. It may restrict the right so as to prevent its exercise from resulting in imminent danger to the public order or threats to its own existence. The test used to determine whether an utterance may be re-

---

(30) Roth v. U.S., 354 U.S. 476.
(31) NAACP v. Alabama, 357 U.S. 449.
(32) Kingsley Books, Inc. v. Brown, 354 U.S. 436.
(33) Robertson v. Baldwin, 165 U.S. 275, 281.
      See, as to injunctions, Gompers v. Buck's Stove Co.,
      221 U.S. 418; Marx Co. v. Watson, 168 Mo. 133;
      Lindsay v. Mont., Fed. Labor 37 Mont. 264.
(34) Schencks v. U.S., 249 U.S. 47.
(35) Kovacs v. Cooper, 336 U.S. 77.

stricted is whether there is a (1) substantial probability
that (2) great harm will result and (3) that freedom of
expression of necessity must be limited to prevent the
harm. In the words of Chief Justice Holmes—"The
question in every case is whether the words used are used
in such circumstances and are of such a nature as to
create a *clear and present danger* that they will bring
about the substantive evils that Congress has a right to
prevent. "It is a question of proximity and degree."

The liability of private individuals for defamatory
spoken or written utterances is dealt with fully in the
article on Torts, Chapter VIII, contained in Volume II
of this work.

A statute limiting free speech may be invalid for one
of two reasons—it may be void on its face, irrespective
of its application in a particular case, or it may be invalid
because of the application in a particular case, though
valid if applied to a different fact situation. A statute is
void on its face where it does not aim specifically at evils
which may be controlled, and hence operates as an over-
hanging threat to free discussion, or where upon its face
it is so vague and indefinite as to permit the punishment
of the fair use of the right of free speech, or where the
sweeping and inexact terms of a statute disclose a threat
to freedom of speech inherent in its existence.

§ 98a. **Freedom and loyalty of employees.** The loyalty programs of the Federal and State governments
within recent years have raised serious questions regarding the constitutional freedom of employees. Thus, to
what extent may an employee, as a condition of his employment, be required to surrender certain constitutional

rights? The question arises in two situations: (1) where there is legislation prohibiting government employees from engaging in certain political activity and (2) where regulations have been designed to keep people of doubtful loyalty from public positions.

It is situations in Class 2 that have given rise to most litigation and will be discussed herein. The validity of loyalty programs requiring oaths has been frequently challenged on grounds that such oaths violate the constitutional guaranties of freedom of thought, speech and religion, that they are unconstitutionally vague, that they violate Article 6 of the Federal Constitution which requires an oath to support the Constitution (the argument being that this oath excludes others) and that they are bills of attainder or ex post facto laws.

Post-loyalty test oath requirements which impose punishment on persons unable to take them solely because of their past associations or conduct prior to the enactment of the requirement, have been struck down by the Supreme Court of the United States as a bill of attainder or ex post facto law. These decisions generally involved Civil War and reconstruction period statutes designed to deny certain rights, activities and privileges to those who had supported the Confederacy (36)! Present anticommunist oath and affidavit legislation which is upheld have been distinguished from the Civil War cases on the grounds that the latter were designed to punish for past acts, while the present legislation is designed to either prevent future action or provides a standard of conduct

---

(36)   Cummings v. Missouri, 4 Wall. 333.

or qualification for public and professional employment and imposes no punishment (37).

Congress, as well as the states, has enacted loyalty oath requirements, varying in their particular items and applicability but generally containing similar provisions: an oath expressed in such terms that the person taking it affirms that he isn't a member of or affiliated with a particular organization or type of organization either designated as the Communist Party or as any other organization teaching the doctrine of the violent overthrow of the government or its overthrow by any other unlawful means, or that the person doesn't believe in such doctrine.

§ 98a-1. Anti-communist oaths and the dismissal of public officers and employees. The discharge of a public employee for his refusal to answer questions of his employer as to his subversive activities has generally been held not to violate due process (38). In these cases, there is generally a state constitutional provision, a statute, or administrative ruling expressly requiring the removal or providing for the termination of employment of specified public officers or employees upon a refusal to testify or to waive immunity in certain types of proceedings or investigations. The basis for the dismissal is that refusal to testify is evidence of incompetency, insubordination, a violation of duty, or unprofessional conduct. The same result has been reached without the aid of rule or statute specifically requiring such testimony (statute may pro-

---

(37)   American Comm. Assoc. v. Douds, 339 U.S. 382;
        Garner v. Board of Public Works, 341 U.S. 716.
(38)   Beilan v. Board of Public Education, 357 U.S. 399.

vide for the dismissal of an employee for conduct unbecoming a person in his position and other good causes) (39).

Where a public employee was discharged for refusing to answer questions propounded by a legislative committee, as distinguished from his employer, there appear to be two lines of authority. The court in Slochower v. Board of Higher Education (40) said that where a municipal statute requires the discharge without notice or hearing of a municipal employee who claimed the privilege of self-incrimination, it violates the due process clause of the Fourteenth Amendment when applied to a municipal employee testifying before a congressional committee investigating matters affecting national security and having no relation to municipal activities. The court pointed out that in effect the statute operated to discharge every municipal employee exercising his constitutional privilege of invoking the Fifth Amendment and was an arbitrary exclusion of a public servant pursuant to a statute and prohibited in Wieman v. Updegraff (see below).

However, the court in Nelson v. Los Angeles County (41) upheld the discharge by the County Board of a public employee who refused to answer questions propounded by the House Unamerican Activities Committee; the grounds for discharge were insubordination (California statute made it mandatory for a public employee to answer questions relating to his subversive

---

(39) Faxon v. School Committee of Boston, 120 N.E. 2d 772.
(40) Slochower v. Board of Higher Education, 350 U.S. 551.
(41) Nelson v. Los Angeles County, 262 U.S. 1.

activities on pain of discharge). The court distinguished
the cases on the ground that in the Nelson case the cause
for discharge was the insubordination of the employee
in failing to give information which the state had a
legitimate interest in securing, but in the Slochower case,
the employee was discharged for invoking the Fifth
Amendment, which amounted to punishment for exercising a constitutional right.

A leading case in this area is Wieman v. Updegraff
(42), which involved an Oklahoma statute. The statute,
which made mandatory a noncommunist oath as a condition of continued employment, contained a clause saying "that within the five years immediately preceding
the taking of this oath . . . I have not been a member of
. . . any agency, party, organization, . . . which has been
officially determined . ... to be a communist front or subversive organization. . . ." The Supreme Court of the
United States struck down the statute as a violation of
due process because it created a conclusive presumption
of disloyalty of one who had been a member of or affiliated with a proscribed organization, regardless of that
person's knowledge at the time of membership of the
purpose and nature of such organization, ". . . membership [in a subversive organization] may be innocent.
A state servant may have joined a proscribed organization unaware of its activities and purposes.

"In recent years, many completely loyal persons have
severed organizational ties after learning for the first
time of the character of the groups to which they had
belonged . . . one of the greatest weaknesses of all Amer-

---

(42)   Wieman v. Updegraff, 344 U.S. 183.

icans, whether Adult or Youth, is to join something . . .
at the time of affiliation, a group may be innocent, only
later coming under the influence of those who would turn
it toward illegitimate ends. Conversely, an organization
formerly subversive and therefore designated as such,,
may have subsequently freed itself from influences which
originally led to its listing, . . . under the Oklahoma Act,
the fact of association alone determines the disloyalty
and disqualification, it matters not whether the association existed knowingly or innocently. To thus inhibit individual freedom of movement is to stifle the flow of
democratic expression and controversy at one of its
chief sources . . .indiscriminate classification of innocent
with knowing activity must fall as an assertion of arbitrary power. The oath offends due process.''

As the court said in Schware v. Board of Bar Examiners (43), just because some party member had illegal
aims and engaged in illegal acts, it can't be automatically
inferred that all members shared their evil purposes or
participated in their evil conduct. (It must be remem-
bered that during the period 1932-1940, the Communist
Party was a lawful political party with candidates on
the ballot in most states.)

A person desiring to run for public office may be required to give a noncommunist or loyalty affidavit (44).
Thus a statute may require a candidate to affirm that he
was not engaged in any way in an attempt to overthrow
the government by force or violence and that he was not
knowingly a member of an organization engaged in such
an attempt.

(43)   Schware v. Board or Bar Examiners, 353 U.S. 232.
(44)   Gerende v. Board of Supervisors, 341 U.S. 56.

§ 98a-2. **Discharge of private employees.** The leading case in this area is Black v. Cutters Laboratories (45), where the question was whether under an employment contract permitting discharge for "just cause," the state courts could deny relief to a person discharged because of Communist Party membership. The Supreme Court of the United States dismissed the writ of certiorari on the ground that no Federal question was presented (thus not on merits). "The court said that the parties to a. collective bargaining agreement may make Communist Party membership 'just cause' for discharge of an employee, and that discharge for that reason is a matter of contract between the union on the one hand and the employee on the other, and that when the contract is enforced, no Federal right is infringed."

§ 98a-3. **Legislative limitations on political activity by government employees.** Congress and the state legislatures have passed legislation designed to restrict the political activity of government employees. The leading case of United Public Workers v. Mitchell (46) involved a provision of the Hatch Act (18 U.S.CA., 1940 ed., Supp. v sec. 61 h) making it unlawful for any employee in the executive branch of the Federal government (with some exceptions) to take an active part in political management or political campaigns. The Supreme Court upheld the provision as applied to a government employee who, after working hours, was a ward committeeman of a political party. Similar state statutes have been upheld (47). Federal legislation prohibiting certain Federal em-

---

(45)   351 U.S. 292.

(46)   330 U.S. 75.

(47)   McAutiffe v. Mayor of New Bedford, 155 Mass. 216.

ployees from making political contributions to other government employees, or receiving such from them, have been upheld. The purpose of such legislation, as succinctly stated by the majority in Ex Parte Curtis (48), is not to forbid all political activity. "It is only partisan political activity that is interdicted. It is active participation in political management and political campaigns. Expressions, public or private, on public affairs, personalities and matters of public interest, not an object of party action, are unrestricted by law so long as the government employee does not direct his activities toward party success."

§ 98b. **Subversive speech and association.** Although the constitutional guarantee of freedom of speech is very broad, its protection does not extend to seditious utterances or those utterances which endanger national security in time of war. The wartime cases (World War I) of Schenck v. U.S. (249 U.S. 47) and Debs v. U.S. (249 U.S. 211) are illustrative of this. Both cases involved the Espionage Act of 1917, which made it punishable by fine and imprisonment to willfully obstruct the recruiting or enlistment or to encourage insubordination, disloyalty or refusal to duty in the Armed Forces. In the Schenck case, the defendants had sent circulars to draftees urging them not to "submit to intimidation" and to assert their opposition to the draft. The lower court had found that the circulars calculated to cause insubordination in the Armed Forces and to obstruct recruiting and enlistment.

_____

(48)   Ex Parte Curtis 106 U.S. 371.

In the Debs case, Debs had spoken to a convention of Socialists approving the conduct of other persons who had been convicted of obstructing the draft. The court here found that the purpose and probable effect of the speech was to affect recruiting, even though incidentally. The Supreme Court affirmed the defendants' conviction in both cases. "We admit that in many places and in ordinary times the defendants in saying all that was said . . . would have been within their constitutional rights. . . . The character of every act depends upon the circumstances in which it is done. . . . When a nation is at war, many things that might be said in time of peace are such a hindrance to its effort that their utterance will not be endured so long as men fight and that no court could regard them as protected by any Constitutional right . . . the question in every case is whether the words used are used in such circumstances and are of such a nature as to create a clear and present danger that they will bring about the substantive evils that Congress has a right to prevent (49)."

However, mere participation in peaceable assembly for lawful discussion cannot be made a crime nor can those who assist in the conduct of such meetings be branded as criminals, even though it is a meeting of the Communist Party, where there is no incitement to violence (50). "The very idea of a government republican in form implies a right on the part of its citizens to meet peaceably for consultation in respect to public affairs and to petition for grievances" (51).

---

(49)   Schenck v. U.S., 249 U.S. 47.

(50)   De Jonge v. Oregon, 299 U.S. 353 (Oregon Criminal Syndicalism Act).

(51)   U.S. v. Cruickshank, 92 U.S. 542.

But in Dennis v. U.S., the court said that a conspiracy to organize the Communist Party for the purpose of teaching and advocating the forcible overthrow of the Government of the United States may present a clear and present danger not protected by the Constitution (52). The court upheld the constitutionality of the Smith Act, saying that Congress has the power to protect the government from armed rebellion, it being sufficient evil for Congress to prevent. The Smith Act did not violate the Constitution because it was aimed at "advocacy," not discussion.

The line of distinction between "discussion" and "advocacy" is thin. The court in Yates v. U.S. (53) attempted to set forth a test. They said that mere advocacy of forcible overthrow of the government, as an abstract doctrine, is not punishable per se under the Smith Act, even though uttered with the hope that it may ultimately lead to violent revolution. It is the advocacy which incites to illegal action that is not protected by the Constitution, as set forth in the Dennis case. "The essence of the Dennis holding was that indoctrination of a group in preparation for future violent action, as well as exhortation to immediate action, by advocacy found to be directed to 'action for the accomplishment' of forcible overthrow, to violence 'as a rule or principle of action,' and employing 'language of incitement,' is not constitutionally protected when the group is of sufficient size and cohesiveness, is sufficiently oriented towards action, and other circumstances are such as reasonably to justify apprehension that action will occur" (54).

---

(52)   Dennis v. U.S., 341 U.S. 494.

(53)   Yates v. U.S., 354 U.S. 298.

(54)   Yates v. U.S., 354 U.S. 298.

In some recent cases involving segregation, the courts have held that an organization's membership list may be immune from state scrutiny because it would inhibit the members' right to freedom of association (55) ". . . (where there is) an uncontroverted showing that on past occasions revelation of the identity of its rank and file members has exposed them to economic reprisals, loss of employment, threats of physical coercion, and other manifestations of public hostility, . . . we think it apparent that compelled disclosure of petitioner's Alabama membership is likely to affect adversely the ability of petitioner and its members to pursue their collective effort to foster beliefs which they admittedly have a right to advocate, in that it may induce members to withdraw from the association and dissuade others from joining it because of fear of exposure of their beliefs shown through their association and of the consequences of this exposure (56)."

·§ 98c. Censorship. The constitutional guarantee of freedom of speech and press is not an unlimited right. Words which are obscene, libelous, or which by their very nature inflict injury or incite to riot are not within the area of constitutionally protected free speech.

Sex and obscenity are not synonymous. Obscene material is material which deals with sex in a manner appealing to prurient interest; i.e., material having a tendency to excite lustful thoughts. The mere portrayal of sex in art, literature and scientific works is not in itself suffi-

---

(55)   N.A.A.C.P. v. Alabama, 357 U.S. 449;
        Bates v. City of Little Rock, 361 U.S. 516.
(56)   Roth v. U.S., 354 U.S. 476 (1957).

cient to deny material the constitutional protection of
freedom of speech and press. ''Sex, a great and myster-
ious motive force in human life, has indisputably been
a subject of absorbing interest to mankind through the
ages; it is one of the vital problems of human interest
and public concern. . . . The freedom of speech and of
the press guaranteed by the Constitution embraces at
least the liberty to discuss publicly and truthfully all
matters of public concern without prior restraint or fear
of subsequent punishment.'' The proper test used to determine whether matter is obscene is whether to the
average person applying contemporary community standards, the dominant theme of the material in question
taken as a whole (rather than the effect of an isolated
passage on the most susceptible persons) appeals to
prurient interests (56a).

Pursuant to its police power, a state may enact censorship legislation. ''Censorship'' means any examination of thought or expression in order to prevent publication of objectionable material or the actual forbidding
of publication in advance of publication (prior restraint)
or punishment for the expression of thought. Both state
(57) and Federal (58) censorship legislation have been
upheld, where the statute in question contains a proper
standard for the regulation of objectionable material.
Thus, a Federal statute providing that obscene, lewd,
lascivious, filthy or indecent material is nonmailable
and that whoever knowingly deposits such material for
mailing or delivery is criminally punishable, has been

(56a) 357 U.S. 449.
(57)   360 U.S. 525.
(58)   184 F2d 153.

upheld (59). Similarly, a California statute making criminally punishable every person who willfully and lewdly writes or otherwise produces obscene or indecent material, or who writes or otherwise produces any notice or advertisement of any such material, has been upheld (60). However, a municipal ordinance making it a criminal offence for any person to have in his possession an obscene or indecent writing or books, in a place of business where books were sold or kept for sale, without knowledge by the defendant of the books' content, for the possession of which he was convicted, was held unconstitutional (61).

§ 98c-1. **Plays and shows.** Moving pictures, like newspapers, magazines, radio, and television are included in the "press" whose freedom is guaranteed by the Federal Constitution. Under its police power, a state has authority to regulate the showing of motion pictures and this authority may be conferred on municipalities, who in turn may delegate it to boards of censors or to a single censor (355 Supreme Court 387). The municipality may require the obtaining of a license before a public showing, but where the authority is vested in a board of censors or individual censors, there must be a definite standard in the ordinance delegating the power, which doesn't give the person authorized to issue the license a wide latitude in the discretion to be used in issuing or refusing to issue a permit. Standards held too vague or indefinite include "sexual immorality" (62), "not ac-

---

(59)   Roth v. U.S., 354 U.S. 476.
(60)   Alberts v. California, 354 U.S. 476.
(61)   Smith v. California, 361 U.S. 147.
(62)   360 U.S. 689.

ceptable to standards of decency, with immorality featured and dialogue unfit'' (63), ''harmful'' (64), ''immoral'' (65), ''sacrilegious'' (66), ''cruel, obscene, indecent or immoral, or such as tend to debase or corrupt morals'' (67).

Plays are also a form of speech and expression protected by state and Federal constitutions. However, the performance of an outright lewd and indecent play or show is not protected by the constitutional guarantee of free speech (Adams Theatre Co. v. Keenan 12 N.J. 267).

§ 98c-2. **Prior restraints.** Generally speaking, any regulation which subjects communications to license infringes the right of free speech, whatever its motive. Further, it is unconstitutional for states to empower courts to issue a permanent injunction against the dissemination of future issues of a publication because prior issues had been found offensive (68). However, every prior restraint is not unconstitutional (69).

In Kingsley Books, Inc. v. Brown (70), it was held that a statute providing for (1) the issuance of a temporary injunction to prevent distribution of obscene matter, (2) a speedy hearing, (3) the issuance of a permanent injunction and destruction of material found obscene, was a valid regulation of obscenity. Further, although a city has the power to impose a system of prior

(63)   355 U.S. 37.
(64)   346 U.S. 587.
(65)   346 U.S. 587.
(66)   Burstyn v. Wilson, 343 U.S. 495.
(67)   350 U.S. 876.
(68)   Near v. Minnesota, 283 U.S. 697.
(69)   Times Film Corp. v. City of Chicago, 81 Sup. Ct. 391.
(70)   354 U.S. 436.

restraints, the procedures it uses may violate the due process clause of the Fourteenth Amendment (71).

§ 98c-3. **Right to picket.** The constitutional guarantee of free speech also embraces the right to picket peacefully so as to inform the public as to the fact of a labor dispute. This guarantee prevents a state from forbidding or enjoining all picketing, regardless of the purpose and circumstances (72) or solely because under the common or statutory law no labor dispute was involved (73) or from making it a criminal offense for a picket to distribute handbills containing information on a labor dispute with an employer on a public street in front of an employer's place of business (74). Nor may picketing be enjoined because of disassociated acts of past violence (75) or other isolated incidents of abuse (76).

The Fourteenth Amendment doesn't make it unconstitutional for a state to regulate or enjoin mass picketing (77), picketing using force and violence (78) (which would otherwise be unlawful) (79) or peaceful picketing, where previous acts of violence neither isolated nor disassociated, by members of the picketing union or their sympathizers give a coercive effect (80). Picketing which is carried on for an illegal purpose may also be enjoined. Examples of picketing for illegal purposes

(71)   Zenith International Film Corp. v. City of Chicago, 291 F2d 785.
(72)   Thornhill v. Alabama, 310 U.S. 88.
(73)   Cafeteria Employees Union v. Angelos, 320 U.S. 293.
(74)   Snyder v. Milwaukee, 308 U.S. 147.
(75)   312 U.S. 287.
(76)   320 U.S. 293.
(77)   310 U.S. 88.
(78)   312 U.S. 287.
(79)   Giboney v. Empire Storage and Ice Co., 336 U.S. 490.
(80)   312 U.S. 287.

are: For the purpose of compelling a store owner to hire Negro clerks in proportion to its Negro customers (81); for the purpose of compelling an employer to force his employees to join the picketing union against the employees' expressed desires not to (82); compelling an employer who conducts his business without any outside help to adopt a union shop and join a union (83).

§ 99. **Right of assembly and petition.** ''[Congress shall make no law abridging] the right of the people peaceably to assemble, and to petition the government for a redress of grievances'' (84). This is a right incident to Federal citizenship, but under the Fourteenth Amendment it has been equated to freedom of speech under the reasoning that such a right is necessarily incident to giving effect to a right of speech. Most of the cases which have arisen in this area deal with municipal or state ordinances requiring a license to speak, assemble or distribute literature. Most states or municipalities have such requirements and they are held invalid if used as a means of prohibition or censorship, or if they give to officials a discretionary power not limited by a reasonable and definite standard as to when and to whom the license may be issued.

Statutes requiring the obtaining of a license to speak, assemble or distribute literature and which give officials a discretionary power as to their issuance have been held invalid as applied to: Distributors of religious handbills (85), door-to-door solicitors of religious converts

---

(81)   Hughes v. Superior Court of California, 339 U.S. 460.

(82)   International Union v. Gazzan, 339 U.S. 532.

(83)   International Brotherhood of Teamsters v. Hanke, 339 U.S. 470.

(84)   Const., Amend. I.

(85)   Lovell v. City of Griffin, 303 U.S. 444.

(86), arbitrary refusal to permit either the use of a park for religious services (87) or use of loudspeakers at an outdoor meeting (88), requiring a union organizer to get a permit before he can speak (89), and door-to-door distribution of religious tracts (90).

However, statutes applied to or requiring commercial solicitors to get a permit (91) or prohibiting the distribution of commercial advertising on any public place within a city (92) have been upheld. Requiring a permit for parades or use of parks where the purpose is just to allow allocation of space or to control traffic) (93), prohibiting certain loudspeaker systems (those instruments emitting loud and raucous noises) from the streets (94), and other similar ordinances containing a definite, ascertainable and reasonable standard have been upheld.

Neither in terms nor in spirit does this provision prevent the government forbidding disorderly assemblages, or those at improper times or places.

§ **100. Right to bear arms.** ''A well regulated militia being necessary to the security of a free state, the right of the people to keep and bear arms shall not be infringed'' (95).

This provision and similar ones in the state constitutions refer only to such keeping and bearing of arms as

---

(86) Cantwell v. Connecticut, 310 U.S. 296.

(87) Niemotko v. Maryland, 340 U.S. 268.

(88) Saia v. New York, 334 U.S. 558.

(89) Thomas v. Collins, 323 U.S. 516.

(90) Martin v. Struthers, 319 U.S. 141.

(91) Beard v. Alexandria, 341 U.S. 622.

(92) Valentine v. Chrestensen, 316 U.S. 52.

(93) Cox v. New Hampshire, 312 U.S. 569.

(94) Kovacs v. Cooper, 336 U.S. 77.

(95) Const., Amend. II.

may be necessary to preserve liberty. It does not prevent the prohibition of weapons usually employed in private affrays, nor the prohibition of carrying concealed weapons altogether (96).

---

(96)   State v. Workman, 35 West Va. 372.

CHAPTER V.

§ 101. **Constitutional history of slavery in United States.** When the Constitution was being framed in 1787, slaves and their labor were of sufficient importance to the southern states to make the existence of slavery a source of disagreement in the Philadelphia convention, and several important clauses of the completed instrument bear witness to the influence of these controversies. Probably some natural feeling of repugnance excluded the words "slave" or "slavery" from the original Constitution and its early amendments, but in several places the institution was obviously referred to by circumlocutions. (See Article I, section 2, §3; section 9, §1; Article IV, section 2, § 3.)

By the Missouri compromise of 1820, by which Missouri was admitted to the Union, Congress forbade the existence of slavery in any of the territories north of 36° 30′ north latitude. The Constitution gave the United States no control over slavery as a domestic institution within a state, and the political controversies over the institution, that marked the generation between 1820 and the Civil war, raged about the policy and power of Congress to prohibit its existence in territory not yet admitted into the Union, and the recovery of fugitive slaves

86

from the free states. In the famous Dred Scott case a majority of the Supreme Court of the United States were of the opinion, though this was not necessary to the decision of the case, that the Missouri Compromise act was unconstitutional in so far as it forbade slave owners from taking their slaves into the territories of the United States. Congress being forbidden to take property without due process of law, it was reasoned that a slave owner was as much entitled to be protected in his slave property in the territories, as if he were the owner of a wagon and mules (1). The Civil war speedily followed, and its first constitutional fruit was the enactment of the Thirteenth Amendment, which prohibited slavery or involuntary servitude, except as a punishment for persons convicted of crime, within the United States or any place subject to their jurisdiction. This amendment became effective December 18, 1865. See §69, above.

§ 102. **What constitutes slavery? Compulsory service of sailor.** There have been few cases judicially construing this amendment. In Robertson v. Baldwin (2), in 1897, the question arose whether a seaman who had voluntarily agreed to complete a voyage could be constitutionally compelled to return to his ship against his will before the completion of the voyage. The question was thus stated by the court:

"Does the epithet 'involuntary' attach to the word 'servitude' continuously, and make illegal any service which becomes involuntary at any time during its exis-

---

(1) Dred Scott v. Sandford, 19 How. 393.
(2) Robertson v. Baldwin, 165 U. S. 275.

tence; or does it attach only at the inception of the servitude, and characterize it as unlawful because unlawfully entered into? . . . The prohibition of slavery in the Thirteenth Amendment is well known to have been adopted with reference to a state of affairs which had existed in certain states of the Union since the foundation of the government, while the addition of the words 'involuntary servitude' were said in the Slaughterhouse cases, 16 Wall. 36, to have been intended to cover the system of Mexican peonage and the Chinese coolie trade, the practical operation of which might have been a revival of the institution of slavery under a different and less offensive name. It is clear, however, that the amendment was not intended to introduce any novel doctrine with respect to certain descriptions of service which have always been treated as exceptional, such as military and naval enlistments; or to disturb the right of parents and guardians to the custody of their minor children or wards.''

The court then showed that the contract of a sailor had always been treated as exceptional and the sailor compellable not to desert during the continuance of the voyage, and therefore decided the Thirteenth Amendment did not apply.

§ 103. Same: **Compulsory service to discharge debt.** In Clyatt v. United States (3), the question was considered whether the Thirteenth Amendment applied to the compulsory enforcement of a person's agreement to

---

(3) 197 U. S. 207.

render service in the discharge of a debt, sometimes called peonage. The court said:

"What is peonage? It may be defined as a status or condition of compulsory service, based upon the indebtedness of the peon to the master. . . . Peonage is sometimes classified as voluntary or involuntary, but this implies simply a difference in the mode of origin, but none in the character of the servitude. The one exists where the debtor voluntarily contracts to enter the service of his creditor. The other is forced upon the debtor by some provision of law. But peonage, however created, is compulsory service, involuntary servitude. A clear distinction exists between peonage and the voluntary performance of labor or rendering of services in payment of a debt. In the latter case the debtor, though contracting to pay his indebtedness by labor or service, and subject like any other contractor to an action for damages for breach of that contract, can elect at any time to break it, and no law or force compels performance or a continuance of the service. We need not stop to consider any possible limits or exceptional cases, such as the service of a sailor, or the obligations of a child to its parents, or of an apprentice to his master, or the power of the legislature to make unlawful and punish criminally an abandonment by an employe of his post of labor in any extreme cases." The court therefore held such involuntary service to be slavery and forbidden by the Constitution.

§ 104. **Same: Imprisonment for breach of labor contract.** At one time, South Carolina had a statute punishing by fine and imprisonment any one who wilfully and without just cause broke a contract to labor on farm land. The Federal district court in South Carolina held this was substantially the same as peonage, because compelling the laborer, under penalty of imprisonment, to continue in involuntary servitude (4). The United States Supreme Court later decided in a case from Alabama that the breach of a contract to render personal service may not be made criminal without violating the Thirteenth Amendment (4a).

§ 104a. **Racial discrimination.**   Statutes upholding segregation have generally been attacked on the basis that there has been a denial of equal protection of the laws. Since every statute involves some classification of persons of different classes receiving different treatment, every law gives, to some extent, unequal treatment. The equal protection clause of the Fourteenth Amendment requires (1) a reasonable basis for the classification, in light of social, economic and historic fact, (2) proper purpose, and (3) that everyone in like circumstances be treated equally.

§ 104b. **Separate but equal doctrine.**   In Plessy v. Ferguson (a case concerned with segregated facilities on railroad carriers) (4b), the court held that segregation per se was not a denial of equal protection of the law because the doctrine applies equally to both parties —the Negroes could not use the white man's facilities and the latter couldn't use the Negroes'. It was only when one race or the other was supplied with less de-

---

(4)   Ex parte Drayton, 153 Fed. 986.
(4a)   Bailey v. Alabama, 219 U.S. 219.
(4b)   Plessy v. Ferguson, 163 U.S. 537.

sirable physical facilities than the other that a denial of equal rights occurred.

This doctrine was subject to gradual erosion through a series of cases (4c), but it was the leading case of Brown v. Board of Education (4d) which sounded its death knell. The court in the Brown case held that the doctrine of separate but equal doesn't apply to public education. The court thus is following Justice Harlan's dissent in Plessy v. Ferguson, where he said: "Our Constitution is color-blind, and neither knows nor tolerates classes among citizens."

The "separate but equal doctrine" has been abolished in public transportation (4e), in the use of public recreational facilities (4f) (such as parks, beaches, golf courses), and bus terminal restaurants (4g). Statutes preventing interracial athletic contests (4h), placing the word "Negro" after a candidate's name on a primary election ballot (4i), designed to prevent integration of public schools (4j), and a statute altering the shape of a city's boundaries so as to remove all but a few Negro votes (4k), have been held unconstitutional.

(4c) 305 U.S. 337 (separate facilities must be provided within the segregating state itself); 339 U.S. 629 (law schools are not equal unless intangible factors such as reputation and tradition are equal); 339 U.S. 637 (once a Negro was admitted to an all-white school, he must be allowed to mingle freely with other students).

(4d) Brown v. Board of Education, 347 U.S. 483.

(4e) Brown v. Gayle, 142 F. Supp. 707, aff. 352 U.S. 903.

(4f) St. Petersburg v. Alsup, 353 U.S. 922.

(4g) Boynton v. Virginia, 264 U.S. 454.

(4h) State Athletic Com. v. Dorsey, 359 U.S. 533.

(4i) Key v. McDonald, 350 U.S. 895 (1955).

(4j) U.S. v. Louisiana, 364 U.S. 500.

(4k) Gomillion v. Lightfoot, 364 U.S. 339 (violated the 15th Amendment).

In Shelley v. Kraemer (4l), state judicial enforcement
of private racially-restrictive covenants as to the ownership of property were held to be (1) state action and (2)
a denial of equal protection of the law. A classification
based on race in determining the ownership of property
within a state is arbitrary and unreasonable. In the
words of Chief Justice Vinson, "It is, therefore, no answer to . . . say that the courts may also be induced to
deny white persons rights of ownership and occupancy
on grounds of race or color. Equal protection of the laws
is not achieved through indiscriminate imposition of in-
equalities. . . ." The Fourteenth Amendment also prohibits a state court from entertaining an action for damages against one who signed but broke a racial restrictive covenant (4m).

In a companion case, Bolling v. Sharpe (District of
Columbia public school) (4n) it was held that the right
not to be segregated in public schools was so fundamental and pervasive, that it was embodied in the concept of due process of law.

The holding of the Brown case was further expanded
in Cooper v. Aaron (4o), where the court refused to delay the enforcement of a local school board's plan to in-
tegrate public schools because of public hostility. "To
yield to such a claim would be to enthrone official lawlessness and lawlessness if not checked is the precursor
of anarchy. On the few tragic occasions in the history

(4l)   334 U.S. 1.

(4m) Barrows v. Jackson, 346 U.S. 249 (1953).

(4n) Bolling v. Sharpe, 347 U.S. 497.

(4o) Cooper v. Aaron, 358 U.S. 1.

of the nation when law was forcibly resisted or systematically evaded, it has signaled the breakdown of constitutional processes of government on which ultimately rest the liberties of all. Violent resistance to law cannot be made a legal reason for its suspension without loosening the fabric of our society.''

The Cooper case establishes the following principles: (1) The Fourteenth Amendment forbids the states to use their governmental powers to bar children on racial grounds from attending schools where there is state participation through any arrangement, management, funds or property; (2) in ending segregation, the school authorities must move ''with all deliberate speed'' and a prompt and reasonable start toward full compliance with the Brown case holding is required; (3) delay in any guise in the integration of public schools is not to be countenanced; (4) constitutional rights of Negro children cannot be nullified openly and directly or indirectly, by the states through their legislative, executive or judicial officers; (5) acts of local school officials are considered state action within the meaning of the Fourteenth Amendment.

It has been held that the refusal of the board of directors of a college to admit qualified Negroes, pursuant to the provisions of the trust fund agreement establishing the college (which granted admittance to ''poor white male orphans'') was unconstitutional state action forbidden by the Fourteenth Amendment, for the board of directors was established by the state's legislature and the settlor named the city of Philadelphia as trustee (4p).

(4p) Pennsylvania v. Board of Directors, 353 U.S. 230.

§ 105. Religious liberty. "Congress shall make no law respecting an establishment of religion, or prohibiting the free exercise thereof" (5).

The constitutional limitations have a dual aspect. They prevent the legal compulsion to accept any creed or the practice of any form of worship on one hand, and, on the other hand, permit the free exercise of a chosen form of religion.

The freedom of religion protected against Federal legislation by the first amendment of the Federal Constitution is also protected against invasion by state action by reason of the Fourteenth Amendment due process clause (6).

What is freedom of religion? It embraces the right to maintain theories of life, of death, and of the hereafter which are rank heresy to followers of the orthodox faiths (7). ". . . (it) allow(s) everyone under the jurisdiction of the United States to entertain such notions respecting his relations to his maker and the duties they impose as may be approved by his judgment and conscience, and to exhibit his sentiments in such form of worship as he may think proper, not injurious to the equal rights of others, and to prohibit legislation for the support of any religious tenets, or the modes of worship of any sect (8)" It means that "neither a state nor the Federal government can set up a church." Neither can they pass laws which aid one religion, aid all religions, or prefer one religion over another. Neither can they force or influence

---

(5)   Const., Amend. I.
(6)   Const. Amend. XIV.
(7)   U.S. v. Ballard, 322 U.S. 78.
(8)   Davis v. Beason, 133 U.S. 33.

a person to go to or remain away from church against his will or force him to profess a belief or disbelief in any religion.

No person can be punished for entertaining or professing religious beliefs or disbeliefs, for church attendance or nonattendance. No tax in any amount, large or small, can be levied to support any religious activities or institutions, whatever they may be called or whatever form they may adopt to teach or practice religion. Neither a state nor the Federal Government can openly or secretly participate in the affairs of any religious organization or group or vice versa (9).

The government cannot finance religious groups or undertake religious institutions, or blend secular and sectarian education, or use secular institutions to force one or some religion on any person (10). The First Amendment has been held not violated by a state statute permitting religious societies to incorporate, (11) nor by exemptions from military service in favor of ministers of religion, theological students, or the members of religious sects whose tenets exclude the moral right to engage in war made by the Selective Service Act of May 18, 1917 (40 Stat 76). The Fourteenth Amendment due process clause was not violated by a state law requiring students at the state university to take a course in military science and tactics (12) nor a state court's denial of an application for admission to the bar because the

(9) Reynolds v. U.S., 98 U.S. 145; Everson v. Board of Education, 330 U.S. 1; Illinois ex rel. McCullum v. Board of Education, 333 U.S. 203.

(10) Zorach v. Clauson, 343 U.S. 306.

(11) Terrett v. Taylor, 9 Cranch 43.

(12) Hamilton v. Univ. of California, 293 U.S. 245.

applicant couldn't take in good faith the required oath to support the state constitution because of a conscientious belief against violence (13).

The religious guaranties of the Constitution weren't violated by state or Federal laws punishing bigamy and polygamy.

"Released Time" arrangements for the religious instruction of public school students were held invalid under a program whereby pupils whose parents signed "request cards" were permitted to attend religious instruction classes conducted during regular school hours in the school building by outside teachers of religion, subject to the approval and supervision of the Superintendent of Schools; attendance records were kept and reported to the school authorities and pupils not attending the religious instruction classes were required to continue their regular secular studies (14). A similar program was upheld where these courses were operated outside the school building at the expense of a duly constituted religious body (15).

Under the Fourteenth Amendment, a state may provide secular textbooks and transportation for parochial as well as public school children (16), but such statutes have been held to violate some state constitutions (17).

The following regulations have been held invalid:

(13)   Re Summers, 325 U.S. 561.
(14)   Illinois ex rel. McCullum v. Board of Education Supra.
(15)   Zorach v. Clauson Supra.
(16)   Everson v. Board of Education, Supra (transportation), Cochran v. the Board of Education, 281 U.S. 370 (textbooks).
(17)   Vesser v. Nooksack Valley School District, 33 Wash. 2d699) (transportation) ; Zelter v. Huff, 55 NM 501.

regulation requiring public school pupils to salute the flag of the United States while reciting a pledge of allegiance where these pupils' religious beliefs command them not to (18); requiring a license for soliciting money or valuables for a religious cause, where the licensing officer is authorized to withhold the license upon his determination that the cause is not a religious one (19); or legislation forbidding distribution on city streets of handbills containing an invitation to participate in a religious activity (20), or requiring a license for carrying out religious activities in public places, or otherwise regulating such distribution (21).

Nevertheless, a state or municipality may reasonably regulate as to time, place, or manner, the sale or other distribution of religious literature pursuant to its police power as long as the regulations are not discriminatory, arbitrary, capricious, and in violation of other constitutional provisions (22). The penal provision of a state's Child Labor Laws have been validly applied where a child engaged in the sale of religious publications (23), and regulations requiring persons using the public streets for a religious parade or procession to procure a license have been upheld (24).

(18)   West Virginia State Board of Education v. Barnette, 319 U.S. 624.
(19)   Cantwell v. Connecticut, 310 U.S. 296.
(20)   Jamison v. Texas, 318 U.S. 413.
(21)   Largent v. Texas, 318 U.S. 418.
(22)   Cantwell v. Connecticut, 310 U.S. 296.
(23)   Prince v. Massachusetts, 321 U.S. 158.
(24)   Ibid.

Sunday Blue Laws have been upheld as not violating the Federal Constitution (25), the court holding that such statutes, as applied to Orthodox Jews, do not violate the constitutional guarantee of the free exercise of religion, even though they impair the ability of certain merchants to earn a living (26). However, Sunday Blue laws have been held to violate the provisions of some state constitutions (27).

---

(25) Cox v. New Hampshire, 312 U.S. 569.
(26) Braunfeld v. Brown, 366 U.S. 599.
(27) Courtesy Motor Sales, Inc. v. Ward, 24 Ill. 2d 82.

CHAPTER VI.

PROTECTION TO PERSONS ACCUSED OF CRIME.

§ 106. Introduction. A considerable number of provisions in the bills of rights of both Federal and state constitutions are designed to afford protection to persons accused of crime. Today we are so familiar with the difficulty of successfully convicting persons charged with serious crime that it is hard to realize that there was a time when alleged criminals found difficulty in securing fair treatment from the government. The elaborate safeguards provided by our constitutions for such persons are due historically to the operation of at least three different circumstances. In the first place, the procedure of the early English criminal law was harsh and oppressive to the defendant. In the second place, a large proportion of all crimes, even of a trivial nature, were punishable by death. Stealing property above the value of five shillings was thus punishable in England into the early part of the nineteenth century. In the third place, the criminal law was often oppressively used by the English government in securing the conviction of its opponents for political crime. When our early constitutions were formed, the abuses and rigor of the English criminal law were fresh in the minds of American statesmen and they sought to prevent the re-occurrence of such things in this country.

SECTION 1. BILLS OF ATTAINDER AND EX POST FACTO LAWS.

§ 107. Bills of attainder. The United States Constitution, Article I, section 9, § 3, prohibits the United States from passing any bill of attainder or ex post facto law. Article I, section 10 forbids any state from doing either of these things. These clauses were inserted in the Constitution in order to protect persons accused of crime from legislative punishment without a trial and from punishment retroactively imposed.

A bill of attainder has been described as "a legislative act which inflicts punishment without a judicial trial"(1).

A statute of West Virginia denied the right to bring certain suits in the courts of that state to persons who were unable to take an oath that they had never supported any government hostile to the United States during the Civil war. This was adjudged by the United States Supreme Court to be invalid as a bill of attainder, in that it was legislative punishment, without a judicial trial, for the offense of engaging in rebellion against the United States (2).

§ 108. Ex post facto laws: Early definition. While there has been but little litigation over the prohibition of bills of attainder, its companion clause, forbidding the enactment of ex post facto laws has been the subject of frequent judicial interpretation. The words "ex post facto" mean, in medieval Latin, "after the fact." Liter-

---

(1)   Cummings v. Missouri, 4 Wall. 277, 323-4.

(2)   Pierce v. Carskadon, 16 Wall. 234.

ally applied, the clause would prohibit retrospective legislation affecting either civil rights or criminal punishments. In its usage in English law the phrase has almost always been restricted to penal statutes, and from the debates in the constitutional convention it appears that this usage was brought to the attention of the members of the convention. In the earliest case construing this clause that came before the United States Supreme Court, a law of Connecticut was challenged as ex post facto which gave a new trial to a party after he had once been finally defeated upon the probate of a will as the law stood at the time of the first trial. That court held that the clause applied only to certain classes of retrospective criminal statutes. Judge Chase said:

"I will state what laws I consider ex post facto laws, within the words and the intent of the prohibition. 1st. Every law that makes an action done before the passing of the law, and which was innocent when done, criminal; and punishes such action. 2d. Every law that aggravates a crime, or makes it greater than it was, when committed. 3d. Every law that changes the punishment, and inflicts a greater punishment than the law annexed to the crime, when committed. 4th. Every law that alters the legal rules of evidence, and receives less or different testimony than the law required at the time of the commission of the offense, in order to convict the offender. . . . But I do not consider any law ex post facto, within the prohibition, that mollifies the rigor of the criminal law; but only those that create, or aggravate, the crime; or increase the punishment, or change the rules of evidence, for the purpose of conviction'' (3).

§ 109. **Same: Later definition.** The classification of ex post facto laws made in Calder v. Bull above has become classic, and has been quoted with approval many times in both state and Federal courts. Like many definitions that have been attempted in advance of a thorough consideration of all possibilities, later decisions have shown it not to be strictly accurate. Some years ago the state of Utah passed a statute for the trial of criminal cases by a jury composed of eight persons. Previously a jury was composed of twelve persons, and several men who were alleged to have committed crimes under the old law were tried for them under the new one before a jury of eight jurors. Although the change of law here obviously did not fall within any one of the four classes enumerated in Calder v. Bull, it was adjudged ex post facto and invalid. The court said a penal statute was ex post facto ''which by its necessary operation and in its relations to the offense or its consequences, alters the situation of the accused to his disadvantage'' (4). Manifestly it was easier to secure the unanimous vote of eight jurors for conviction than of twelve, and so the situation of the accused was altered to his disadvantage.

§ 110. **What is a mitigation of punishment?** Nice questions may sometimes be raised as to whether a law changing the punishment of crime really mitigates it or not, for if the change is a lessening of the severity of the

---

(3)   Calder v. Bull, 3 Dallas, 386.

(4)   Thompson v. Utah, 170 U. S. 343, 351, 353.

punishment it is unobjectionable. In New York in 1860 the legislature changed the punishment for various crimes from death to life imprisonment. The New York court of appeals held this change to be ex post facto, because it was such an entirely different kind of punishment that they were unable to say that it was less severe. The determination of what kind of punishment would generally be preferred by criminals ought not to be left to the opinion of the judges (5). On the other hand the Massachusetts supreme court held such a change to be clearly a mitigation of the punishment and so valid (6). Probably the correct view of a change in the manner of punishment is stated by Judge Peckham in a later New York case as follows:

"I think that where a change is made in the manner of punishment, if the change be of that nature which no sensible man could by any possibility regard in any other light than that of a mitigation of the punishment, the act would not be ex post facto where made applicable to the offense committed before its passage" (7).

§ 111. Changes in procedure. Legislatures frequently make changes in procedure that affect the trial of men for crimes already committed. Interesting questions of constitutionality are sometimes raised by such statutes. In Missouri, at the time a certain murder was committed, the law forbade the use in evidence of other writings of the prisoner in order to show whether or not same docu-

---

(5) Shepherd v. People, 25 N. Y. 406.

(6) Commonwealth v. Wyman, 12 Cush. 237.

(7) People v. Hayes, 140 N. Y. 484, 492.

ment in the case was in his handwriting. Before trial, the legislature altered this rule and permitted such comparison of handwritings to be made. This was held valid, the court saying:

"The statute did nothing more than remove an obstacle arising out of a rule of evidence that withdrew from the consideration of the jury testimony which, in the opinion of the legislature, tended to elucidate the ultimate, essential fact to be established, namely, the guilt of the accused. Nor did it give the prosecution any right that was denied to the accused. It placed the state and the accused upon an equality; for the rule established by it gave to each side the right to have disputed writings compared with writings proved to the satisfaction of the judge to be genuine. Each side was entitled to go to the jury upon the question of the genuineness of the writing upon which the prosecution relied to establish the guilt of the accused" (8).

Similarly statutes changing the place of trial, changing the number of the appellate judges, requiring more intelligent jurors, and so forth, are valid. They do not necessarily change the situation of the accused to his disadvantage. On the contrary, they are quite as likely to operate to his advantage as to that of the state, and therefore they deprive him of no substantial right (8a).

§ 112. **Retroactive qualifications for a profession.** In 1878 one Hawker was convicted in New York of the crime of abortion, and served a term in the penitentiary there-

---

(8) Thompson v. Missouri, 171 U. S. 380, 387-8.

(8a) But see Ex parte McCardle, 7 Wall. 506; Mallett v. N. C., 181 U. S. 587.

for. Afterwards he lawfully practiced medicine in New York until the enactment in 1895 of a statute forbidding any person after conviction of felony to practice medicine in the state. Hawker was indicted for practicing medicine in New York in violation of this statute, and after conviction took his case to the United States Supreme Court, claiming the law was ex post facto. The court said:

"On the one hand it is said that defendant was tried, convicted and sentenced for a criminal offense. He suffered the punishment pronounced. The legislature has no power to thereafter add to that punishment. The right to practice medicine is a valuable property right. To deprive a man of it is in the nature of punishment, and after the defendant has once fully atoned for his offense a statute imposing this additional penalty is one simply increasing the punishment for the offense, and is ex post facto.

"On the other, it is insisted that within the acknowledged reach of the police power, a state may prescribe the qualifications of one engaged in any business so directly affecting the lives and health of the people as the practice of medicine. It may require both qualifications of learning and good character, and, if it deems that one who has violated the criminal laws of the state is not possessed of sufficiently good character, it can deny to such a one the right to practice medicine, and, further, it may make the record of a conviction conclusive evidence of the fact of violation of the criminal law and of the absence of the requisite good character. . . . We are of the opinion that this argument is the more applicable and must control the answer to this question'' (9).

§ **113. Same: Ex post facto if unreasonable.** On the other hand, just after the Civil war, Missouri adopted a constitution disqualifying all persons who took any part in the Rebellion from holding an office in any corporation in the state, being professors or teachers in any educational institution, acting as attorneys at law, or acting as priests or clergymen of any religious denomination, under penalties of fine and imprisonment. The conviction of a priest, obtained under this statute, was set aside by the United States Supreme Court. The court said:

''Among the rights reserved to the states is the right of each state to determine the qualifications for office, and the conditions upon which its citizens may exercise their various callings and pursuits within its jurisdiction. . . . It by no means follows that, under the form of creating a qualification or attaching a condition, the states can in effect inflict a punishment for a past act which was not punishable at the time it was committed. . . .

''Qualifications relate to the fitness or capacity of the party for a particular pursuit or profession. Webster defines the term to mean 'any natural endowment or any acquirement which fits a person for a place, office, or employment, or enables him to sustain any character, with success.' It is evident from the nature of the pursuits and professions of the parties, placed under disabilities by the constitution of Missouri, that many of the acts, from the

(9) Hawker v. New York, 170 U. S. 189, 191-2.

taint of which they must purge themselves, have no possible relation to their fitness for those pursuits and professions. There can be no connection between the fact that Mr. Cummings entered or left the state of Missouri to avoid enrolment or draft in the military service of the United States and his fitness to teach the doctrines or administer the sacraments of his church; nor can a fact of this kind or the expression of words of sympathy with some of the persons drawn into the Rebellion constitute any evidence of the unfitness of the attorney or counsellor to practice his profession, or of the professor to teach the ordinary branches of education, or of the want of business knowledge or business capacity in the manager of a corporation, or in any director or trustee'' (10).

The doctrines of these two cases show very clearly where the line is to be drawn between laws imposing conditions that amount to punishment for past acts, and laws that impose reasonable qualifications for future occupations.

SECTION 2. SELF-INCRIMINATION.

§ 114. **General scope of privilege.** The Fifth Amendment of the Constitution declares that no person shall be compelled in any criminal case to be a witness against himself. Though this provision applies only to the United States government, and not to the states, most of the states have in their own constitutions a similar provision.

The provision means not only that a person cannot be compelled to testify against himself in an actual prosecu-

---

(10) Cummings v. Missouri, 4 Wall. 277, 319-20.

tion against himself, but that he shall not be required, as a witness in any proceeding whatever, to give testimony that may afterwards be used in that jurisdiction in a criminal prosecution against him.

The majority of courts do hold that the admission of real evidence does not violate the privilege against self-incrimination. Thus, a suspected offender may be compelled to: Grow a beard (11), try on certain clothes worn by the person who committed the crime (11a), wear a mask (11b), display a limp (11c), or other muscular action, submit to a physical examination (11d), display scars (11e), give his fingerprints (11f), palm prints (12), or footprints (12a), give a handwriting specimen (12b), participate in a police ''lineup'' (12c), and give up documents or other objects in his possession (12d). This list is illustrative, not exhaustive.

The reasoning of the majority of the courts in upholding the admissibility of such evidence without violating the privilege against self-incrimination was succinctly put in People v. Sallow (12e), a case allowing compulsory fingerprinting. The court in that case said, ''It has

---

(11)   Ross v. State, 209 Ind. 281.

(11a) Barrett v. State, 190 Tenn. 366.

(11b) Ross v. State, 209 Ind. 281.

(11c) Funderburgh v. State, 144 Texas cr. 35.

(11d) Green Lake County v. Domes, 247 Wisc. 903.

(11e) State v. Ah Chuey, 14 Nev. 79.

(11f) U.S. v. Kelly, 55 F 2d 67.

(12)   83 A.L.R. 127.

(12a) State v. Rodgers, 64 S.E. 2nd 572.

(12b) Beltram v. Sampson and Jose, 53 Philippine Islands 570.

(12c) Meriwether v. State, 63 Ga. App. 667.

(12d) People v. Richter's Jewelers, 291 N.Y. 161.

(12e) People v. Sallow, 165 N.Y.S. 915.

always . . . been permissible to put in evidence for the purpose of identification of the defendant, testimony as to his personal appearance, his hair, his eyes, his complexion, marks . . . his hands and the like. Fingerprints are but the tracing of physical characteristics for the lines upon the fingers . . . the witness does not testify . . . the physical facts speak for themselves; no fear, no hope, no will of the prisoner to falsify or exaggerate could produce or create a resemblance of her fingerprints or change them. . . . There is no danger of error being committed or untruth told. The taking of fingerprints is not a violation of the spirit or purpose of the constitutional inhibition. The scope of the privilege in history and in principle . . . includes only the process of testifying by word of mouth or in writing. . . . It has no application to such physical evidential circumstances as may exist on the witness's body or about his person.''

§ 115. **Purely personal.** The privilege is confined wholly to the person whose conduct may later be made the subject of criminal charge, and it may not be pleaded by that person's agents. Even in the case of a corporation, which of course can act in no other way than by agents, the rule is the same. The agents of the corporation, including the president and the highest officials, may be required to give testimony that may afterwards be used in a criminal case against the corporation. This privilege, which in this case is virtually non-existent because a corporation cannot testify itself, cannot be made use of by its officers (13).

§ 116. **Protects only against criminal prosecution.**

---

(13) Hale v. Henkel, 201 U. S. pp. 66-70. See Wilson v. U. S., 221 U. S. 361.

The immunity given by this provision applies only to testimony that may actually expose a person to prosecution for crime, whether such testimony is given in a civil or criminal proceeding (State v. Byington, 200 P2d 723). It is further recognized that any fact which is a necessary or essential part of the crime, which, if testified to by a witness, would tend to incriminate him is privileged. "It is not declared that he may not be compelled to testify to facts which may impair his reputation for probity, or even tend to disgrace him, but the line is drawn at testimony that may expose him to prosecution. If the testimony relate to criminal acts long since past, and against the prosecution of which the statute of limitations has run, or for which he has already received a pardon or is guaranteed an immunity, the amendment does not apply" (14).

§ 117. **Secures immunity only in the immediate jurisdiction.** The immunity guaranteed, by statute or otherwise, need not extend outside of the jurisdiction of the state granting it, in order to make a witness compellable to testify within it. Of course a state statute cannot give immunity against prosecution by the United States or by other states, and it may well happen that, in answering fully the questions asked by the state, information may incidentally be given that might be used in prosecutions by the Federal or other state governments. Protection against these possibilities, however, is not within the scope of this constitutional provision (15). However a Federal statute may grant immunity from both state and Federal prosecution.

---

(14)   Hale v. Henkel, 201 U. S. pp. 66-67.

(15)   Hale v. Henkel, 201 U. S. pp. 68-69.

SECTION 3. UNREASONABLE SEARCHES AND SEIZURES.

§ 118. General scope of privilege. The Fourth Amendment of the Constitution provides: "The right of the people to be secure in their persons, houses, papers, and effects, against unreasonable searches and seizures, shall not be violated, and no warrants shall issue, but upon probable cause, supported by oath or affirmation, and particularly describing the place to be searched, and the persons or things to be seized."

It has been said that this provision is applicable to criminal proceedings only (16), and it has been decided that it has no reference to civil proceedings for the recovery of debts where a search warrant is not used (17). The intimate relation between the Fourth and Fifth Amendments has been judicially noticed. It has been said:

"They throw great light on each other. For the 'unreasonable searches and seizures' condemned in the Fourth Amendment are almost always made for the purpose of compelling a man to give evidence against himself, which in criminal cases is condemned in the Fifth Amendment; and compelling a man 'in a criminal case to be a witness against himself,' which is condemned in the Fifth Amendment, throws light on the question as to what is an 'unreasonable search and seizure, within the meaning of the Fourth Amendment. And we have been unable to perceive that the seizure of a man's private books and papers to be used in evidence against him is substantially different from compelling him to be a witness against himself. We think it is within the clear intent and meaning of those terms" (18).

---

(16) In re Strouse, 1 Sawyer 605.

(17) Murry v. Hoboken Land Co., 18 How. 272, 285.

(18) Boyd v. United States, 116 U.S. 616.

Some later cases reflect the views of high Federal courts in recent years. For instance, in *Trupiano* v. *United States*, 334 U.S. 699, decided in 1948, FBI men long suspecting defendants of illegally rectifying spirits entered their premises lawfully and through a hole in the wall saw one of them operating a still. The agents arrested him, the crime having been committed in their presence, and seized some of the articles used in its commission. The majority of the Supreme Court, Justice Douglas and others, held the seizure illegal since the agents had abundant time to procure a warrant. Dissenting were Chief Justice Vinson and Justices Black, Reed, and Burton on the ground that the articles were seized in the course of a valid arrest and that they were in plain sight of agents who saw them being used in illegal operation of the still.

This dissent was followed in *Rabinowitz* v. *United States*, 339 U.S. 56 (1950), where defendant was arrested under a valid warrant for possessing forged and altered postage stamps which were, no search warrant having been issued, finally uncovered, seized and used by the officers in securing defendant's conviction. On appeal, the Supreme Court held both the arrest and the search and seizure lawful. The search and seizure, the Court said through Justice Minton, were incident to a valid arrest and the reasonableness and validity of such search and seizure did not depend on whether or not the officers had time to procure a warrant. Even if they had time, they were not bound to procure one. In this connection the Court said: "To the extent that *Trupiano* v. *United States*, 334 U.S. 699, requires a search warrant solely upon the basis of the practicability of procuring it rather than upon the reasonableness of the search after a lawful arrest, that case is overruled. The relevant test is not whether it was reasonable to procure a search warrant but whether the search was reasonable.''

In *Steeber* v. *U.S.*, decided by the United States Court of Appeals, Tenth Circuit, in 1952, and reported in 198 F. 2d 615, the defendant has been tried and found guilty of violation of the Internal Revenue laws pertaining to the manufacture and possession of intoxicating liquors. It appeared here that certain premises leased by the defendant but not occupied by him as a dwelling house had been searched and a large amount of nontax-paid whiskey seized without a warrant. It also appeared that the defendant had stated to the officers that he had subleased the premises. He was not arrested until the day after the search. On appeal the Circuit Court observed that the premises were admittedly searched and the contraband seized without a warrant and such search and seizure could be justified only as an incident to a lawful arrest or under exceptional circumstances making it impractical to secure a search warrant through orderly procedure, citing *U.S.* v. *Rabinowitz*. The Court held that the search was not an incident to the appellant's arrest, and that there was nothing in the evidence tending to show any extraordinary or exceptional circumstances making it impractical to secure a search warrant.

In Wolf v. Colorado, 338 U.S. 25 decided in 1949, defendant was a practicing physician. He had been tried and convicted of conspiracy to commit an abortion and sentenced to imprisonment. The conviction was obtained largely by evidence procured by officers on the staff of the State's attorney, who, without a warrant, had gained entrance to defendant's office and seized some daybooks.

The conviction was affirmed by the Colorado Supreme
Court on the ground that though the evidence was illegally seized it might be used against Wolf in the criminal proceedings.

On appeal to the United States Supreme Court, the
judgment of conviction by the Colorado Court was affirmed. The majority opinion, by Justice Frankfurter,
held that evidence obtained by an unconstitutional search
and seizure was admissible in State courts although it
might be inadmissible in the Federal courts under the
holding of *Weeks* v. *U.S.* It was held that there was no
departure from basic standards by permitting a State
to limit enforcement of a constitutionally-protected right
of privacy to a private suit for damages.

Two leading cases involving search and seizure evidently turned on the point whether there was such invasion by state police of personal privacy and security as to
shock the conscience. In *Rochin* v. *California*, 342 U.S.
165, decided in 1952, deputy sheriffs, suspecting appellant
of selling narcotics, went to the building where he lived
with his common-law wife and other members of his
family. They found the outside door open and entered,
proceeding to the second-floor room occupied by Rochin
and his wife. They forced open the door and spied some
suspicious looking capsules on a stand beside the bed on
which appellant was sitting. Rochin, anticipating their
movement, seized the capsules and swallowed them despite bodily preventive measures used by the officers. They
then handcuffed him and took him to a hospital where at
their directions his stomach was forcibly pumped and by
these means two morphine capsules recovered. With this

evidence a conviction was secured which was affirmed by a divided California Supreme Court. On certiorari to the United States Supreme Court, the majority voted for a reversal. Justice Frankfurter in his majority opinion used this significant language: "We are compelled to conclude that the proceedings by which this conviction was obtained do more than offend some fastidious squeamishness or private sentimentalism about combating crime too energetically. It is conduct that shocks the conscience. . . . They are methods too close to the rack and screw to permit of constitutional differentiation."

In *Irvine* v. *California,* 347 U.S. 128, decided in 1954, the same court affirmed a judgment of conviction for violation of antigambling laws based on evidence procured by police who, without obtaining a search warrant, duplicated defendant's house key and secretly placed microphones in several rooms.

Two cases decided by the U.S. Supreme Court in 1960 have substantially altered the law in this area.

In Elkins v. U.S., 364 U.S. 206, the Supreme Court held that evidence obtained by state officers during a search which if conducted by Federal officers would have violated the Fourth Amendment is inadmissible in a Federal criminal trial, even though there was no Federal participation in obtaining the evidence.

In Mapp v. Ohio, 367 U.S. 643, it was held that evidence obtained by a search violating the Fourth Amendment is inadmissible in a state court.

In the Mapp case, the Cleveland police, without a search warrant, broke into the appellant's apartment after she refused to admit them and seized some contraband material. Appellant's conviction by the state court based on evidence obtained through the illegal search was set aside. The court held that the individual's right of privacy under the Fourth Amendment was protected against state action through the due process clause of the Fourth Amendment.

§ 119. **Extends to the mails.** The same protection extends to sealed packages going through the mails. "Letters and sealed packages of this kind in the mail are as fully guarded from examination and inspection, except as to their outward form and weight, as if they were retained by the parties forwarding them in their own domiciles. The constitutional guaranty of the rights of the people to be secure in their papers against unreasonable searches and seizures extends to their papers, thus closed against inspection, wherever they may be. Whilst in the mail, they can only be opened and examined under like warrant, issued upon similar oath or affirmation, particularly describing the thing to be seized, as is required when papers are subjected to search in one's own household. No law of Congress can place in the hands of officials connected with the postal service any authority to invade the secrecy of letters and such sealed packages in the mail; and all regulations adopted as to mail matter of this kind must be in subordination to the great principle embodied in the Fourth Amendment of the Constitution" (18a).

§ 120. **Forbids general warrants.** When the warrant provided for in the Fourth Amendment is issued for the arrest of a person it must specifically name or describe

---

(18a) Ex parte Jackson, 96 U. S. p. 733.

him. A warrant without other description, giving a fic-titious name for the accused, or one by which he has never been known, or a so-called blank or "general" warrant, does not comply with the constitutional provision and is invalid. (19). The subject is fully treated in the article on Criminal Procedure §§ 9-11. in Volume III of this work.

SECTION 4. JURIES.

§ 121. Definition of a trial jury. The United States Constitution provides that in the Federal courts all crim-inal trials shall be by jury, and also all civil trials in suits at common law where the value in controversy shall ex-ceed $20 (20). There is no requirement under the Fed-eral Constitution that any case or controversy in a state court be tried by a jury, but similar provisions are found in most of our state constitutions. This requirement of a jury means not merely a body of men of indefinite num-ber, who may decide questions by a majority or other fractional vote, but refers to the particular kind of a jury known to the English law with which the colonists were familiar. It is a jury of twelve men, no more and no less, who must find a unanimous verdict. "The word 'jury' and the words 'trial by jury' were placed in the Constitution of the United States with reference to the meaning affixed to them in the law as it was in this coun-try and in England at the time of the adoption of that in-strument; . . . which required a trial by a jury composed of not less than twelve persons." "The Seventh Amend-

---

(19)   West v. Cabell, 153 U. S. 78.
(20)   Art. III., Sec. 2; Amend. VI and VII.

ment secured unanimity in finding a verdict as an essential feature of a trial by jury in common law cases, and Congress could not . . . change the constitutional rule'' (21).

§ 122.   Constitutional function of judge in jury trials. Of the function of the judge in respect to jury trials it has been said: '' 'Trial by jury,' in the primary and usual sense of the term at the common law and in the American Constitution, is not merely a trial by a jury of twelve men before an officer vested with authority to cause them to be summoned and empanelled, to administer oaths to them and to the constable in charge, and to enter judg‹ ment and issue execution on their verdict; but it is a trial by a jury of twelve men, in the presence and under the superintendence of a judge empowered to instruct them on the law and to advise them on the facts, and (except on acquittal of a criminal charge) to set aside their verdict if in his opinion it is against the law or the evidence'' (22).

§ 123.   Waiver of trial by jury.   At common law, an accused in a felony case could not waive his right to a trial by jury. This rule prevails in jurisdictions where the constitutional provisions for jury trial are mandatory.

In many jurisdictions, however, a jury trial may be waived whether the case involves a felony or a misdemeanor (23). The holding of the jurisdictions following this view is that an accused may waive the right to a trial by jury whether the right is constitutional or given by

---

(21)   Thompson v. Utah, 170 U. S., 343, 350; Springville v. Thomas, 166 U. S. 707.

(22)   Capital Traction Co. v. Hof, 174 U. S. pp. 13-14.

(23)   Patton v. U.S., 281 U.S. 276.

statute, since a jury trial is not jurisdictional (24). For an interesting discussion of the evolution of the law in this area see People v. Spegal, 5 Ill. 2d 211, 125 N.E. 2d 468, 51 A.L.R. 2d 1337.

§ 124. **Diversities of constitutional requirement.** The guaranty of trial by jury contained in the Federal Constitution has no application to proceedings in the state courts. But, as stated previously, the various state constitutions have similar provisions. However, among the various states there are considerable diversities as to form and procedural detail concerning juries. In some jurisdictions, the jury may consist of less than twelve persons or the verdict need not be unanimous. What the correct procedure is and whether the right to trial by jury even exists in a given case depends upon the type of case and the constitutional requirement of the particular jurisdiction. The common law power of the judge in the conduct of the trial has also been substantially limited and altered in a number of states. See Criminal Procedure, Sections 72-75 in Volume 3 of this work.

§ 125. **Grand juries.** The Fifth Amendment of the Constitution provides that no person shall be held to answer for a capital or otherwise infamous crime, unless on a presentment or indictment of a grand jury, except in cases arising in the land or naval forces, or in the militia, when in actual service in time of war or public danger. The principal question that may arise regarding these provisions is what constitutes an infamous crime. A capital crime is of course one punishable by death. An infamous crime has been decided to be one for which an infamous punishment may be inflicted. Imprisonment

---

(24)   People v. Lobb, 17 Ill. 2d 287, 161 N.E. 2d 325.

in a state prison or penitentiary is an infamous punishment, also deprivation of ordinary civil or political privileges. Perhaps also are punishments that have come to be regarded by public opinion as infamous though not so regarded formerly, like whipping or putting in the stocks (25).

SECTION 5. MISCELLANEOUS RIGHTS.

§ 126. **Notice. Witnesses. Counsel.** "[In all criminal prosecutions the accused shall enjoy the right] to be informed of the nature and cause of the accusation; to be confronted with the witnesses against him; to have compulsory process for obtaining witnesses in his favor, and to have the assistance of counsel for his defense" (26).

These topics are fully considered in the article upon Criminal Procedure in Volume III of this work.

§ 127. **Excessive bail and fines.** The Eighth Amendment to the Constitution provides: "Excessive bail shall not be required, nor excessive fines imposed, nor cruel and unusual punishments inflicted." This is a limitation upon the Federal government only, though most of the state constitutions contain similar provisions applicable to the state governments.

Very serious offences which are punishable by death or life imprisonment, are ordinarily not bailable. It has recently been held that the Eighth Amendment does not require that aliens awaiting deportation as communists be allowed bail (27). When the offence is bailable, the

(25)   Ex parte Wilson, 114 U. S. 417.
(26)   Const., Amend. VI.
(27)   Carlson v. London, 342 U.S. 524 (1952).

amount of bail that may properly be required under this provision of the Constitution is to be determined by a consideration both of the magnitude of the offence and of the ability of the defendant to give bail. A wide latitude in determining these questions must necessarily be allowed to the magistrate to whom application is made. The same considerations doubtless apply in determining what is an excessive fine.

§ 128. **Cruel and unusual punishments.** What is a cruel and unusual punishment must be determined with respect to the prevailing usages of government and the condition of public opinion at the time the question arises. In earlier and more barbarous ages, torture and mutilation were common punishments, and perhaps could not then have been denominated cruel and unusual. Such punishments, in the present state of public opinion, would undoubtedly violate the Constitution (28).

A punishment is not unconstitutional merely on account of its novelty, unless it is also cruel. For instance, the execution of the death penalty by means of electricity, instead of hanging, is not a cruel punishment in the constitutional sense. It does not shock public opinion as would torture (29).

On the other hand, chaining a prisoner by the neck with a trace-chain and padlock so that he could neither lie nor sit, and leaving him thus chained in darkness for several hours is a cruel and unusual punishment (30).

---

(28) In re Kemmler, 136 U. S. 436.

(29) Kemmler v. Durston, 119 N. Y. 569.

(30) Re Birdsong, 39 Fed. 599.

It has been held that the deprivation of United States citizenship for desertion in time of war is a cruel and unusual punishment (30a).

Where a defendant has committed a number of minor offences, which are slight in themselves, but the penalties for which in the aggregate are very heavy, it is a debated question whether the infliction of the aggregate penalties is unconstitutional or not. In one case a city ordinance punished the destruction of plants in the public square by a fine of $10 or imprisonment for 30 days. The defendant was convicted upon 72 charges of this offence, all committed within the space of one hour and forty minutes, making a total fine of $720 or six years in jail. This fine was held excessive and the punishment cruel and unusual, the reasoning turning in part upon the fact that the offences were not really separate but continuous, inasmuch as one was charged for each minute and a half of the time (31).

On the other hand, a defendant was convicted in Vermont of sending out from his store, upon separate orders, 307 different consignments of liquor in violation of the prohibition law. The offenses were committed during a period of three years and each one was punishable by a fine of $20 and imprisonment for one month, making a total fine of over $6,000 and imprisonment for over twenty-five years. The sentence was upheld, the court saying:

(30a) Trop v. Dulles, 356 U.S. 86 (1958).

(31)   State v. Whittaker, 48 La. Ann. 527.

"If he has subjected himself to a severe penalty, it is simply because he has committed a great many such offences. It would scarcely be competent for a person to assail the constitutionality of the statute prescribing a punishment for burglary, on the ground that he had committed so many burglaries that, if punishment for each were inflicted on him, he might be kept in prison for life. The mere fact that cumulative punishments may be imposed for distinct offenses in the same prosecution is not material upon this question. If the penalty were unreasonably severe for a single offense, the constitutional question might be urged; but here the unreasonableness is only in the number of offenses which the respondent has committed" (32).

§ 129. **Double jeopardy.** "Nor shall any person be subject for the same offense to be twice put in jeopardy of life or limb" (33).

This topic is fully discussed in the article upon Criminal Procedure, §§52-53, in Volume III of this work.

---

(32)   State v. O'Neil, 58 **Vt.** p. 165.

(33)   **Const., Amend. V-**

CHAPTER VII.

DUE PROCESS AND EQUAL PROTECTION OF LAW: PROCEDURE.

SECTION 1. DUE PROCESS OF LAW.

§ 130. General requisites of due process in procedure.
The Fifth Amendment forbids the United States government to deprive any person of life, liberty, or property without due process of law. The Fourteenth Amendment enacts the same prohibition against the states. This general prohibition, as we shall see, applies not only to matters of procedure, but to matters of substantive right, independently of the procedure employed; but in this section we consider the meaning of the phrase only as concerns procedure.

"The essential elements of due process of law, already established, are singularly few, though of wide application and deep significance. We are not here concerned with the effect of due process in restraining substantive laws, as, for example, that which forbids the taking of private property for public use without compensation. We need notice now only those cases which deal with the principles which must be observed in the trial of criminal and civil causes. Due process requires that the court which assumes to determine the rights of parties shall have jurisdiction, and that there shall be notice and opportunity

111

for hearing given the parties. Subject to these two fundamental conditions, which seem to be universally prescribed in all systems of law established by civilized countries, this court has up to this time sustained all state laws, statutory or judicially declared, regulating procedure, evidence, and methods of trial, and held them to be consistent with due process of law'' (1).

§ 131. **Jurisdiction.** Whether a tribunal has jurisdiction to render a given judgment or not depends upon the kind of judgment sought and what control the court has over the person, thing, or relation to be affected thereby. Thus, if a judgment is sought against X personally, that he pay money or do some act, the court must have gained control over the person of X. This it is considered to have when X, whether domiciled (resident) within the limits of the state or not, is served there with the court's process, or consents to subject himself to its jurisdiction. That he leaves the state afterwards before judgment is rendered makes no difference. Service of process upon a non-resident by publication is therefore invalid, and a personal judgment based upon this is of no effect, even where rendered, because not due process of law (2). If the object to be affected by the judgment is corporeal property, it must be within the territorial limits of the state. Thus a state may, by appropriate legislation, validly confer upon its courts power to dispose of the interests of non-resident owners of domestic land, or of the property of persons who have been absent and unheard of

(1)   Twining v New Jersey, 211 U S. 78, 110-111.
(2)   Pennoyer v. Neff, 95 U. S. 714.

for seven years (3). Where a relation between two per
sons is to be affected, it likewise must be subject to appropriate control where the proceedings are held.   Thus, the
garnishment of a debt may be made where the debtor
alone is, because it can there be made effective by compelling the debtor to pay it (4).   Compare the jurisdictional requirement for taxing a debt as property, or taxing
its transfer (§§176, 184, below).   When the relation to be
affected is the marriage bond, there is no jurisdiction to
dissolve it in a state where neither party is domiciled (5).
The requirements of jurisdiction to make judgments of
various kinds valid, outside of the state where rendered,
are discussed in Conflict of Laws, Chapter VI, in Volume
IX of this work. Of course, whatever satisfies these requirements is due process of law where rendered, within
the Fourteenth Amendment.

§ 132. **Any procedure giving notice and fair hearing
is valid.** In addition to jurisdiction, due process of law,
in point of procedure, ordinarily requires a fair hearing
before some impartial tribunal (not necessarily a court),
with due notice to parties to be affected, opportunity to
be heard, and a trial according to some orderly course of
proceedings. If these essentials be afforded, in any case to
which they may be appropriate, the requirements of due
process are fulfilled, even though the precise procedure
be in other respects wholly novel. For instance, before
1879 California required, in accordance with prevailing

---

(3) Arndt v. Griggs, 134 U. S. 316; Cunnius v. Reading School
Dist., 198 U. S. 458.

(4) Chicago, etc. Ry. v. Sturm, 174 U. S. 710.

(5) Bell v. Bell, 181 U. S. 175.

American usage, that persons charged with serious crime
be indicted by a grand jury before they could be put on
trial. The new state constitution adopted in that year
permitted criminals to be charged with crime by information lodged before a magistrate. To the objection that
this procedure was not due process, because so different
from the English and Californian usage before 1879, the
Supreme Court said that while procedure sanctioned by
settled usage in England and this country was due process, it by no means followed that nothing else was. To
hold otherwise "would be to deny every quality of the
law but its age, and to render it incapable of progress or
improvement. It would be to stamp upon our jurisprudence the unchangeableness attributed to the laws of the
Medes and Persians. . . .

"The Constitution of the United States was ordained,
it is true, by descendants of Englishmen, who inherited
the traditions of English law and history; but it was made
for an undefined and expanding future, and for a people
gathered and to be gathered from many nations and of
many tongues. And while we take just pride in the principles and institutions of the common law, we are not to
forget that in lands where other systems of jurisprudence
prevail, the ideas and processes of civil justice are also
not unknown. Due process of law, in spite of the abso-
lutism of continental governments, is not alien to that
code which survived the Roman Empire as the foundation
of modern civilization in Europe. . . . There is nothing in Magna Charta, rightly construed as a broad charter
of public right and law, which ought to exclude the best

ideas of all systems and of every age; and as it was the characteristic principle of the common law to draw its inspiration from every fountain of justice, we are not to assume that the sources of its supply have been exhausted. On the contrary, we should expect that the new and various experiences of our own situation and system will mould and shape it into new and not less useful forms" (6).

Upon the same principle it has been held that a state may abolish jury trials in both civil and criminal cases, without violating the requirement of due process of law, provided that the new proceeding affords a fair trial (7). Similarly, statutes forbidding the sale of liquor may be made enforceable by injunctions in courts of equity, instead of by jury trials in common law courts (8).

"It is clear that the Fourteenth Amendment in no way undertakes to control the power of a state to determine by what process legal rights may be asserted or legal obligations be enforced, provided that the methods of procedure adopted for this process give reasonable notice and afford fair opportunity to be heard before the issues are decided" (9).

§ 133. **Procedure according to settled usage is valid.** In addition to procedure that secures a fair hearing, any other procedure that is according to the settled usage of England and of the American colonies is due process of

---

(6) Hurtado v. California, 110 U. S. 516, 529, 530-31.

(7) Maxwell v. Dow, 176 U. S. 581.

(8) Eilenbecker v. Plymouth County, 134 U. S. 31.

(9) Iowa Central Railway v. Iowa, 160 U. S. 389, 393.

law, even though not involving a hearing. An act of
Congress provided that when a Federal revenue collector
was found indebted to the United States by the Treasury
Department his property could be seized and sold to satisfy this claim, without any notice or hearing. The Supreme Court held this historically to be due process of
law. It said:

"The article is a restraint on the legislative as well
as on the executive and judicial powers of the government, and cannot be so construed as to leave Congress
free to make any process 'due process of law,' by its
mere will. To what principles, then, are we to resort
to ascertain whether this process, enacted by Congress, is
due process? To this the answer must be two-fold. We
must examine the Constitution itself, to see whether this
process be in conflict with any of its provisions. If not
found to be so, we must look to those settled usages and
modes of proceeding existing in the common and statute
law of England, before the emigration of our ancestors,
and which are shown not to have been unsuited to their
civil and political condition by having been acted on by
them after the settlement of this country. . . .

"Tested by the common and statute law of England
prior to the emigration of our ancestors, and by the laws
of many of the states at the time of the adoption of this
amendment, the proceedings authorized by the act of 1820
cannot be denied to be due process of law, when applied to
the ascertainment and recovery of balances due to the
government from a collector of customs. . . . For,
though 'due process of law' generally implies and in-

cludes, actor, reus, judex (10), regular allegations, opportunity to answer, and a trial according to some settled course of judicial proceedings, yet this is not universally true. . . . Though, generally, both public and private wrongs are redressed through judicial action, there are more summary extra-judicial remedies for both. An instance of extra-judicial redress of a private wrong is, the recapture of goods by their lawful owner; of a public wrong, by a private person, is the abatement of a public nuisance; and the recovery of public dues by summary process of distress, issued by some public officer authorized by law, is an instance of redress of a particular kind of public wrong, by the act of the public through its authorized agents'' (11).

§ 134. **Summary destruction of personal property.** Similar principles apply to the power of government summarily to destroy a person's property used for illegal purposes or which has become a nuisance. A New York statute authorized the summary destruction of nets used in illegal fishing, and was upheld, although the destruction preceded any judicial inquiry regarding the guilt of the owner. The Supreme Court said:

''Where the property is of little value, and its use for the illegal purpose is clear, the legislature may declare it to be a nuisance, and subject to summary abatement. Instances of this are the power to kill diseased cattle; to pull down houses in the path of conflagrations; the de-

---

(10) Plaintiff, defendant, judge.

(11) Murray v. Hoboken Land Company, 18 How. 272, 276-7, 278, 280.

struction of decayed fruit or fish or unwholesome meats, or infected clothing, obscene books or pictures, or instruments which can only be used for illegal purposes. . . .

"Nor is a person whose property is seized under the act in question without his legal remedy. If in fact his property has been used in violation of the act, he has no just reason to complain; if not, he may replevy his nets from the officer seizing them, or, if they have been destroyed, may have his action for their value. In such cases the burden would be upon the defendant to prove a justification under the statute" (12).

§ 135. **Exercise of legislative power by boards.** When the legislature passes a law, it is of course not necessary to the validity of the law that it be preceded by a notice or hearing to persons who will be affected by it. A legislature may, for instance, forbid the killing of certain kinds of game at certain seasons, or may regulate the hours in certain occupations, and so forth, and, if what it does is really not unreasonable or arbitrary, its acts are not invalid merely because no hearing is afforded to parties affected by its legislation. Wherever the legislative power of regulation may be exercised more effectively in regard to details by delegating it to a commission, this is ordinarily upheld. Where the delegation of power is valid the commission to which it is delegated may ordinarily exercise it in the same manner as the legislature can, and therefore need not give a hearing to interested parties before making its regulations.

---

(12)   Lawton v. Steele, 152 U. S. 133, 140-42.

A Massachusetts statute provided that where the fish in streams were of sufficient importance to warrant the regulation of the discharge of sawdust into streams where it materially injured the fish, the fish commission might make an order regulating or forbidding this disposal of sawdust. The fish commission acting under this statute, ordered one Sisson not to discharge sawdust into the Konkapot river, acting upon their own investigation and without giving any hearing to Sisson. The Massachusetts Supreme Court upheld the order, saying:

"In our opinion the action of the board in the case at bar was the working out of details under a legislative act. The board is no more required to act on sworn evidence than is the legislature itself, and no more than in case of the legislature itself is it bound to act only after a hearing or to give a hearing to the plaintiff when he asks for one; and its action is final, as is the action of the legislature in enacting a statute. And being legislative, it is plain that the questions of fact passed upon by the commissioners in adopting the provisions enacted by them cannot be tried over by the court" (13).

§ 136. Proper procedure for taxation and eminent domain. Where property is to be taken by the government, whether under its power of eminent domain or of taxation, the proceedings thereto must comply with the requirements of due process of law. These requirements, however, are not necessarily the same in such cases as in other controversies. "In judging what is 'due process of

---

(13) Commonwealth v. Sisson, 189 Mass, p. 252.

law' respect must be had to the cause and object of the taking, whether under the taxing power, the power of eminent domain, or the power of assessment for local improvements, or some of these; and if found to be suitable or admissible in the special case, it will be adjudged to be 'due process of law,' but if found to be arbitrary, oppressive, and unjust, it may be declared to be not 'due process of law' " (14).

"Of the different kinds of taxes which the state may impose, there is a vast number of which, from their nature, no notice can be given to the tax-payer, nor would notice be of any possible advantage to him, such as poll taxes, license taxes (not dependent upon the extent of his business), and generally, specific taxes on things, or persons, or occupations. In such cases the legislature, in authorizing the tax, fixes its amount, and that is the end of the matter. If the tax be not paid, the property of the delinquent may be sold, and he be thus deprived of his property. Yet there can be no question, that the proceeding is due process of law, as there is no inquiry into the weight of evidence, or other element of a judicial nature, and nothing could be changed by the hearing of the taxpayer. No right of his is, therefore, invaded. . . .

"But where a tax is levied on property not specifically, but according to its value, to be ascertained by assessors appointed for that purpose upon such evidence as they may obtain, a different principle comes in. The officers in estimating the value act judicially; and in most of the

---

(14)   Davidson v. New Orleans, 96 U. S. 97, 107.

states provision is made for the correction of errors committed by them . . . The law, in prescribing the time when such complaints will be heard, gives all the notice required, and the proceeding by which the valuation is determined, though it may be followed, if the tax be not paid, by a sale of the delinquent's property, is due process of law'' (15).

In any case where the amount of the tax is made to depend upon questions of fact, like those of value, benefit, amount of property, and the like, a fair hearing must be granted at some stage of the proceeding in order to satisfy the requirements of due process (16). Similar rules apply to the exercise of the power of eminent domain. No hearing can be required upon legislative questions involved, like the necessity of the taking (see § 212, below) but one must be given to ascertain the value of the property taken.

§ 137. **Procedure in matters over which government has absolute control.** Wherever the government has absolute control over a certain class of acts, or may wholly prohibit them under its legislative powers, it may permit them conditionally. In such a case the fulfillment of the terms of the conditions exacted may be determined by an administrative officer without even a hearing to those interested. The power absolutely to forbid carries with it the lesser power to permit upon hard terms. Some instances of this are to be found in the practice of the United States regarding admission to this country of for-

(15) Hagar v. Reclamation District, 111 U. S. 701, 709-10.
(16) Norwood v. Baker, 172 U. S. 269.

eign imports and aliens. Congress may absolutely exclude these, but instead it has chosen to admit them on certain terms that do not always require a fair hearing upon the questions involved. A United States statute provided that a board should establish certain standards for imported tea, and that any such tea falling below such standards should be rejected by the examiners, and if not shipped out of the country within six months from the time of rejection should be destroyed. Certain tea imported by one Buttfield was rejected and destroyed, according to the statute, by the collector of the port of New York. He was sued therefor by Buttfield, who alleged, among other things, that he was not accorded a hearing regarding the quality of his tea when it was examined; but the procedure established by the statute was upheld (17).

§ 138. Judicial tribunal not necessary. Even in cases where due process of law requires a fair hearing, this hearing need not be before a judge, or court, or other strictly judicial tribunal. There is nothing in the nature of a fair hearing which requires that in every case it need be before a court. In the absence of other constitutional provisions especially requiring particular tribunals, like courts or juries, a state may commit the determination of litigated controversies of all kinds to boards, commissions, inspectors, or other officers. Due process of law does not even necessarily require that the officers who discharge judicial functions shall not also be connected

---

(17) Buttfield v. Stranahan, 192 U. S. 470. See also Oceanic S Nav. Co. v. Stranahan, 214 U. S. 320.

with other departments of government. That is, it does not require a separation of the three great departments of government, executive, legislative and judicial. This is required, if at all, by other parts of our constitutions. ''Suppose a state, by its constitution, grants legislative functions to the executive, or to the judiciary, what provision of the Federal Constitution will nullify the action?'' (18).

Today an ever increasing number of controversies are arising between the government, represented by various boards, commissions, or administrative officers, on one side, and private individuals on the other. These questions, when not of a criminal nature, are coming to be known as ''administrative questions'' and they are frequently required by law to be settled by administrative officers without permitting any appeal to the courts. Among such matters that may be wholly committed to administrative determination, provided only that there be no fraud or other abuse of authority, are the following: The administration of the public land system, the determination of lands benefited by irrigation schemes, the value of property taken by the state for public use, the classification of the mail and the exclusion of fraudulent matter therefrom, and the appraisal of imported goods (19).

---

(18)   Michigan Central Railway v. Powers, 201 U. S. 245, 294. See also Dreyer v. Ill., 187 U. S. 71, 83-84.

(19)   Fall Brook Irrigation District v. Bradley, 164 U. S. pp. 167-70; Clearing House v. Coyne, 194 U. S. 497; Hilton v. Merritt, 110 U. S. 97.

One of the most striking applications of this principle is found in the case of the United States v. Ju Toy. The United States excluded alien Chinese from the United States and gave to the executive officers of the Department of Commerce the exclusive right to decide all questions of fact relating to the right of Chinese to enter the United States. When Ju Toy sought to enter the country, and alleged that he was a native-born citizen of the United States who had temporarily left the country and now wished to return, the executive officer of the Department of Commerce decided that he was not a citizen and excluded him; whereupon he applied to the Federal courts, alleging that so important a fact as American citizenship could not be conclusively decided against him without an appeal to the courts. His claim was denied by the Supreme Court, saying: "If we assume that the Fifth Amendment applies to him and that to deny entrance to a citizen is to deprive him of liberty, we nevertheless are of the opinion that with regard to him due process of law does not require a judicial trial. . . . The decision may be entrusted to an executive officer and . . . his decision is due process of law" (20). Compare the article on Public Officers, §105, in Volume IX of this work.

§ 139. **Kind of notice required.**   Where the proceeding is one for which notice is required, as in ordinary litigation, the contents of the notice must apprise the defendant of the nature of the proceeding against him, it must be given in such a manner as to come to the attention of a person of reasonable diligence, and it must afford a sufficient opportunity to make an answer. Where service of process is not necessary to acquire jurisdiction (§ 131, above), as where the action is in rem regarding property in the state, the notice may be served by publication, especially on non-residents. It is customary, though probably not necessary, to send actual notice to the defendant also, if his residence is known. Where a notice to defend a suit in Texas, regarding land there, was served on a defendant in Virginia, which gave but five days in which to appear and answer the suit, this time was held too short to afford due process (21). From four to eight weeks are usually given under such circumstances.

§ 140. **Erroneous and fraudulent decisions.** If the parties to a litigation have been given a fair hearing in their case, in a manner appropriate to the occasion, neither can complain that his property has been taken without due process merely because a court has erroneously decided against him. Due process does not assure a correct decision, but only a fair hearing (22). Similarly, an erroneous decision in criminal cases does not deprive the defendant of liberty without due process (23).

The requirement of due process does, however, entitle a litigant to an honest, though not a learned tribunal. If a litigant is injured through the corruption or fraud of the court or other body disposing of his case, he is entitled

---

(21) Roller v. Holly, 176 U. S. 398.

(22) Central Land Company v. Laidley, 159 U. S. 103.

(23) In re Converse, 137 U. S. 624. The tribunal must not be mentally incompetent. Jordan v. Mass., 225 U. S. 167.

to redress under this section of the Constitution (24).

§ 141. **Denying or hindering access to the courts upon the question of due process itself.** The courts may ultimately decide that the decisions of administrative officers, with or without a hearing according to circumstances, are due process of law, but the final decision of this ultimate question cannot be conclusively confided to any non-judicial tribunal. Any legislative attempt to do this, whether by direct denial of access to the courts upon this question, or by hindering such access by making resort to the courts upon it difficult, expensive, or hazardous, all alike violate the constitutional provision.

Some years ago the Minnesota legislature created a railway commission upon which it attempted to confer the power of fixing railway rates and determining conclusively, without any hearing, that they were lawful and reasonable. The United States Supreme Court held the statute unconstitutional. It said:

"In the present case, the return alleged that the rate of charge fixed by the commission was not equal or reasonable, and the supreme court held that the statute deprived the company of the right to show that judicially. The question of the reasonableness of a rate of charge for transportation by a railroad company, involving as it does the element of reasonableness both as regards the company and as regards the public, is eminently a question for judicial investigation, requiring due process of

---

(24) Fall Brook Irrigation District v. Bradley, 164 U. S. pp. 167-70; Louisville & Nashville Railway Co. v. Kentucky, 183 U. S. pp. 515-16; C. B. & Q. Railway v. Babcock, 204 U. S. 585.

law for its determination. If the company is deprived of the power of charging reasonable rates for the use of its property, and such deprivation takes place in the absence of an investigation by judicial machinery, it is deprived of the lawful use of its property, and thus, in substance and effect, of the property itself, without due process of law and in violation of the Constitution of the United States'' (25).

Still more recently this principle was affirmed in another case from Minnesota. A state statute prescribed certain railroad rates and made each separate act of disobedience thereto, by charging a higher rate, a felony, subject to imprisonment for a period not exceeding five years and a fine not exceeding $5,000. The court held these penalties invalid. It said:

"When the penalties for disobedience are by fines so enormous and imprisonment so severe as to intimidate the company and its officers from resorting to the courts to test the validity of the legislation, the result is the same as if the law in terms prohibited the company from seeking judicial construction of laws which deeply affect its rights.

"It is urged that there is no principle upon which to base the claim that a person is entitled to disobey a statute at least once, for the purpose of testing its validity without subjecting himself to the penalties for disobedience provided by the statute in case it is valid. This is not an accurate statement of the case. Ordinarily a law

---

(25) Chicago, etc., Ry. v. Minnesota, 134 U. S. p. 458.

creating offenses in the nature of misdemeanors or felonies relates to a subject over which the jurisdiction of
the legislature is complete in any event. In the case,
however, of the establishment of certain rates without any
hearing, the validity of such rates necessarily depends
upon whether they are high enough to permit at least
some return upon the investment (how much it is not now
necessary to state), and an inquiry as to that fact is a
proper subject of judicial investigation'' (26).

§ 142. **Self-incrimination not forbidden. Confronting
witnesses not required.** Most constitutions now contain
provisions shielding a person accused of crime from being compelled to testify against himself. The Fifth
Amendment lays this prohibition upon the United States
government, but it is not expressly prohibited to the
states in the national Constitution. Recently it was urged
that due process required that a defendant in a criminal
case should not be compelled to testify against himself,
but this was denied in an able opinion by the United
States Supreme Court (27). It was shown historically
that the provision requiring due process of law was in
Magna Charta, while the practice of compulsory incrim-
ination existed in the English courts for four or five hundred years thereafter, that it secured a foothold in the
colonies, and was not forbidden by the New York constitution until 1821, nor by Rhode Island until 1842.

The same has been held regarding the ordinary con-

---

(26)   Ex parte Young, 209 U. S. 123, 147-8.
(27)   Twining v. New Jersey, 211 U. S. 78.

stitutional provision that persons accused of crime must be confronted with the witnesses against them (27a).

SECTION 2. EQUAL PROTECTION OF THE LAWS.

§ 143. **Discriminatory exclusion from jury service.** One of the clauses of the Fourteenth Amendment, section 1, forbids a state to deny to any person within its jurisdiction the equal protection of the laws. Most of the cases that have interpreted this clause have involved laws that attempted arbitrarily to discriminate between persons in respect to matters of substantive right, rather than those of procedure. Of the few cases that have arisen where procedure was held to be improperly discriminating, the leading one is Strauder v. West Virginia (28). The laws of West Virginia made colored men ineligible for jury service. A negro was tried and convicted by a jury from which all persons of his race were thus excluded, and he carried the case to the United States Supreme Court. The court said:

"The words of the amendment, it is true, are prohibitory, but they contain a necessary implication of a positive immunity, or right, most valuable to the colored race —the right to exemption from unfriendly legislation against them distinctively as colored. . . . That the West Virginia statute respecting juries—the statute that controlled the selection of the grand and petit jury in the case of the plaintiff in error—is such a discrimination ought not to be doubted. Nor would it be if the persons

---

(27a)   West v. Louisiana, 194 U. S. 258.

(28)   Strauder v. West Virginia, 100 U. S. 303.

excluded by it were white men. . . . The statute of West Virginia, discriminating in the selection of jurors, as it does, against negroes because of their color, amounts to a denial of the equal protection of the laws to a colored man when he is put upon trial for an alleged offense against the state.''

The same has been held regarding the exclusion of negroes from the grand jury (29).

The equal protection of the laws, however, does not require that any part of a jury trying a negro shall necessarily be composed of negroes. It only requires that they shall not be excluded on account of their color from having a fair opportunity of being drawn to serve on a jury (30). Nor does the Constitution forbid the exclusion from juries of any general class of persons who through age, sex, alienage, or incapacity, may reasonably be thought not well qualified for such service (31). Also persons engaged in various occupations may be excluded from jury duty so as not to interrupt their regular work for the community. Lawyers, ministers, doctors, teachers, engineers, etc., are frequently excluded on this ground (32).

---

(29)   Carter v. Texas, 177 U. S. 442.
(30)   Virginia v. Rivers, 100 U. S. 313.
(31)   Ex parte Virginia, 100 U. S. 339, 367.
(32)   Rawlins v. Georgia, 201 U. S. 638.

CHAPTER VIII.

DUE PROCESS AND EQUAL PROTECTION OF LAW: POWERS OF REGULATION.—POLICE POWER.

Section 1. General Conceptions.

§ 144. **Fundamental guarantees apply to rights as well as procedure.** In Chapter VII, above, we have discussed the limitations upon procedure imposed by the constitutional requirements of due process and equality of law. But these provisions include much more. The very substance of individual rights to liberty and property may not be arbitrarily impaired, no matter how fair the procedure. For instance, suppose a state should pass a law providing that in each township the person best able to bear the burden should pay the entire expense of local government, or should be deprived of one-half of his property, or that persons having more than $100,000 of property should be forbidden to acquire more. The fairest possible procedure might be provided to ascertain the persons affected by these laws, and to administer their provisions, but this would be unavailing. Our present constitutions prohibit the objects sought by such laws, regardless of methods of procedure.

In the next three chapters we shall consider at some length the scope of these limitations upon the principal governmental powers of the states and the nation.

131

§ 145. **They apply to all departments of government.**
Regarding the history and present meaning of the phrase
"due process of law" the United States Supreme Court
has said:

"The equivalent of the phrase 'due process of law,' according to Lord Coke, is found in the words 'law of the
land,' in the Great Charter, in connection with the writ
of habeas corpus, the trial by jury, and other guarantees
of the rights of the subject against the oppression of the
crown. In the series of amendments to the Constitution
of the United States, proposed and adopted immediately
after the organization of the government, which were dic-
tated by the jealousy of the states as further limitations
upon the power of the Federal government, it is found
in the Fifth, in connection with other guarantees of personal rights of the same character. . . . It is easy
to see that when the great barons of England wrung from
King John, at the point of the sword, the concession that
neither their lives nor their property should be disposed
of by the crown, except as provided by the law of the land,
they meant by 'law of the land' the ancient and customary
laws of the English people, or laws enacted by the Parliament of which those barons were a controlling element.
It was not in their minds, therefore, to protect themselves
against the enactment of laws by the Parliament of England. But when, in the year of grace 1866, there is placed
in the Constitution of the United States a declaration that
no state shall deprive any person of life, liberty, or property without due process of law,' can a state make anything due process of law which, by its own legislation, it

chooses to declare such? To affirm this is to hold that the prohibition to the states is of no avail, or has no application where the invasion of private rights is effected under the forms of state legislation. It seems to us that a statute which declares in terms, and without more, that the full and exclusive title of a described piece of land, which is now in A, shall be and is hereby vested in B, would, if effectual, deprive A of his property without due process of law, within the meaning of the constitutional provision (1).

"In this country written constitutions were deemed essential to protect the rights and liberties of the people against the encroachments of power delegated to their governments, and the provisions of Magna Charta were incorporated into bills of rights. They were limitations upon all the powers of government, legislative as well as executive and judicial. . . . Applied in England only as guards against executive usurpation and tyranny, here they have become bulwarks also against arbitrary legislation; but, in that application, as it would be incongruous to measure and restrict them by the ancient customary English law, they must be held to guarantee, not particular forms of procedure, but the very substance of individual rights of life, liberty, and property" (2).

The requirement of equal protection of the laws has been similarly interpreted and applied.

§ 146. **Meaning of liberty.** As applied to the regulative powers of government, the constitutional prohibi-

---

(1) Davidson v. New Orleans, 96 U. S. 97, 101-2.

(2) Hurtado v. California, 110 U. S. 516, 531-32.

tion against depriving persons of liberty without due process of law (3) means that they may not be deprived arbitrarily and without some reasonable ground of either their personal liberty, or of their freedom to make contracts, to engage in occupations, or to acquire and use property.

The word "liberty" in Magna Charta and other early English political documents (whence it came into our constitutions) doubtless referred only to liberty of the person (4). The same process that enlarged the application of the phrase "due process of law" (see § 145, above) has also widened the meaning of "liberty." Louisiana attempted to forbid any person from doing any act within the state to insure property in the state in any marine insurance company which had not complied with Louisiana law. The Supreme Court held the statute invalid as applied to a person who mailed a notice in the state to an outside company to effect insurance previously contracted for elsewhere. The prohibition of such acts was held to have no reasonable relation to any legitimate public policy of the state. The court said:

"The liberty mentioned in that amendment means not only the right of the citizen to be free from the mere physical restraint of his person, as by incarceration, but the term is deemed to embrace the right of the citizen to be free in the enjoyment of all his faculties; to be free to use them in all lawful ways; to live and work where he will;

---

(3) Const., Amend. V and XIV.

(4) C. E. Shattuck in 4 Harvard Law Review, 365.

to earn his livelihood by any lawful calling; to pursue any livelihood or avocation, and for that purpose to enter into all contracts which may be proper, necessiry, and essential to his carrying out to a successful con lusion the purposes above mentioned'' (5).

§ 147. **Meaning of deprivation of property.** Deprivation of property may take place in a variety of ways besides sheer confiscation. The state may place such restrictions upon the possession, use, or the transfer of property as to amount to a deprivation of some or all of its essential incidents. Legislation may attempt to change the character of an owner's title to property, or to compel special expenditures on account of the ownership or control of certain kinds of property, or to enlarge the owner's liability for damage resulting from the condition or use of property, or to limit the owner's remedies for infringement of property rights. If such and similar interferences with property rights are merely arbitrary, and do not serve any reasonable or legitimate public purpose they may be declared unconstitutional. Many specific illustrations of this appear in succeeding subsections of this chapter. The rights protected by the guarantees of liberty and of property blend together at certain points, as for instance where an owner is forbidden to make a certain use of his property. This may be regarded as invading his liberty of action or as limiting his property rights. It is usually not important to distinguish closely between the two, and courts frequently do not do so.

---

(5) Allgeyer v. Louisiana, 165 U. S. 578, 589.

§ **148. Meaning of equal protection of the laws.** The
Fourteenth Amendment guarantees the equal protection
of the laws to all persons within the jurisdiction of a state.
Obviously this provision does not mean that all persons,
property, or occupations must be treated alike by the
state.   Insane persons may be treated differently from
sane ones, bricks differently from dynamite, and rail-
roading differently from farming.   For the public welfare, persons, property, and occupations must be classified and subjected to differing and appropriate regulations. ''Regulations for these purposes may press with
more or less weight upon one than upon another, but they
are designed not to impose unequal or unnecessary restrictions upon any one, but to promote, with as little
individual inconvenience as possible, the general good.
Though, in many respects, necessarily special in their
character, they do not furnish just ground of complaint
if they operate alike upon all persons and property under
the same conditions and circumstances.   Class legislation, discriminating against some and favoring others,
is prohibited; but legislation which, in carrying out a public purpose, is limited in its application, if within the
sphere of its operation it affects alike all persons similarly situated, is not within the amendment'' (6).

Nor is it objectionable that the state chooses to regulate
the evils in one kind of business, while it permits the
evils of other kinds of business to go unregulated.   A
legislature is not obliged to reform everything in order

(6)   Barbier v. Connolly, 113 U. S. 27, 31-32.

constitutionally to reform anything. "Specific regulations for one kind of business, which may be necessary for the protection of the public, can never be the just ground of complaint because like restrictions are not imposed upon other business of a different kind. The discriminations which are open to objection are those where persons engaged in the same business are subjected to different restrictions, or are held entitled to different privileges under the same conditions" (7). Thus, a California statute forbidding the sale of corporation stock on margin, or for future delivery, was upheld although similar sales of other property were not forbidden. This particular form of speculative gambling being easy and prevalent, as compared with other forms, furnished a proper reason for treating it differently (8).

On the other hand, an Illinois statute was held invalid which forbade all combinations to fix prices or restrict competition except those of producers and raisers regarding farm products or live stock. The excepted classes were so numerous and important that no good reason appeared why they alone should be permitted to combine against the public interest (9). All classification for purposes of regulation "must always be based upon some difference which bears a reasonable and just relation to the act in respect to which the classification is proposed, and can never be made arbitrarily and without such basis." This was said in declaring invalid a statute re-

(7)   Soon Hing v. Crowley, 113 U. S. pp. 708-9.
(8)   Otis v. Parker, 187 U. S. 606.
(9)   Connolly v. Union Sewer Pipe Co., 184 U. S. 540.

quiring railroad companies alone to pay costs when defeated in litigation (10).

A statute may be valid on its face and yet the administration of it may be so arbitrary as to be unconstitutional. Thus, the requirement that laundries in wooden buildings must obtain special licenses on account of the danger from fire is a valid classification, but if the laundries of white men are uniformly licensed while those of Chinese similarly situated are not, this administration of the ordinance is invalid (11).

§ 149. **Application of these guaranties to corporations.** The constitutional provisions under discussion apply to persons, not merely to citizens. They clearly include all natural persons, even though aliens, and have been held to cover corporations also, these being artificial persons (12). The peculiar nature of a corporation, however, deprives it of much of the protection against arbitrary and unequal legislation enjoyed by natural persons.

A corporation derives all its powers of action from some law, state or Federal. If it is incorporated or employed by the United States, or if its business is solely interstate or foreign commerce, a state may not interfere with these activities. (See § 296, below). The same is true if it has an irrepealable charter or contract or license to do business in a state. (See § 230, below). With these exceptions, a state may determine absolutely what corporations shall or shall not do business within it, and what

---

(10)   Gulf, etc., Railroad Co. v. Ellis, 165 U. S. 150.

(11)   Yick Wo v. Hopkins, 118 U. S. 356.

(12)   Pembina Co. v. Pennsylvania, 125 U. S. 181.

powers they shall exercise. Permission to do business not made part of a contract, can be withdrawn at any time by the state; and from these principles it results that the liberty clauses of our constitutions are scarcely applicable to corporations (13). The requirement of the equal protection of the laws applies only to persons "within the jurisdiction." A corporation, not within the excepted classes mentioned above, cannot exist within the jurisdiction of a state without its permission, because the artificial corporate entity has no existence except where sustained by law. A state may thus arbitrarily exclude corporations, or, when admitted, it may arbitrarily put them out unless they submit to new conditions (14). But generally, conditions cannot be imposed which require relinquishment of rights protected by the Federal Constitution.

Although corporations are popularly supposed to occupy positions of great privilege in this country, they are more vulnerable to legislative attack than individuals. Their essential strength is economic rather than legal.

§ 150. **Definition of police power.** The various powers of government overlap in their exercise to such an extent that a rigorous classification of them is scarcely practicable. A few of them are sufficiently distinct from the remainder to have acquired distinguishing names, like the powers of war, of taxation, and of eminent domain. There is no general agreement regarding the classification of other governmental powers, though they may be

---

(13) Western Turf Association v. Greenberg, 204 U. S. 359.

(14) Philadelphia Fire Association v. New York, 119 U. S. 110; National Council v. State Council, 203 U. S. 151. But see W. U. Tel. Co. v. Kansas, 216 U. S. 1; So. Ry. Co. v. Greene, 216 U. S. 400.

divided roughly into such groups as those regulating procedure and the forms of remedies, those defining private
rights and duties between individuals, and those regulating conduct in the interest of the public welfare. This
latter group is perhaps today more frequently called the
police power, though the name is a vague one constantly
applied by judges and writers to powers included in the
other groups mentioned (15). The powers discussed in
this chapter are chiefly those falling in the third group,
regulation for the public welfare, with a few that perhaps
belong in the second group as mainly concerning rights
between individuals.

§ 151. **Classification of subjects of police power.** The
subjects of the police power in its narrower sense may be
divided roughly into three classes: 1. Legislation designed to promote the social welfare of the public. 2.
Legislation designed to promote the economic interests of
the public. 3. Administrative regulations the better to
secure these ends. The principal topics in each of these
classes will be briefly dealt with.

SECTION 2. REGULATION OF SOCIAL INTERESTS (16).

§ 152. **Public health.** Very great latitude is allowed
government in its bona fide efforts to protect the health
of persons or animals. Direct sanitary legislation, bear-

---

(15) See Freund, Police Power, §§ 1-3.

(16) The outline of this and succeeding sections of this chapter
follows the analysis of the subject made by Professor Ernst Freund,
of the University of Chicago Law School, in his excellent work, The
Police Power.

ing any reasonable relation to the matter, is of course valid, as are also many restrictions upon occupations and the use of property that indirectly promote these objects. Thus, a state may require all slaughtering of cattle in a large city to be conducted under the control of a single corporation, which is given a monopoly of the business, in order to secure more effective sanitary control of the business; the manufacture and sale of oleomargarine may be wholly forbidden if much of that sold is unhealthful; persons may be forbidden to labor more than eight hours a day in underground mines; and women may be restricted to ten hours a day of work in public laundries (17).

Where the court thinks that the alleged health law bears no reasonable relation to the avowed purposes of its creation, it is invalid. A noteworthy instance of this was the annulling of a New York statute forbidding more than ten hours a day of labor in bakeries, the court not being persuaded that this occupation was sufficiently unhealthful to make such a regulation reasonable (18). Obviously the determination of such questions depends more upon a knowledge of the pertinent facts than upon legal learning, and reputable courts may readily disagree upon close questions (19).

§ 153. **Public morals.** The immense importance of

---

(17) Slaughter House Cases, 16 Wall. 36; Powell v. Pennsylvania, 127 U. S. 678; Holden v. Hardy, 169 U. S. 366; Muller v. Oregon, 208 U. S. 412.

(18) Lochner v. New York, 198 U. S. 45.

(19) Compare People v. Marx, 99 N. Y. 377, with Powell v. Pennsylvania, above.

this subject justifies a correspondingly wide legislative control. The principal subjects of regulation have been gambling in its varied forms, intoxicating liquors, and sexual vice. Betting may be forbidden, even upon games wholly of skill, lotteries and the common forms of gambling are almost everywhere illegal, and even business transactions of a more highly speculative character may be forbidden. Thus, option contracts for the future delivery of grain may be made illegal, as may sales of stock upon margin (20).

Attempts to control the liquor traffic in this country have produced a vast amount of legislation and litigation. As a result it has been definitely settled that the admitted evils of the traffic justify absolute prohibition of the manufacture, keeping, or sale of intoxicating liquor, and that this prohibition may constitutionally apply to places of manufacture or to liquor legally owned in a state before the prohibitory law took effect (21). This is one of the most notable instances of legislative power to render property virtually useless and almost valueless in the public interest, without compensation. Of course the right to forbid includes the lesser right to license upon stringent conditions, and at least one state (South Carolina) has legally made the selling of liquor a government monopoly (22).

Measures designed to prevent or limit sexual immorality are seldom held invalid. It has even been suggested

---

(20)   Booth v. Illinois, 184 U. S. 425; Otis v. Parker, 187 U. S. 606.

(21)   Mugler v. Kansas, 123 U. S. 623.

(22)   Vance v. Vandercook Co., 170 U. S. 438.

that a state may restrict the location of houses of ill fame to certain districts, without infringing the constitutional rights of property owners in such districts (23).

§ 154. **Public safety.** The rapidly increasing bulk of state and municipal legislation for the public safety indicates its importance. Dangerous property and businesses may be required to adopt appropriate measures for the protection of employees, patrons, or the public generally; and precautionary steps may be required in order that property or occupations shall not become dangerous. Regulation of factories, mines, railroads, navigation, construction of buildings, and many other matters are common instances. The principal questions here are what parties may be made to bear the expense of measures for the public safety. This is discussed in § 165, following.

§ 155. **Public order and comfort. Esthetics.** The state may regulate the use of streets and other public places, may secure quiet at night and on Sundays, and may forbid acts offensive either to the senses or the feelings of the public.

Comprehensive zoning ordinances are a valid exercise of the state's police power and do not violate the due process clause of the Fourteenth Amendment as long as there is a reasonable classification, for a proper governmental purpose, and they are properly applied (24). As the court said in Berman v. Parker, 348 U.S. 26, "Public safety, public health, morality, peace and quiet, law and order . . . these are some of the more conspicuous ex-

---

(23) L'Hote v. New Orleans, 177 U. S. 587.

(24) Euclid v. Ambler Realty Co., 272 U.S. 365.

amples of the traditional application of the police power to municipal affairs. Yet they merely illustrate the scope of the power and do not delimit it. . . . Miserable and disreputable housing conditions may do more than spread disease and crime and immorality. They may also suffocate the spirit by reducing the people who live there to the status of cattle. They may indeed make living an almost insufferable burden. They may also be an ugly sore, a blight on the community which robs it of charm, which makes it a place from which men turn. The misery of housing may despoil a community as an open sewer may ruin a river.

"We do not sit to determine whether a particular housing project is or is not desirable. The concept of the public welfare is broad and inclusive . . . the values it represents are spiritual as well as physical, aesthetic as well as monetary. It is within the power of the legislature to determine that the community should be beautiful as well as healthy, spacious as well as clean, well-balanced as well as carefully patroled."

Statutes have been upheld which require interstate railroads to abolish grade crossings (24a) and replace the grade crossing with a street underpass (25), without regard to cost or financial ability; and which require the destruction of diseased trees to prevent their infection of other trees (26).

§ 156. **Licensing occupations.** Not only may licenses be required for occupations that may be forbidden altogether, like selling liquor, but "if the occupation or calling be of such a character as to require a special course of

---

(24a) Lyford v. New York, 140 f2d 840.

(25)   A.T. and S.F. Co. v. Public Utilities Com., 346 U.S. 346.

(26)   Miller v. Schoene, 276 U.S. 272.

study or training or experience to qualify one to pursue such occupation or calling with safety to the public interests, no one questions the power of the legislature to impose such restraints and prescribe such requirements as it may deem proper for the protection of the public against the evils resulting from incapacity and ignorance'' (27). The requirement of appropriate qualifications, to be evidenced by licenses, has been upheld in respect to a great variety of occupations including many of those involving professional skill, fiduciary relation, or a likelihood of fraud or public disorder occurring in connection with the business. But the qualifications required must be appropriate to the business. Requiring a barber to be a citizen is invalid (28). The examination and licensing cannot be required in occupations where this is not reasonably necessary to the public protection, such as horseshoeing, and undertaking (29).

§ 157. **Domestic relations. Dependent, delinquent and defective persons.** The control of the state over marriage and divorce is discussed in the article on Domestic Relations in Volume II of this work. This power to prescribe qualifications and formalities for marriage is doubtless much wider than any previous exercise of it in this country; and the power to prescribe the conditions of divorce is practically absolute. In the absence of express constitutional restrictions a state legislature may even grant divorces in individual cases (30).

---

(27)   Singer v. Maryland, 72 Md. 464.
(28)   Templar v. State Board, 131 Mich. 254.
(29)   Besette v. People, 193 Ill. 334; People v. Ringe, 125 App. Div. (N.Y.), 592.
(30)   Maynard v. Hill, 125 U.S. 190.

Minor children, insane persons, and those with abnormal tendencies markedly injurious to the social order, like habitual criminals, vagrants, and truants may be cared for by the state in an appropriate manner. The education of children may be made compulsory, and the state may care for them if their parents are unable or unwilling to do so. Insane and otherwise defective persons may be treated in state institutions such as asylums, hospitals, reformatories, etc., wherever public care seems likely to secure better results than private care.

SECTION 3. ECONOMIC INTERESTS.

§ **158. In general.** It is noticeable that the courts have allowed the legislature less latitude in regulations affecting economic, than in those dealing with social, interests. This has been particularly marked in the case of legislation designed to restrict competition. Unfair methods of competition may in many instances be successfully forbidden, but, eliminating these, the "free struggle for life" has been carefully protected. It may be that this century will witness such a change in the essential conditions of this struggle that much of the older economic reasoning will be abandoned by the courts.

§ **159. Protection against fraud.** Fraud, as a means of competition, it is everywhere agreed may be forbidden. Laws against short weights, imitations, and even harmless adulterations, inspection laws, regulations to secure the fidelity of fiduciaries and the regulation of other kinds of business where fraud is likely to appear are common instances of this. Under the guise of such legislation, however, it is not permissible unreasonably to restrict competition. For instance, if the prohibition of oleo-margarine cannot reasonably be attributed to a purpose to protect health and prevent fraud, it cannot be sustained upon the ground of protecting the butter interests of a state from competition (31). Similarly, laws against merchants giving premiums with their goods have been held invalid (32). The courts, however, influenced, perhaps, by changing social and economic conditions, have since upheld so-called "unfair practice acts" which prohibit this and other trade practices, including discrimination in price, considered unfair.

§ 160. **Protection against oppression.** Where the economic superiority of certain classes of persons in their dealings with other classes or with the public is so marked that oppressive terms are likely to be frequently exacted, the weaker party may be protected by legislation which either regulates particular contracts or methods of organization, that give undue economic advantages. Debtors and laborers have been the two classes commonly protected by the regulation of their contracts. Excessive interest and annoying practices in the collection of debts are forbidden in most states; and bankruptcy acts may even discharge honest or unfortunate debtors altogether. The latter subject is dealt with at length in the article on Bankruptcy in Volume X of this work.

Legislation regulating the more important elements of labor contracts, to prevent economic oppression have, in the past, generally been held invalid. It has been held that hours of work cannot be restricted except to protect health or morals, that employees cannot be protected from

(31)   People v. Marx, 99 N. Y. 377.
(32)   People v. Gillson, 109 N. Y. 389.

arbitrary discharge, for instance, because they are members of a union (33), and that the rate of wages cannot be regulated. But in West Coast Hotel Co. v. Parrish (34), the United States Supreme Court upheld a minimum wage law for women and minors. And in National Labor Relations Board v. Jones & Laughlin Corporation (34a), the same court held valid the National Labor Relations Act of 1935, which declares it to be an unfair labor practice to discriminate against employees in order to encourage or to discourage membership in labor organizations.

Various incidents of the contract of employment may be regulated, such as requiring full payment when a servant is discharged and forbidding payment in store orders instead of in cash (34b). The blacklisting of employees by combinations of employers may be forbidden. Combinations in restraint of trade may be prohibited. The states' power with respect to these is greater than against individual action (35).

§ 161. Business affected with a public interest. Various businesses that render important services to the community may be regulated in great detail by the legislature. These businesses are often said to be clothed or affected with a public interest, and in recent years the more important ones have generally been collectively called "public utilities," or "public service businesses." They include the furnishing of transportation, telegraph and

---

(33)   Lochner v. New York, 198 U. S. 45; Adair v. United States, 208 U. S. 161.

(34)   300 U. S., 379, 108 A.L.R. 1330.

(34a)   301 U. S., 1, 108 A.L.R. 1352.

(34b)   Knoxville Iron Co. v. Harbison, 183 U. S. 13.

(35)   Aikens v. Wisconsin, 195 U. S. 194. § 160 revised by publisher's editorial staff.

telephone service, gas, water, and electricity, and other important public services. It is difficult to state any single test by which to distinguish public service businesses from others. Probably there are several different principles of inclusion. Businesses discharging governmental functions, like transportation, may be regulated; businesses requiring public franchises, as for the use of the streets, may be regulated; and perhaps any business of vital importance which either legally or economically has become a virtual monopoly may be regulated. The general characteristics and obligations of such occupations are fully treated in the article on Public Service Corporations in Volume VIII of this work.

Regulation of these businesses may prescribe maximum charges and equality of service and may specify the details of the service to be supplied. The principal limitation upon the regulation of charges is that they must permit the earning of a fair return upon the business. As to railroad rates the Supreme Court has said:

"We hold, however, that the basis of all calculations as to the reasonableness of rates to be charged by a corporation maintaining a highway under legislative sanction must be the fair value of the property being used by it for the convenience of the public. And in order to ascertain that value, the original cost of construction, the amount expended in permanent improvements, the amount and market value of its bonds and stock, the present as compared with the original cost of construction, the probable earning capacity of the property under particular rates prescribed by the statute, and the sum required to meet operating expenses, are all matters for consideration, and are to be given such weight as may be just and right in each case. We do not say that there may not be other matters to be regarded in estimating the value of the property" (36).

Under our dual system of government, internal state rates may be regulated by the state alone, and interstate rates by the United States alone; and in determining what is a fair return upon the value of the property, the income from internal transportation must alone be considered in fixing the internal rates, and vice versa. See § 293, below. Governmental regulation of public service business is fully discussed in the article upon Public Service Corporations in Volume VIII of this work.

Banks and insurance companies are usually the subject of rather stringent regulations in order to protect their patrons from loss due to unwise or dishonest management.

§ 162. Regulation of corporations. As has been explained elsewhere (see § 149, above), corporations owe their existence and powers entirely to legislation and they are therefore subject to much more stringent and arbitrary regulation than are individuals. As a condition of the grant of a corporate charter the corporation may be required to consent in advance to exactions that could not be required of it under ordinary legislative powers. Thus, it may validly agree to carry passengers at rates too low to make a fair profit (37). See also §§ 291, 296, below. The Federal Constitution may forbid the enforceability

---

(36) Smyth v. Ames, 169 U.S. 466, 546-7.

(37) Grand Rapids, etc. R. R. Co. v. Osborne, 193 U. S. 17.

of some terms even in a franchise grant, as for instance
an agreement not to remove suits into the Federal courts;
but though the state may not specifically enforce such an
agreement it may punish the corporation by expelling it
from the state for breach of it (38).

§ 163. **Regulation of ownership of property.** The state
may regulate the future creation of interests in property,
as by forbidding perpetuities or long time leases of agricultural lands. The use and appropriation of certain
peculiar kinds of property may also be regulated, such
as running water, game, fish, natural gas, and oil. The
wanton waste of these substances may be forbidden in the
interest of the public, though otherwise private rights in
them may be left untouched. The public control over
game, fish, and navigable waters is very extensive, and
their taking for private purposes may be forbidden, or allowed subject to qualifications (39). The prohibition of
the wasteful destruction of natural gas or forest trees by
private owners has been upheld (40).

§ 164. **Compelling joint action to improve property.**
Where property is so situated that it cannot be most
beneficially enjoyed by its owners acting separately, the
legislature may compel some of the owners, upon receiving compensation, to submit to measures enabling the
others to obtain the most beneficial use of the joint property, provided that this result is of considerable public

---

(38) Home Ins. Co. v. Morse, 20 Wall. 445; Security Ins. Co. v.
Prewitt, 202 U. S. 246.

(39) Geer v. Connecticut, 161 U. S. 519; Hudson Water Co. v.
McCarter, 209 U. S. 349.

(40) Ohio Oil Co. v. Indiana, 177 U. S. 190; Opinion of Justices,
103 Me. 506.

benefit. Thus, where a large water power can be developed from a stream by damming it and flooding the upper riparian land, the legislature may authorize such a dam and compel the upper owner to submit to flooding upon being paid therefor by the owner of the dam (41). Similarly, when land is held by several tenants in common or joint tenants, the legislature may authorize a compulsory partition and sale in order to secure the more beneficial use of the property.

Much the same principle is involved where the property of several owners is so situated that all must concur to obtain some important public improvement such as a land irrigation or drainage system. All of the owners whose land is benefited may be required to contribute to a common system (42). A compulsory sharing of the expense of party walls is in some states treated similarly.

§ 165. Special liabilities due to nature of business. If the nature of the business requires special supervision, or exposes other persons and property to special hazard, even when carefully conducted, the cost of such supervision and the burden of such hazard may be placed wholly upon the business occasioning them. Thus, the railroads of a state may be made to pay the expense of a railroad commission; coal mines must pay for mine inspectors; and so on (43). Railroads may be made absolutely liable for fire from their engines, or for the injuring of passengers, even though all proper precautions are

---

(41) Head v. Amoskeag Co., 113 U. S. 9.
(42) Wurts v. Hoagland, 114 U. S. 606.
(43) Railroad Co. v. Gibbes, 142 U. S. 386.

used to prevent these accidents; and a liquor seller may be made liable for damage done by intoxicated persons to whom he has sold liquor. The businesses themselves are hazardous and may be made to bear the expense of their hazards (44). Similarly, a business may be made to bear the expense of guarding against injuries likely to occur in its conduct; for instance, railroads must pay for fencing their tracks, for the installation of safety devices, and for track elevation in populous districts (45).

§ 166. **Special liabilities due to natural condition of property.** At common law a landowner was not liable for a nuisance occasioned on his premises by the ordinary operation of natural causes, such as stagnant water in a natural swamp, or the springing up of noxious weeds injurious to the crops of his neighbors (46). But by statute he may be required to remedy these defects at his own expense, unless the trouble and expense of doing so is unreasonably great. Thus he may be required to fill up a city lot to a grade fixed so as to prevent the accumulation of stagnant water (47), or to cut noxious weeds, or kill diseased animals (48); but he cannot be required to free his farm land from ground squirrels and similar refractory vermin, where the expense and burden is excessive as compared with the public benefit (48). Compulsory public improvements on a large scale, requiring the united efforts of the landowners of a district, are discussed in § 164, above.

(44) St. Louis, etc., Ry. v. Mathews, 165 U. S. 1; Chicago, R. I & P. Ry. v. Zernecke, 183 U. S. 582; Howes v. Maxwell, 157 Mass. 333

(45) New York, etc., Ry. v. Bristol, 151 U. S. 556.

(46) Roberts v. Harrison, 101 Ga. 773; Giles v. Walker, 24 Q. B. D. 656.

(47) Nickerson v. Boston, 131 Mass. 306.

(48) Ex parte Hodges, 87 Cal. 162.

§ 167. **Retroactive laws.** Retroactive laws that affect prejudicially persons charged with crime, or which impair the obligations of contracts are dealt with elsewhere in this article as ex post facto laws and laws impairing the obligations of contracts. (See Chapters VI and XI.) Other retroactive laws, however, may be passed by the legislature which will be invalid if they amount to a taking of property without due process of law. A statute enacting merely that land now owned by A should become the property of B would of course be invalid. But suppose A purports to convey land to B by a deed which is invalid for some formal defect, and the legislature by statute validates the deed. This also takes the title from A and puts it in B, but it is "due process" because it carries out the intention of the parties so as to produce a just result. The general rule for such cases has been thus stated in a leading decision: "When a statute is expressly retroactive, and the object and effect of it is to correct an innocent mistake, remedy a mischief, execute the intention of the parties, and promote justice, then, both as a matter of right and of public policy affecting the peace and welfare of the community, the law should be sustained" (49).

This principle is frequently invoked to sustain curative laws validating not only acts between private parties, but those of public officials and of municipal corporations (50). Of course no act can be thus validated which could not have been originally authorized. The legislative

---

(49) Mechanics' Savings Bank v. Allen, 28 Conn. 97.

(50) Mitchell v. Clark, 110 U. S. 633; New Orleans v. Clark, 95 U. S. 644.

validation of a void mortgage is binding not only between the parties, but as against attaching creditors of the mortgagor, who knew of the existence of the void mortgage (51). Doubtless such retroactive validation would not be good against third parties who were purchasers for value without notice.

When a right of action has been barred by the statute of limitations it is generally held that it cannot be revived against the debtor by a retroactive statute; nor, when it is not a matter of curing defective proceedings, can a cause of action or a defense to an action be abrogated by a retroactive statute, except when the action or defense is based upon some purely arbitrary rule of law (52). There is much difference of opinion regarding the validity of "betterment laws," which permit one who in good faith has spent money upon property which he thinks he owns to recover the value of his improvements when ejected by the real owner. In law the improvements become the property of the owner of the land, and opinions differ about the justice of making him pay for what he has not requested to be done (53). Retroactive laws validating marriages and legitimating children have been upheld (54).

Great latitude is given to the state in making retroactive changes in the remedies for wrongs. The forms and incidents of actions, rules of evidence, and methods of pro-

(51)　McFaddin v. Evans-Snider-Buel Co., 185 U. S. 505. But see Steger v. Trav. Men Bldg. Assn., 208 Ill. 236, contra.

(52)　Bd. of Ed. v. Blodgett, 155 Ill. 441; Plummer v. Northern Pacific Ry., 152 Fed. 206.

(53)　See 14 Harvard Law Rev. 385.

(54)　Goshen v. Stonington, 4 Conn. 209.

cedure before and after judgment may all be changed after a cause of action has arisen, provided that such alterations are not mere colorable devices for unjustly and arbitrarily depriving persons of their rights.

SECTION 4. ADMINISTRATIVE REGULATIONS.

§ 168. **In general.** Many regulations incidental to those directly concerning the public welfare are enacted in order to secure uniformity, certainty, and administrative efficiency in enforcing the law. Of this character are most laws fixing standards, laying down prima facie rules of evidence, and forbidding certain acts or conduct regardless of their effect or tendency in particular cases.

§ 169. **Illustrations.** Thus, all women may be forbidden to work in factories more than ten hours a day, even though a considerable number of particular women may be able to work more than this length of time without injury (55); the sale of all game of a certain kind may be forbidden during the closed season in a state, even though some of the game offered for sale may have been lawfully killed elsewhere (56); the sale of all oleomargarine artificially colored to resemble butter may be forbidden, even though no effort be made to sell it as butter (57); and nonproducing sellers of milk may be made absolutely liable for selling milk containing less than a certain percentage of milk solids, while a dairy owner may escape liability by proving that his cows actually gave milk with a smaller percentage of solids (58).

---

(55) Muller v. Oregon, 208 U. S. 412.
(56) Silz v. Hesterberg, 211 U. S. 31.
(57) Plumley v. Massachusetts, 155 U. S. 461.
(58) St. John v. New York, 201 U. S. 633.

It is evident that all of these provisions, though not necessary in particular cases, do in general substantially aid the enforcement of the law where it is needed. It would be difficult to determine the strength or endurance of any particular woman; or to prove that game offered for sale was killed within the state; and if the sale of butter-colored oleomargarine is permitted at all, some dealers will sell it for butter. In the milk case, the dairyman's cows may be tested, while it is much more difficult to trace the source of milk sold by non-producers.

§ 170. **Prima facie rules of evidence.** Of a similar character are many so-called prima facie rules of evidence, which make the proof of some fact, if unexplained, a sufficient ground for conviction of an offense with which the proven fact is ordinarily closely connected. Thus, a statute may make the possession of policy slips prima facie evidence of the illegal playing of policy (59); or the drinking of liquor in a shop prima facie evidence that it was sold there (60). The fact upon which the presumption is to rest must have some fair relation to, or natural connection with the act which is made criminal; and in any case of this kind the defendant may rebut the presumption by explaining the fact that is made prima facie evidence, and thus showing his innocence.

A statute which provided that the finding of intoxicating liquors in the possession of any person by means of a search warrant should be prima facie evidence that such person had possession for the purpose of selling without first obtaining a license therefore, was held un-

(59)   Adams v. New York, 192 U. S. 585.
(60)   Board of Excise v. Merchant, 103 New York 143.

constitutional in State v. Kelly (61) because the mere possession of intoxicating liquor furnishes no logical basis for an inference of an illegal intent. In its opinion the court quoted with approval from Mobile, J. & K. C. R. Co. v. Turnipseed (62) as follows:

"That a legislative presumption of one fact from evidence of another may not constitute a denial of due process of law or a denial of the equal protection of the law, it is only essential that there shall be some rational connection between the fact proved and the ultimate fact presumed, and that the inference of one fact from proof of another shall not be so unreasonable as to be a purely arbitrary mandate. So, also, it must not, under guise of regulating the presentation of evidence, operate to preclude the party from the right to present his defense to the main fact thus presumed.

"If a legislative provision not unreasonable in itself, prescribing a rule of evidence, does not shut out from the party affected a reasonable opportunity to submit to the jury in his defense all of the facts bearing upon the issue there is no ground for holding that due process of law has been denied him."

And from Tot v. United States (63):

"Under our decisions, a statutory presumption cannot be sustained if there be no rational connection between the fact proved and the ultimate fact presumed, if the inference of the one from proof of the other is arbitrary because of lack of connection between the two in common experience. This is not to say that a valid presumption may not be created upon a view of relation broader than that a jury might take in a specific case. But where the inference is so strained as not to have a reasonable relation to the circumstances of life as we know them it is

---

(61) State v. Kelly, 218 Minn. 247, 162 A. L. R. 477.
(62) Mobile, J. & K. C. R. Co. v. Turnipseed, 219 U. S. 35.
(63) Tot v. United States, 319 U. S. 463.

not competent for the legislature to create it as a rule governing the procedure of courts.''

Some of the grounds upon which the validity of Statutes making certain facts prima facie evidence of other facts in criminal cases have been questioned are: That they violate the guarantees of due process of law, equal protection of the laws and trial by jury. That they encroach on the powers of the judiciary. That they compel the accused to testify against himself and that they deprive the accused of the presumption of innocence. Generally speaking, if a statute establishing a prima facie evidence rule can satisfy the tests set out above it will be upheld notwithstanding these objections. Statutes, however, which undertake to establish conclusive presumptions with respect to material facts are held unconstitutional on the ground that they deprive the accused of due process of law (64).

---

(64)   Caroline Products Co. v. McLaughlin, 365 Ill. 62.

CHAPTER IX.

DUE PROCESS AND EQUAL PROTECTION OF LAW: TAXATION.

§ 171. General requisites. The fundamental guaran tees of the Fifth and Fourteenth Amendments regarding due process and equality restrict the powers of taxation of both Federal and state governments. They prohibit legislation that is arbitrary and unreasonable in respect to taxation, just as they restrict such legislation in other fields. Other specific restrictions upon the taxing powers of the states and the United States, not included under the fundamental guarantees of due process of law and equal protection of the laws, will be discussed elsewhere. See §§ 314-17, below.

The principal requisites, with respect to taxation, enforced by these constitutional provisions are as follows:

(a) The taxing power must have jurisdiction of the subject of taxation.

(b) The tax must be levied for a public purpose.

(c) The tax must not be arbitrarily discriminatory, nor disproportionate, nor confiscatory, as respects the standards proper for any particular case.

SECTION 1. JURISDICTION FOR PURPOSES OF TAXATION.

§ 172. Object taxed must have situs in jurisdiction. When a government levies a tax upon property, it is not

158

valid unless the property is located, *for purposes of taxation,* within the territorial jurisdiction of the taxing power; that is, it must have a situs, as it is called, in the jurisdiction. Similarly, when it taxes occupations, or privileges, or the doing of acts, the occupation must be pursued, or the privilege exercised, or the act done, inside the jurisdiction of the taxing power. Otherwise, it is not taxation at all, but is confiscation (1).

§ 173. **Real estate and chattels.** It has always been admitted that real estate is taxable only in the jurisdiction where it is located. Where the tax is upon the tangible land itself this is perfectly clear, but the rule is the same even when the right is an intangible one connected with the land, a so-called "incorporeal hereditament," such as a right of way over the land of another, or a right to ferry from the shore of a river. Such rights can be taxed only where the land is to which they are attached (1a). A mortgage on land is an interest in land taxable where the land is (2).

The same rule applies to tangible personal property, chattels. If permanently kept in one place they can be taxed as property there only, although their owner may live elsewhere. The state where hè lives cannot tax them (3). Where an owner employs the same article of property part of the time in the state where he lives and a part of the time elsewhere, it may be taxed as property

---

(1) State Tax on Foreign-held Bonds, 15 Wall. 300, 319.

(1a) Louisville & Jeffersonville Ferry Co. v. Kentucky, 188 U. S. 385.

(2) Savings & Loan Society v. Multnomah County, 169 U. S. 421.

(3) D., L. & W. R. R. Co. v. Pennsylvania, 198 U. S. 341.

where he lives (4). But where a refrigerator company domiciled outside of Colorado ran its cars irregularly in the state according to the demands of business, so that there was an average of forty-one cars in the state, though composed of constantly changing cars, it was held that Colorado could tax the company upon the value of forty-one cars (5). This average amount of property received the protection of the state, and so might fairly be taxed there.

§ 174. **Corporate assets.** Suppose a corporation, doing business wholly in Illinois, has issued $1,000,000 worth of stock, owes $500,000 worth of bonds, and has $750,000 worth of tangible property, real and personal, in the state. What is the total property value of this corporation? Evidently it is not merely the value of its tangible property, for its stock alone is worth more than this, and in addition to the stock value it is able to sustain the value of $500,000 worth of bonds that it has issued. The value of the corporation as a going concern is fairly indicated by the value of its stock and bonds together, for if the bonds were paid all of the stock would be worth approximately that much more. It is the various intangible values connected with the corporation that account for this great difference between the $750,000 of tangible property and the $1,500,000 gross value of the corporation. These intangible values consist of franchises, contracts, the good-will of an established business, the business ability of its managers, and like elements upon

(4) New York v. Miller, 202 U. S. 584.
(5) American Refrigerator Co. v. Hall, 174 U. S. 70.

which are based the expectations of dividends. These intangible values may be taxed by the state just like any other property, and the method of determining them by adding together the market value of the stock and bonds of the corporation is valid (6).

§ 175. **Corporate assets in several states.** Suppose, however, that the corporation in question is not doing business in Illinois alone, but in several states, although its home office is in Illinois. May these other states also tax a share of these intangible values of the corporate assets, or are they restricted to such tangible property as they can find belonging to it within their respective limits? The Adams Express Company had altogether $16,000,000 worth of corporate assets. About $4,000,000 of these consisted of tangible real and personal property. In Ohio it had about $67,000 of property, including money and credits. About 1-30 of its mileage and business was in the state of Ohio. Ohio taxed express companies upon such part of their entire capital stock as was proportional to their mileage and amount of business done in Ohio. On this basis the property of the Adams Company in Ohio was assessed at $533,000. This was upheld by the United States Supreme Court, which said:

"But where is the situs of this intangible property? The Adams Express Company has, according to its showing, in round numbers $4,000,000 of tangible property scattered through different states, and with that tangible property thus scattered transacts its business. By the

---

(6) State Railway Tax Cases, 92 U. S. 575.

business which it transacts, by combining into a single use
all these separate pieces and articles of tangible property,
by the contracts, franchises, and privileges which it has
acquired and possesses, it has created a corporate property of the actual value of $16,000,000. Thus, according
to its figures, this intangible property, its franchises,
privileges, etc., is of the value of $12,000,000, and its
tangible property of only $4,000,000. Where is the situs of
this intangible property? Is it simply where its home
office is, where is found the central directing thought which
controls the workings of the great machine, or in the state
which gave it its corporate franchise; or is that intangible
property distributed wherever its tangible property is
located and its work is done? Clearly, as we think, the
latter. Every state within which it is transacting business and where it has its property, more or less, may
rightfully say that the $16,000,000 of value which it pos-
sesses springs not merely from the original grant of corporate power by the state which incorporated it, or from
the mere ownership of the tangible property, but it springs
from the fact that that tangible property it has combined
with contracts, franchises, and privileges into a single
unit of property, and this state contributes to that aggregate value not merely the separate value of such tangible
property as is within its limits, but its proportionate
share of the value of the entire property'' (7).

The same rule of taxation, commonly called the ''unit
rule'' has been applied similarly to other kinds of busi-

---

(7)   Adams Express Co. v. Ohio, 166 U. S. 185, 223-4.

ness extending over several states, such as telegraph companies, railroads, and sleeping-car companies. The proportion of intangible values to be localized in any particular state may be ascertained in any fair manner, which is usually by taking a part of it proportional to the mileage or business done in the taxing state.

The only limits that have thus far been suggested upon the principle of the "unit rule" are that the value of the property outside of the state, not directly used by the company in its general business, like bonds held for investment, must be deducted; and that a fair part of disproportionately valuable property held outside of the state, like great railroad terminals, must be deducted in ascertaining the mileage value of the road in states where there is no property of a corresponding character (8).

§ 176. Debts. Suppose A, living in Vermont, owes $100 to X living in New York. The contract right to recover this $100 from A is unquestionably valuable property, and as such is protected in many ways by the constitutional guarantees respecting property. Where is this property located for purposes of taxation? The property consists of an intangible relation between A and X, created by law in consequence of their agreement, by which X is entitled to compel A to pay him $100. It is difficult to see how this relation can be property where the debtor lives, for his obligation to pay is quite the reverse of being valuable to him, and, for similar reasons, the obligation does seem to be property where the creditor

---

(8) Fargo v. Hart, 193 U. S. 490.

lives. This common sense view of the matter has been accepted by the courts, and it is generally held that a debt, pure and simple, is not taxable *as property* at the residence of the debtor (9). On the other hand, generally speaking, debts are taxable as property at the residence of the creditor (10).

§ 177. **Documentary evidence of debts or property.** Suppose, in the case put in the preceding section, that A had given X a promissory note or acknowledgment as evidence of the debt, and that X had kept this in Connecticut, his own residence still being in New York. Could Connecticut tax this evidence of debt as property at the full value of the debt? In a recent case the United States Supreme Court denied that this could be done, at least if the evidence of the debt were a document other than a bond or a bank-note, and if no business of any character were transacted in Connecticut with the credits represented by the documents (11). As regards bonds and bank-notes they have historically been treated as if they were themselves property and not merely evidence of it. Originally, if the owner of a bond (a contract under seal) lost it he could not recover the debt; and bank-notes, payable to bearer, have always passed from hand to hand in ordinary use as money. Bank-notes will probably be regarded as taxable only where they are, like tangible property; and it is perhaps doubtful what will be held in re-

---

(9)   State Tax on Foreign-held Bonds, 15 Wall. 300.

(10)   Kirtland v. Hotchkiss, 100 U. S. 491.

(11)   Buck v. Beach, 206 U. S. 392.

gard to bonds when an actual case arises in the Federal courts.

Warehouse receipts for goods outside of a state also may not be taxed by the state at the full value of the goods, at least unless only the transfer of the receipt could transfer the title to the goods. The ordinary warehouse receipt merely represents the goods for purposes of trade convenience, and the goods themselves may be dealt with independently of it (12).

§ 178. **Credits employed in business.** If intangible credits are employed by the owner in business outside of the state where he lives, they acquire a situs for taxation at the place where they are thus employed, even though the documents representing them are most of the time kept elsewhere. A New York insurance company made loans in Louisiana to its policyholders, upon the security of their policies. The business was done through a local agent in Louisiana, and the notes given by the debtors and the policies held as securities were sent to New York until they were paid, when they were sent back to be delivered to the debtors. The Supreme Court held these loans were taxable in Louisiana, saying:

"Here the loans were negotiated, the notes signed, the security taken, the interest collected, and the debts paid within the state. The notes and securities were in Louisiana whenever the business exigencies required them to be there. . . . We are not dealing here merely with a single credit or a series of separate credits, but with a business.

---

(12) Selliger v. Kentucky, 213 U. S. 200.

The insurance company chose to enter into the business of lending money within the state of Louisiana, and employed a local agent to conduct that business. It was conducted under the laws of the state. The state undertook to tax the capital employed in the business precisely as it taxed the capital of its own citizens in like situation. For the purpose of arriving at the amount of capital actually employed, it caused the credits arising out of the business to be assessed. We think the state had the power to do this, and that the foreigner doing business cannot escape taxation upon his capital by removing temporarily from the state evidences of credits in the form of notes. Under such circumstances they have a taxable situs in the state of their origin'' (13).

§ 179. **Shares of stock.** When a corporation is organized, the artificial corporate entity thus created is the legal owner of all the corporate property. The taxation of this property, tangible and intangible, is governed as to situs by the same rules as if the owner were an individual. The stockholders of the corporation have an interest in it, a step removed from the actual legal ownership of the corporate property. Their right is to receive the dividends from the corporation, if any are earned by the corporate management, and to share in what is left after the payment of debts when the corporation is dissolved. The interest of the stockholders in the corporation is sufficiently different from the corporation's ownership of its property, so that each may be taxed separately

---

(13) Metropolitan Insurance Co. v. New Orleans, 205 U. S. 395, 402-3.

although the same property or business really give value
to both. "It is well settled by the decisions of this court
that the property of the shareholders in their shares and
the property of the corporation in its capital stock are
distinct property interests, and, where that is the legislative intent clearly expressed, that both may be
taxed" (14).

This interest of the shareholders in a corporation not
only is property, separate from the property of the corporation, but apparently it may be treated as having a
taxable situs not only where the stockholder lives, but
also where the corporation does business. A Michigan
stockholder in a New York corporation may be taxed in
Michigan upon the full value of his New York stock, even
though all of the corporate property and business are outside of Michigan (15). On the other hand, shares of
stock may also be treated as having a business situs
where the corporation is located or does business, and may
be taxed there as the property of non-resident share-
holders (16). Presumably, however, a state where the
stock certificates were merely kept could not tax them,
provided both the owner and the corporation were domiciled elsewhere (17).

§ 180. Franchises. A franchise is a privilege grant-
able by the government at its pleasure, which cannot be

---

(14) New Orleans v. Houston, 119 U. S. 265, 277.

(15) Bacon v. Tax Commissioners, 126 Mich. 22.

(16) Tappan v. Merchants' National Bank, 19 Wall. 490.

(17) See Matter of Enston, 113 N. Y. p. 181; and Matter of James,
144 N. Y. p. 12.

exercised without such a grant. The right to purchase property against the will of the owner by eminent domain is an instance. So is the right to become a corporation and exercise corporate powers. So is the right to take tolls for a public highway or ferry or railroad, or to occupy public streets with pipes or conduits or poles, as for gas, electric wires, and trolley lines.

All franchises have a situs for taxation wherever they are exercised. The most striking illustrations of this are cases of corporate franchises. When a corporation is chartered, it is given a variety of franchises. One of these is the franchise of corporate capacity—to be a corporation. Others are its franchises to exercise certain powers. The corporation chartered to run a railroad has different corporate powers from one chartered to conduct a bank, though each has corporate capacity. These various franchises may be taxed as privileges irrespective of their property values, in any place where they are exercised; and they may also be taxed as property, at their fairly ascertained value, either separately, or in common with all other corporate assets. In every state in which a corporation does business it exercises its franchise to be a corporation and its franchises to do its particular kind of business, and these may be taxed as property wherever it does business.

"For the transaction of its business it goes into various states, and wherever it goes as a corporation it carries with it the franchise to be. But the franchise to be is only one of the franchises of a corporation. The franchise to do is an independent franchise, or rather a combination of franchises, embracing all things which the corporation is given power to do, and this power to do is as much a thing of value and a part of the intangible property of the corporation as the franchise to be. Franchises to do go wherever the work is done. The Southern Pacific Railway Company is a corporation chartered by the state of Kentucky, yet within the limits of that state it is said to have no tangible property and no office for the transaction of business. The vast amount of tangible property which by lease or otherwise it holds and operates, and all the franchises to do which it exercises, exist and are exercised in the states and territories on the Pacific slope. Do not these intangible properties—these franchises to do—exercised in connection with the tangible property which it holds, create a substantive matter of taxation to be asserted by every state in which that tangible property is found?" (18). See § 291, below.

The Western Union Telegraph Company, which has a New York franchise, may be taxed upon a fair share of the value of this under the "unit rule" by Missouri when it does business there (19). See § 175.

§ 181. **Situs of property for inheritance taxes.** A kind of taxation adopted in many states, and of increasing importance, is the so-called inheritance tax—a tax upon the right to succeed to property, whether by inheritance or by will, upon the death of its owner. Obviously this right can be exercised only when the state has jurisdiction over the right to succession, and this right.

---

(18) Adams Express Co. v. Ohio, 166 U. S. 185, 224-5.

(19) Western Union Telegraph Co. v. Missouri, 190 U. S. 412.

being intangible, presents various nice problems as to
its situs. It will be convenient to divide the discussion of
these into four parts:

(a)   Property in a state owned by a resident decedent.

(b)   Property out of the state owned by a resident decedent.

(c)   Property in the state owned by a non-resident
decedent.

(d)   Property out of the state owned by a non-resident decedent.

§ 182.   Same: **Domestic property of resident decedent.**
Example: A, a citizen of Illinois dies, leaving land and
chattels in Illinois, and debts due him from Illinois
debtors.

Clearly the descent of all this property upon A's death
is governed solely by the law of Illinois, and, for the
privilege of permitting its descent to A's heirs or persons
named in his will, Illinois may exact a tax. As to this
there is no controversy.

§ 183.   Same: **Foreign property of resident decedent.**
Example: A, a citizen of Illinois, dies leaving land and
chattels situated in Ohio, and debts due him from Ohio
debtors. What succession tax can be collected by Illinois?

As regards land, the succession has always been controlled by the state where it is located. Illinois cannot
confer or take away anybody's right to succeed to land
in Ohio, and so there is nothing for Illinois to tax (20).
The personal property in Ohio might stand differently.
At common law, each state permitted personal property

---

(20)   Matter of Swift, 137 N. Y. 77.

within its borders to descend according to the law of the residence of the owner, upon the latter's death. If this is still the law of Ohio, then it would seem Illinois might tax the recipients of the personal property in Ohio for exercising in their favor the privilege permitted to Illinois by Ohio (21). In such a case both Illinois and Ohio might levy an inheritance tax; Ohio for permitting the law of Illinois to govern, and Illinois for permitting particular persons to succeed to the property. On the other hand, Ohio might pass a statute providing specifically how personal property in the state should descend upon the owner's death, regardless of his domicile. In this case there would be nothing that could be controlled by Illinois, and so Illinois could levy no inheritance tax.

The United States Supreme Court, however, has taken the view that when a state permits property within its borders to descend according to the law of the state in which the deceased owner resided, it thereby adopts the law of that state as its own. The Supreme Court, therefore, holds that the domiciliary state has no power to impose a tax. Hence, even in the absence of an Ohio Statute, Illinois could not levy an inheritance tax (22).

§ 184. Same: Domestic property of non-resident decedent. Example: A, a citizen of Ohio, dies leaving land and chattels situated in Illinois, stock in an Illinois corporation, and debts due him from Illinois debtors. He also owns stock in an Indiana corporation, and notes and bonds due him from Indiana debtors. These latter

---

(21) (See note 20.)

(22) Frick v. Pennsylvania, 268 U. S. 473.

stock, notes and bonds are kept in Illinois, though neither creditor, debtor, nor corporation is in that state. What property is subject to an Illinois succession tax?

As regards the land and chattels in Illinois, Illinois can control the succession to them and so has the right to tax the succession. The right as regards the Illinois debt and the stock in the Illinois corporation is not so clear, but according to recent decisions, Illinois can impose the tax, even though Ohio is also imposing the same kind of tax. But Illinois cannot tax the transfer of the stock in the Indiana Corporation nor the bonds and notes due from Indiana debtors.

§ 185. **Same: Reasons.** The power to tax is based upon power or control over the object taxed, at least so far as tangible property is concerned. The state in which real property is located certainly has control over it and over the process of transfer whether inter-vivos, by will or by operation of the laws of descent and distribution. The same is true with almost equal force in the case of tangible personal property.

With respect to intangible personal property, like stocks, bonds, notes, credits and bank deposits, the matter is more complicated. Such property grows out of personal obligations and relationships. They may be represented by documents of various kinds, but control over them results from control over the persons out of whose relationships they grow. Since the persons involved may be subject to the control of more than one State, it follows that more than one state may have such power or control over such property as to give a right to impose succession taxes.

Perhaps the original view was that intangible personal property follows the person and for purposes of taxation has its situs only at the home of the owner. But gradually it became the practice for succession taxes on such property to be imposed both at the home of the owner and at the home of the debtor, or, in the case of corporate stock, at the home of the corporation. This practice was approved by the United States Supreme Court in Blackstone v. Miller (23). It continued to be lawful until 1930, when Blackstone v. Miller was overruled, and it was held that, because of the due process clause of the Fourteenth Amendment, no more than one state could impose succession taxes, and that state, in the case of intangible personal property, which could have no actual situs, was the domicile of the owner at the time of his death (24). In 1939, a case arose in which the Supreme Court questioned the validity of the doctrine that the Fourteenth Amendment precluded taxation of intangibles in more than one state, and held that under the circumstances of that case, more than one state had power to impose succession taxes on the same intangibles (25). This was followed in 1942 by State Tax Commissioner v. Aldrich (26), which specifically overruled First National Bank v. Maine (27), and held that a state can impose a succession tax on stock in a domestic corporation owned by a nonresident, even though it is subject to a similar tax at the domicile of the owner.

SECTION 2.   WHAT IS A PUBLIC PURPOSE FOR TAXATION?

§ **186. Discharge of governmental functions.** The power of taxation may be validly used to assist in the discharge

---

(23)   188 U. S. 189, decided in 1903.

(24)   Farmers Loan and Trust Co. v. Minnesota, 280 U. S. 204, decided in 1930; First National Bank v. Maine, 284 U. S. 312, decided in 1932.

(25)   Curry v. McCanless, 307 U. S. 357, decided in 1939.

(26)   State Tax Commissioner v. Aldrich, 316 U. S. 174.

(27)   See (24) above.

of any governmental function, whether the function be exercised directly by public officers, or by private persons who are permitted to make a profit from the discharge of these functions. Governmental activities connected with making, interpreting, and enforcing laws are the commonest illustrations of functions discharged directly by public officers. They include all of the machinery by which laws are made and enforced, public order kept, and justice administered. A considerable extension of public functions beyond these essentials is increasingly noticeable. Public schools and charitable institutions are everywhere maintained; parks and public amusements are increasingly provided; gas, electricity, and water are in many places furnished directly by the public; drainage and irrigation works are coming to be likewise maintained; and the public health and safety are increasingly made the subject of direct public action. As regards any activity really benefiting the public, and which may reasonably be thought to be more advantageously conducted by the public than by private enterprise, it is difficult to pronounce it not a public purpose. Especially is this true of all supervisory, regulative, and administrative activities. The legitimate scope of these will constantly expand with the complex needs of society.

At present several functions that are fairly governmental in their nature are generally permitted to be supplied by private enterprise, subject to public regulation. Of this character are railroads, street railways, telegraph and telephone, express service, and in many places the furnishing of light, heat, and water. An analogous activity, the transportation of mail, has in this country always been a government monopoly. Banking and insurance are activities that in some countries are and in all countries doubtless could be assumed by the government. All of these functions may be assisted by public taxation, even though they are carried on by private persons for profit. They do not cease to be public functions merely because the government for the time being thinks private enterprise a more advantageous method of conducting them. Early in our history public aid was not uncommonly given to railroads, canals, and banks, and such aid has almost uniformly been upheld (28).

§ 187. **Objects not in fact of public benefit.** If money raised by taxation is given to a single individual to be used by him as he pleases, or for some purpose really not public, as to build himself a house, this is invalid. Taxes thus exacted for purely private purposes take property without due process of law. "To lay with one hand the power of the government on the property of a citizen, and with the other to bestow it upon favored individuals to aid private enterprises and build up private fortunes, is none the less a robbery because it is done under the forms of law and is called taxation" (29).

§ 188. **Demoralizing public benefits.** Suppose instead of revenue derived from taxation being paid to a single private individual or a few such, that it is divided among a great many; a sufficient number of persons being thus

---

(28)   Sharpless v. Philadelphia, 21 Pa. 147; Railroad Co. v. Otoe, 16 Wall. 667.

(29)   Loan Association v. Topeka, 20 Wall. 655, 664.

benefited so that it can fairly be regarded as a public benefit. Does this make the proceeding valid? It may be argued that the number of persons benefited can make no difference, for the benefit to each one is private. Plainly this is not so, however, in many cases. A city could not validly levy taxes to supply free drinking water for a single individual; it may readily do so to supply public drinking fountains. The only difference here consists in the number of persons at liberty to use the city's bounty. Similarly, a city could not supply a private golf course to one of its citizens, but it may equip courses in its parks. Even though a city may not give $5 to a single individual to use as he pleases, why may it not raise by general taxation enough to give everyone $5? A few will of course contribute much more than others in producing this fund, which all share equally; but the same thing is true of a public golf course. Those who contribute the most probably never use it at all. And it is surely a public benefit that everyone should have $5.

The answer seems to be that, owing to the likelihood of abuse, certain kinds of public benefits are excluded from the legal definition of a public purpose for which money raised by taxation may be used. Particular purposes which the experience of mankind has found to be ultimately demoralizing or oppressive are not valid public purposes, even though temporarily beneficial to large numbers of individuals. Therefore the distribution per capita or by families of money raised by public taxation is unconstitutional (30). The same was held in another

---

(30) Hooper v. Emery, 14 Me. 375.

case where the situation appealed much more to public sympathy. Just after the great Boston fire the Massachusetts legislature authorized the city to issue $20,000,-000 of bonds for money to be loaned to owners of burned buildings, secured by mortgages on their land, to enable them to rebuild. This was held invalid, the Massachusetts supreme court saying:

"The incidental advantage to the public, or to the state, which results from the promotion of private interests, and the prosperity of private enterprises or business, does not justify their aid by the use of public money raised by taxation, or for which taxation may become necessary. It is the essential character of the direct object of the expenditure which must determine its validity, as justifying a tax, and not the magnitude of the interests to be affected, nor the degree to which the general advantage to the community, and thus the public welfare, may be ultimately benefited by their promotion" (31).

§ 189. **Supplying needs for which private enterprise is inadequate.** When we come to consider activities that neither historically nor in the present state of public opinion can be called governmental, by what test can it be determined which may be aided by public taxation? Consider, for instance, a private iron works in Topeka, Kansas, a hotel in Milwaukee, Wisconsin, and a steam gristmill in a small frontier village. Which of these industries may be aided by public taxation?

The iron works is seeking a location, it will employ a

---

(31) Lowell v. City of Boston, 111 Mass. 454, 461.

considerable amount of labor, it will add much to the business of the city, it will increase taxable values. Even under these circumstances it is generally held that such an enterprise may not be assisted by public taxation (32). On the other hand public assistance to the grist-mill was upheld, grist-mills being required by statute to serve all customers according to certain regulations (33). A hotel is also required by law to serve the public according to certain regulations, without discrimination, but public aid to a hotel was held invalid in Weeks v. Milwaukee (34). The principle involved in such cases has been thus discussed by a New Hampshire judge:

"What is it that settles the character of a given purpose, in respect to its being public or otherwise? . . . Why is the building of roads to be regarded as a public service, while many other things equally necessary for the upholding of life, the security of property, the preservation of learning, morality, and religion, are by common consent regarded as private, and so left to the private enterprise of the citizens? The answer to this question, surely, is not to be found in any abstract principle of law. It is essentially a conclusion of fact and public policy, the result of an inquiry into the individual necessities of every member of the community (which in the aggregate show the character and urgency of the public need), and the likelihood that those necessities will be supplied without interference from the state. . . . Should it be

---

(32)   Loan Association v. Topeka, 20 Wall. 655.
(33)   Burlington v. Beasley, 94 U. S. 310.
(34)   10 Wis. 242.

found by experience that no person in the state would, voluntarily and unaided, establish and carry on any given trade or calling, necessary, and universally admitted to be necessary, for the upholding of life, the preservation of health, the maintenance of decency, order and civilization among people, would not the carrying on of such necessary trade or calling thereupon become a public purpose, for which the legislature might lawfully impose a tax?

"Experience shows that highways would not be built, or, if built, would not be located in the right places with reference to convenient transit between distant points, nor kept in suitable repair, but for the control assumed over the whole matter by the state; and so the state interferes, and establishes a system, and imposes an enormous burden upon the people in the shape of taxes, compelling them to supply themselves with what they certainly need, but need no more than they need shoes or bread—and nobody ever complained that the interference was unauthorized, or the purpose other than a public one" (35).

Private capital will readily supply the iron works in Topeka, or a hotel in Milwaukee if there is any public need for these. The same may not be said, perhaps, of a steam grist-mill in a small isolated place. It could not be said, perhaps, of a hotel located in some place where there was but a small though very necessary amount of travel, such as carrying the mail overland to parts of

---

(35)   Perry v. Keene, 56 New Hampshire 514, 532, 533.

Alaska. Under this view of the matter what is a proper purpose for taxation changes with economic and social conditions.

§ 190. **Influence of historical considerations.** As in most governmental matters, history and experience have more weight than logic in determining the limits of legit-imate public purposes. "It may not be easy to draw the line in all cases so as to decide what is a public purpose and what is not. . . . And in deciding whether, in the given case, the object for which the taxes are as-sessed falls upon the one side or the other of this line, they must be governed mainly by the course and usage of the government, the objects for which taxes have been customarily and by long course of legislation levied, what objects or purposes have been considered necessary to the support and for the proper use of the government, whether state or municipal. Whatever lawfully pertains to this, and is sanctioned by time and the acquiescence of the people, may well be held to be of public use, and proper for the maintenance of good government, though this may not be the only criterion of rightful taxation" (36).

§ 191. **Tax exemptions.** It may be urged with much force that the exemption of certain property from taxa-tion is equivalent to assisting it by public taxation to this extent, as other property must pay somewhat more in consequence. Where the property exempted is that of a class, rather than of an individual, the question really becomes one of proper classification for purposes of

---

(36)   Loan Association v. Topeka, 20 Wall. 655, 664, 665.

taxation, rather than one as to a public purpose. The two run into each other, however, as where a constitution forbids state aid to any church or religious sect. The payment of money derived from taxation to a church is certainly invalid under this provision, but tax exemptions of the property of churches and religious bodies are almost everywhere upheld, probably because historically these exemptions have generally been made.

Where the tax exemption is granted in an individual case, because of the public benefit supposed to be derived from the establishment of a new industry, the decisions are conflicting. The Mississippi constitution expressly permits it, and the United States Supreme Court apparently denies that the Fourteenth Amendment prohibits this (37). A practical distinction between granting monetary aid and giving a tax exemption is that the latter is closely limited in amount and so not susceptible of great abuse.

Any indirect benefits to private business from the operation of tax laws, as by a protective tariff for instance, are valid under other governmental powers, like that to regulate foreign commerce.

§ 192. **Discharging moral obligations of government** In the absence of express constitutional restrictions, a government may use its revenue from taxation to discharge not only obligations that would be legally enforceable between individuals but also moral obligations. If

---

(37) Held invalid, Brewer Brick Co. v. Brewer, 62 Me. 62; and valid in Franklin Needle Company v. Franklin, 65 N. H. 177. See Mississippi Const. of 1890, §§ 182, 192; and Florida Central Ry. Co. v. Reynolds, 183 U. S. p. 476.

public bonds are invalid through some informality, the legislature may validate them (38). Claims barred by the statute of limitations may still be paid. Perhaps the strongest case upon moral obligations arose out of the Federal sugar bounty of 1890. Congress provided a bounty to sugar growers in lieu of a protective tariff, and when the bounty was repealed it was provided that bounties already earned should be paid. The payment was attacked as an unconstitutional grant to a private business. The court held that whether the original sugar bounty law was unconstitutional or not, Congress owed a moral obligation to persons who in good faith had relied upon it, and might discharge this by the subsequent law. The court said:

"These parties cannot be held bound, upon the question of equitable or moral consideration, to know what no one else actually knew, and what no one could know prior to the determination, by some judicial tribunal, that the law was unconstitutional. . . . We are of the opinion that parties, situated as were the plaintiffs in this case, acquired claims upon the government of an equitable, moral, or honorary nature. . . . Under the provisions of the Constitution Congress has power to lay and collect taxes, etc., to pay the debts of the United States. . . . The term 'debts' includes those debts or claims which rest upon a merely equitable or honorary obligation, and which would not be recoverable in a court of law if existing against an individual" (39).

---

(38)   New Orleans v. Clark, 95 U. S. 644.

(39)   United States v. Realty Co., 163 U. S. 427, 438-40.

§ 193. **Pensions.** The ground of moral obligation is sufficient to support pensions granted after the event to persons who have rendered conspicuous public services or to persons who have rendered services of unusual hazard, even though in humble positions. Soldiers, sailors, firemen, and policemen are common instances of the latter. Such pensions may be paid not merely to the person rendering the service, but to his family and other dependents (40). Of course an agreement may be made with any public officers for future pensions as part of the compensation for present services.

§ 194. **Public charity.** The relief of actual paupers is of course a valid governmental function, and the temporary relief of persons suffering from sudden calamity seems of the same general character. Both are designed to remove pressing needs not likely to be directly provided for by private means. A state appropriation has been upheld for expenditures made in burying the dead, caring for the injured, and cleaning up debris after a cyclone (41). An appropriation was upheld in North Dakota to purchase grain for a considerable number of farmers whose credit had been exhausted by a succession of bad crops, farming being the principal industry in that state (42).

---

(40)   United States v. Hall, 98 U. S. 343; Opinion of Justices, 175 Mass. 599. See Opinion of Justices, 190 Mass. 611.

(41)   State v. Davidson, 114 Wis. 563.

(42)   North Dakota v. Nelson County, 1 N. D. 88; contrary, State v. Osawkee, 14 Kan. 418.

SECTION 3. CLASSIFICATION OF OBJECTS FOR TAXATION.

§ 195. **In general.** As was observed in § 171, above, the constitutional guarantees of due process and equality require in regard to taxation that it shall not be arbitrarily discriminatory, nor disproportionate, nor confiscatory, as respects standards proper to be observed in any particular case. Broadly speaking, the problem here, except in the case of wholesale confiscation under the guise of taxation, is one of classification. The objection that a tax is discriminatory, or disproportionate is really leveled at the classification employed, either with respect to the territory within which the tax is laid, the objects upon which it falls, or the method in which its amount is ascertained.

§ 196. **General municipal taxation.** "It is for the state to determine its political subdivisions, the number and size of its municipal corporations and their territorial extent. These are matters of a local nature, in which the nation, as a whole, is not interested, and in which, by the very nature of things, the determination of the state authorities should be accepted as authoritative and controlling" (43). If there are no local constitutional provisions upon the matter, a state is not obliged to create any political or municipal subdivisions at all, but may govern itself altogether as a single political unit. In this case, it could doubtless levy taxes upon property in the state generally, and spend the money for needed improvements in any parts of the state the government

(43) Forsyth v. Hammond, 166 U. S., 506, 518.

chose. State-wide taxation could be used to raise the money and build a bridge or pave a street in a single city. The extraordinary inconvenience of such a system makes it extremely unlikely that any state will ever adopt it. The operation of the principle involved, however, may be seen in cases where the boundaries of municipal corporations have been enlarged and general taxes levied over its entire extent to furnish the money for public improvements located within the municipality but so far distant from some of the property taxed as to be of no benefit to it whatever. For instance, Pennsylvania annexed to the city of Pittsburg a township containing a large amount of farm land, as yet usable for agricultural purposes only. The land was not laid off into lots, nor were any streets run through it, nor was it supplied by the municipality with water or gas. This farm land was subject to the same general taxation as the rest of the city of Pittsburg, the tax being used, among other purposes, to supply water and gas and maintain streets in the more thickly settled parts of the city. This procedure was upheld by the Supreme Court (44).

§ 197. **Municipal taxing district may be created for special purpose.** The general principle is that taxation over the entire territory of any municipal subdivision is valid, even though the proceeds be applied to improvements in the subdivision that leave many persons and much property unbenefited. It is not necessary that the municipal subdivision throughout which the tax is levied should be one existing for general governmental pur-

(44)   Kelly v. Pittsburg, 104 U. S., 78.

poses, like a city, town, or county. It may be created solely for the purpose of raising money for some specific improvement, and its boundaries may be determined by a commission appointed by the legislature, as well as by the legislature itself. In California a law authorized the creation of irrigation districts by commissioners who were authorized to include within the boundaries of a district all lands which in their natural state would be benefited by irrigation and susceptible of it by one system, regardless of the fact that the proposed system would be useless to city buildings or land already sufficiently irrigated within the district. All property in the district was to be taxed equally according to its value, and regardless of the benefit to it from the irrigation works. Persons owning city property and lands already irrigated which would not be actually benefited by the proposed system objected, but the law was upheld. The court said:

"The legislature thus in substance provides for the creation not alone of a public corporation, but of a taxing district whose boundaries are fixed, not by the legislature, but, after a hearing, by the board of supervisors, subject to the final approval by the people in an election called for that purpose. It has been held in this court that the legislature has power to fix such a district for itself without any hearing as to benefits, for the purpose of assessing upon the lands within the district the cost of a local, public improvement" (45).

§ 198. **Illustrations. Limits of doctrine.** Nor is it

---

(45)   Fall Brook Irrigation District v. Bradley, 164 U. S., 117, 174.

an objection that the public improvement, for the creation of which a taxing district has been established, will also benefit persons and property outside of the taxing district. For instance, the state may create a taxing district out of a single village for building a state normal school there, to which students will come from all parts of the state; or such a district may be created out of a certain part of a city for grading a street and moving a railroad therein (46). The only limit suggested upon this doctrine is in such gross cases as were put by the court:

"For instance, if the general expenses of the government of the state, or of one of its municipal divisions, should be levied upon the property of an individual or set of individuals, or perhaps upon a particular district. Cases of this description might be imagined in which an act would fall within the express prohibitions of the constitution. But to raise the constitutional question would require an extreme case, where . . . one district should be confessedly and arbitrarily required to pay for benefits conferred upon others who bore no proportion of the burden. No such question arises where a tax is imposed upon a particular locality to aid in a public purpose which the legislature may reasonably regard as a benefit to that locality as well as to the state at large" (47).

Of course it is not necessary that the improvement for

(46) Gordon v. Cornes, 47 N. Y., 608; Litchfield v. Vernon, 41 N. Y., 123.

(47) Gordon v. Cornes, 47 N. Y., 608, 612.

which a district is taxed be located within the district,
provided that the district obtains a reasonable amount
of benefit from it. A state may by taxation build a railroad to it even through another state; but taxation of
one district for improvements located in and substantially beneficial only to another district would be
invalid (48).

§ 199. · **Theory of local assessments.** If the legislature
has not created or authorized the creation of some special municipal subdivision or taxing district, which can
be treated as a unit for fiscal purposes irrespective of
benefits to the persons or property taxed; nevertheless,
taxes may be levied upon a part of the property included
in any existing municipality upon the principle of "local
assessments." These go upon the ground that property
specially benefited by a public improvement may fairly
be required to pay the amount of this special benefit, in
addition to the general tax which it pays in common with
all other similar property in the municipality. A New
Jersey opinion upon this point has been quoted with approval by the Supreme Court:

"But while it is thus clear that the burden of a particular tax may be placed on any political district to
whose benefit such tax is to enure, it seems to me it is
equally clear that, when such burden is sought to be imposed on particular lands, not in themselves constituting a political subdivision of the state, we at once ap-
proach the line which is the boundary between acts of

---

(48)   Walker v. Cincinnati, 21 Ohio 14; Farris v. Vannier, 6 Dakota.
186.

taxation and acts of confiscation. . . . If a statute should direct a certain street in a city to be paved, and the expense of such paving to be assessed on the houses standing at the four corners of such street, this would not be an act of taxation, and it is presumed that no one would assert it to be such. If this cannot be maintained, then it follows that it is conceded that the legislative power in questiton is not completely arbitrary. It has its limits; and the only inquiry is, where that limit is to be placed. . . . . .

"In our judgment, the exaction from the owner of private property of the cost of a public improvement in substantial excess of the special benefits accruing to him is, to the extent of such excess, a taking, under the guise of taxation, of private property for public use without compensation. We say 'substantial excess' because exact equality of taxation is not always attainable, and for that reason the excess of cost over special benefits, unless it be of a material character, ought not to be regarded by a court of equity when its aid is invoked to restrain the enforcement of a special assessment" (49).

Where therefore the cost of opening a new street was assessed upon the abutting owners, without inquiry as to the amount of their benefits therefrom, the assessment was held invalid.

§ 200. Same: Exceptions and qualifications. Although a local or special assessment may not exceed the amount of the benefits, yet it is probably prima facie valid when levied by the "front-foot rule," provided it

---

(49)   Norwood v. Baker, 172 U. S., 269, 282-83, 278-79.

is reasonably clear that ordinarily the tax does not exceed benefits under this rule. For instance, the cost of a curbing, a pavement, or a branch sewer usually benefits abutting property about in proportion to its frontage; and so a law imposing a local assessment according to this rule is prima facie valid, even though it does not make a special inquiry as to particular benefits in the case of each lot. If any particular lot is, under this rule, benefited substantially less than it is taxed, it may obtain relief; but the tax law as a whole is valid (50).

It is not a valid objection to a local assessment that considerable property actually benefited is not taxed; provided that the property taxed *is* benefited by the amount of the tax (51). Persons on adjoining streets are often benefited by improvements on one street, but they need not be required to contribute to these improvements. Probably a very gross or unusual discrimination would be invalid, as, for instance, if the people of only one side of a street were taxed for the entire pavement. They might be benefited as much as it cost, but the people on the other side of the street are so exactly in the same situation that their exemption is purely arbitrary.

It is generally held that an abutting owner may be made to bear the entire expense of a sidewalk in front of his premises regardless of benefits. "A sidewalk has, always in the laws and usages of this state, been regarded as an appendage to, and a part of, the premises

---

(50) Norwood v. Baker, 172 U. S., 269. 279; French v. Barber Asphalt Co., 181 U. S., 324.

(51) State v. Patterson, 42 N. J. L., 615.

to which it is attached, and is so essential to the beneficial use of such premises, that its improvement may well be regarded as a burden belonging to the ownership of the land, and the order or requisition for such improvement as a police regulation. On this ground I conceive it to be quite legitimate to direct it to be put in order at the sole expense of the owner of the property to which it is subservient and indispensable'' (52). Likewise, in most states he may be required to bear the expense of keeping his sidewalk clean, irrespective of benefits to him.

§ 201. **Different kinds of taxes.** Taxation, being designed to raise a revenue for the purposes of government, has at various times been exercised upon the most diverse classes of objects. Some of the commonest kinds have been: an ad valorem property tax, as one of 2% on the value of all or certain kinds of property; an excise tax on property, as one of $2 on each automobile, regardless of value; a license tax, either of a fixed amount on certain occupations, like the ordinary license taxes, or a tax graded according to receipts or profits; an income tax; privilege taxes levied either at a fixed or graded rate upon the exercise of certain privileges, such as franchises, suffrage, and the inheritance of property; taxes on persons, as a capitation tax; taxes on acts, such as drawing a check, or making a deed, or giving a receipt; and taxes upon documents and various steps in business or legal proceedings.

§ 202. **Legislative discretion in selecting objects of**

---

(52) State v. Newark, 37 N. J. L., p. 423.

taxation. A very wide discretion is possessed by legislative bodies in determining the objects of taxation, both of property and of business. Within what limits this power extends may be seen from the quotations which follow:

"A tax may be imposed only upon certain callings and trades, for, when the state exerts its power to tax, it is not bound to tax all pursuits or all property that may be legitimately taxed for governmental purposes. It would be an intolerable burden if a state could not tax any property or calling unless, at the same time, it taxed all property or all callings (53).

"The provision in the Fourteenth Amendment, that no state shall deny to any person within its jurisdiction the equal protection of the laws, was not intended to prevent a state from adjusting its system of taxation in all proper and reasonable ways. It may, if it chooses, exempt certain classes of property from any taxation at all, such as churches, libraries, and the property of charitable institutions. It may impose different specific taxes upon different trades and professions, and may vary the rates of excise upon various products; it may tax real estate and personal property in a different manner; it may tax visible property only, and not tax securities for payment of money; it may allow deductions for indebtedness, or not allow them.

"All such regulations, and those of like character, so long as they proceed within reasonable limits and general usage, are within the discretion of the state legislature,

(53)   Connolly v. Union Sewer Pipe Co., 184 U. S., 540. 562.

or the people of the state in framing their constitution. But clear and hostile discriminations against particular persons and classes, especially such as are of an unusual character, unknown to the practice of our governments, might be obnoxious to the constitutional prohibition'' (54).

''The power of the legislature over the subject of taxation, except as limited by constitutional restrictions, is unbounded. It is for that body, in the exercise of its discretion, to select the objects of taxation. It may impose all the taxes upon lands, or all upon personal property, or all upon houses or upon incomes. It may raise revenue by capitation taxes, by special taxes upon carriages, horses, servants, dogs, franchises, and upon every species of property and upon all kinds of business and trades'' (55).

''While a tax upon a particular house, or horse, or the houses or horses of a particular man, or on the sale thereof, would obviously invade a constitutional right; still a tax upon all houses, leaving barns and business buildings untaxed, or upon all horses or the sale thereof, leaving sheep and cows untaxed, however unwise, would be within the power of the legislature. This is true of a tax on all houses with 'more than one chimney,' or 'with more than one hearthstone,' or on all race-horses'' (56).

§ 203. Same: Limitations. ''While the legislature has wide latitude in classification, its power in that regard is

(54)   Bell's Gap Railroad Co. v. Pennsylvania, 134 U. S., 232.
(55)   Matter of McPherson, 104 N. Y., 306, 316-17.
(56)   People v. Reardon, 184 N. Y., 431, 445.

not without limitation, for the classification must have some basis, reasonable or unreasonable, other than mere accident, whim or caprice. There must be some support of taste, policy, difference of situation or the like, some reason for it even if it is a poor one. While the state can tax some occupations and omit others, can it tax only such members of a calling as have blue eyes or black hair? We have said that it could tax horses and leave sheep untaxed, but it does not follow that it could tax white horses and omit all others, or tax the sale of certificates printed on white paper and not those on yellow or brown. While one class may be made of horses and another of sheep, or even a class made of race-horses, owing to the use made of them, without a shock to common sense, a classification limited to white horses would be so arbitrary as to amount to tyranny, because there would be no semblance of reason for it. A classification of dealers in cigarettes into those selling at wholesale without the state and those selling at retail within the state was sustained on the ground that the two occupations are distinct, but could dealers in any commodity be classified according to age, size, or complexion? A classification of sales into those made in an exchange and those made elsewhere was sustained in another case, but could exchanges be so classified as to tax only such sales as are made in those carried on in brick buildings? . . . A similar fate met an act of another state, which provided that a certain tax should be imposed only upon those taxable inhabitants of a school district who had not paid a tax assessment in the year 1871. Even if a tax on farms according to acreage might be sustained, it is obvious that a tax on farms according to the number of fields into which they are divided would not be valid. Such classification would not treat all in the same class alike, and would impose a heavier burden upon one farm than upon another of the same size, situation, and value'' (57).

§ 204. **Same: Illustrations.** Louisiana imposed a tax upon persons carrying on the business of refining sugar and molasses, but excepted from the tax planters and farmers grinding and refining their own sugar and molasses. The United States Supreme Court held the classification valid, saying that the discrimination was founded upon a reasonable distinction in principle. Governments frequently exempt producers from taxation of the methods employed to put their products upon the market, and, refined sugar being the natural product of the cane, the steps taken to perfect such a product were incidental to the original growth or production (58).

The greater freedom accorded the legislature in classifying for taxation, as compared with classifying for regulation, is seen by comparing the above case with another, in which an Illinois statute was held invalid which forbade all combinations in restraint of trade except those between producers of agricultural commodities and raisers of live stock. This discrimination in favor of producers as a matter of *regulation* was held to rest upon

---

(57) People v. Mensching, 187 N. Y., 8, 18, 19.
(58) American Sugar Co. v. Louisiana, 179 U. S., 89, 92.

no reasonable basis, despite the previous case holding it a
valid discrimination for purposes of *taxation* (59).

"A tax of two cents on every check, regardless of the
amount for which it was drawn, and of five cents on a
written contract, whether it covered a transaction involving hundreds or thousands, may be referred to as
examples of what has been done without serious question
in the imposition of excise taxes. A poll tax does not
depend upon the income or earning capacity of the persons subjected to it. A tax on carriages, guns, and
watches does not rest on the value of the subjects taxed.
They are counted, not appraised. . . . The same is
true of an excise tax on legal process, domestic animals,
vocations, and the like, of which there have been many
instances during the history of the nation and the different states" (60).

§ 205. **Progressive taxation.** Property taxes in this
country, when levied according to the value of the property taxed, have usually been levied at the same rate
(disregarding certain small exemptions), irrespective of
the amount of property owned by a single owner. Econ-
omists have frequently urged that a tax whose rate increased with the amount of property held by a single
owner would be a just one, because a large estate can
afford to pay a heavier percentage tax than can a smaller
one. It is doubtful whether this principle, for the present
at least, would be approved as constitutional. In at least

---

(59)   Connolly v. Union Sewer Pipe Co., 184 U. S., 540.
(60)   People v. Reardon, 184 N. Y., 431.

one case this has been intimated (61). Probably the
same would be held regarding very large exemptions
from a general property tax. A progressive income tax
prior to the sixteenth amendment might have suffered
the same fate, though this is more doubtful. The
field where progressive taxation has been most frequently applied and upheld is that of inheritance taxes.
A differing rate of taxation here has been upheld as
between lineal descendants, collateral relatives, and persons unrelated to the decedent; as between legacies of
different amounts; and even life estates have been taxed
at a different rate according to the relation to the decedent of the person who takes the remainder. Exemptions as high as $20,000 have been held valid (62).
Whether the rate may constitutionally be increased with
the size of the entire estate, instead of according to the
size of the legacy given, has not yet been decided by the
Federal courts. It has been admitted to be open to
question there, and some state courts have decided this
method of progression unconstitutional (63). Considering that the inheritance tax may be viewed either as a tax
upon the power to transmit property or to receive it,
it would seem that a progressive rate upon the former,
measured by the entire value of the estate, would be as
valid as a progressive rate upon the latter, measured
by the amount of each individual legacy.

---

(61) Magoun v. Illinois Trust & Savings Bank, 170 U. S., p. 302.

(62) Magoun v. Illinois T. & S. Bank, 170 U. S., 283; Billings v.
Illinois, 188 U. S., 97.

(63) Knowlton v. Moore, 178 U. S., 41, 77; Black v. State, 113 Wis.,
205.

§ 206. **Confiscatory taxation.** It has often been said that "the power to tax is the power to destroy." Doubtless wherever property may be taken outright by the government without compensation, or where an occupation may be prohibited for the public good, the power of taxation may be resorted to to accomplish the same results. All of the cases where confiscatory taxation have been upheld are of this character. Where the right of confiscation or of prohibition does not exist upon other grounds, it is believed that taxation may not be used indirectly to accomplish such results (64).

---

(64) McCray v. United States, 195 U. S., 27, 64; Minot v. Winthrop, 162 Mass., 113, 117.

CHAPTER X.

DUE PROCESS AND EQUAL PROTECTION OF LAW: EMINENT DOMAIN.

§ 207. **Power of eminent domain and guarantees respecting it.** The right of a government to take or destroy private property for the public welfare has been universally recognized as one of the inherent powers of sovereignty, and has been exercised by governments from time immemorial. This power has been commonly known as that of "eminent domain" from the Latin name (eminens dominium) given it by a writer, Grotius, in the seventeenth century. Writers upon the subject have recognized that the government owed a moral obligation to make compensation for property taken under this power, and civilized governments in modern times have ordinarily made legal provision for this. The Federal Constitution and most of the state constitutions contain express provisions making this moral obligation legally binding upon their respective governments. The language of the Federal Constitution is typical of all of these—"Nor shall private property be taken for public use without just compensation" (1).

This clause, however, is a prohibition upon the Federal government only, and there is no corresponding clause

---

(1) Amend. V.

in the Constitution expressly forbidding the states to take private property without compensation. When the Fourteenth Amendment was adopted it forbade the states to "take property without due process of law." In 1896 the United States Supreme Court decided that the taking by a state of private property for the private use of another was not due process of law, and hence forbidden by the Fourteenth Amendment (2).

The next year it was held that it was also not due process of law to take private property for public use without just compensation. "Due process of law as applied to judicial proceedings instituted for the taking of private property for public use means, therefore, such process as recognizes the right of the owner to be compensated if his property be wrested from him and transferred to the public. The mere form of the proceeding instituted against the owner, even if he be admitted to defend, cannot convert the process used into due process of law, if the necessary result be to deprive him of his property without compensation" (3). By this interpretation of the Fourteenth Amendment all of the states, as well as the United States, become legally obliged by the Constitution to make compensation for private property taken for public use.

§ 208. **Various interferences with property distinguished from eminent domain.** In a number of instances property may be rendered valueless, destroyed, or even taken for governmental use without this action

---

(2)   Missouri Pacific Railway Co. v. Nebraska, 164 U. S., 403.

(3)   C. B. & Q. Railway v. Chicago, 166 U. S., 226, 236-37.

being considered an exercise of the power of eminent domain, for which compensation must be made. The use of property may be so regulated as to make it of little value to its owner, as where the owner of a brewery is forbidden to manufacture beer by a state prohibition law. The keeping of some kinds of property, like fire works, may be absolutely forbidden; diseased cattle may be destroyed against the will of the owner; property may be destroyed to prevent the spread of a conflagra-tion; and property upon the scene of active hostilities may be seized and used by military officers. In none of these cases is compensation required, the first three be-ing justified under the regulative powers of the state, the fourth under the right to preserve other property of much greater value in the face of a pressing danger; and the last under the war power.

§ 209. **What is a public use?** The power of eminent domain can be exercised only in taking property for pub-lic use. To take property from A and give it to B for private purposes is mere confiscation, and a taking of property without due process of law. This is illustrated by a Nebraska case, where the state vainly attempted to compel a railroad company to permit private persons to erect private grain elevators upon its right of way (4).

Perhaps the leading case upon the question of what constitutes a public use for the purpose of eminent do-main is Talbot v. Hudson. A Massachusetts statute had previously authorized riparian owners having good mill sites to erect dams for the purpose of providing water

---

(4)   Missouri Pacific Railroad Co. v. Nebraska, 164 U. S., 403.

power, and it authorized the necessary flooding of adjacent lands in consequence, upon making compensation for such damage. Under this statute a large dam and valuable mill buildings had been erected upon the Concord river and hundreds of acres of low-lying meadow land had been flooded. When this statute was enacted the creation of water power was of more public utility in the state than was the preservation of these low lands. Later, with the increase of population, the use of these lands became relatively more valuable than the water power, and another statute required the taking down of the dam upon payment of compensation for the ensuing loss to the mill owner. The legislation was upheld, the court saying:

"In many cases, there can be no difficulty in determining whether an appropriation of property is for a public or private use. . . . But there are intermediate cases where public and private interests are blended together, in which it becomes more difficult to decide within which of the two classes they may be properly said to fall. There is no fixed rule or standard by which such cases can be tried and determined. Each must necessarily depend upon its own peculiar circumstances. In the present case there can be no doubt that every owner of meadow land bordering on these rivers will be directly benefited to a greater or less extent by the reduction of the height of the plaintiff's dam. The act is, therefore, in a certain sense for a private use, and enures directly to the individual advantage of such owners. But this is by no means a decisive test of its validity. Many enterprises of the highest public utility are productive of great and immediate benefits to individuals. . . . The act would stand on a different ground, if it appeared that only a very few individuals or a small adjacent territory were to be benefited by the taking of private property. But such is not the case here. . . .

"It has never been deemed essential that the entire community or any considerable portion of it should directly enjoy or participate in an improvement or enterprise, in order to constitute a public use, within the true meaning of these words as used in the constitution. Such an interpretation would greatly narrow and cripple the authority of the legislature, so as to deprive it of the power of exerting a material and beneficial influence on the welfare and prosperity of the state. In a broad and comprehensive view, such as has been heretofore taken of the construction of this clause of the declaration of rights, everything which tends to enlarge the resources, increase the industrial energies, and promote the productive power of any considerable number of the inhabitants of a section of the state, or which leads to the growth of towns and the creation of new sources for the employment of private capital and labor, indirectly contributes to the general welfare and to the prosperity of the whole community" (5).

As noted above, the traditional definition of eminent domain is in terms of public use and formerly contemplated only the use to which the property is put after it has been taken (for schools, streets, parks, etc.). The traditional concept of use as the keystone of eminent

---

(5) Talbot v. Hudson, 16 Gray (Mass.), 417, 423, 425.

domain has been enlarged in modern thought and cases, to be described as "public purpose." The variation from the term "use" to "purpose" indicates a progression in thought. The idea is that the taking itself as distinguished from the subsequent use of the property may be required in the public interest. The taking of title to real estate for the public purpose of eliminating or preventing slums is within the power of eminent domain, even though the use to which the property is put after seizure is not a public use, provided that: (1) The seizure of the title is necessary to the elimination of the slum or (2) the proposed disposition of the title may reasonably be expected to prevent the otherwise probable development of a slum (5a).

§ 210. **Same: Illustrations.** In the arid parts of the United States individual land owners may be authorized to exercise the power of eminent domain in securing a right of way for ditches across the lands of their neighbors, where this is necessary to enable them to irrigate their fields. In parts of the country where no such necessity exists, such a statute would doubtless not be valid (6). Similarly, a statute may authorize the condemnation of land in an arid district by a water company for reservoirs and ditches used by it in supplying water for irrigation in the neighborhood (7).

Those public purposes for which public money may be raised by taxation will equally permit the exercise of the power of eminent domain. Among these may be

---

(5a)   Berman v. Parker, 348 U.S. 26.

(6)   Clark v. Nash, 198 U. S., 361.

(7)   Fall Brook Irrigation District v. Bradley, 164 U. S., 112.

mentioned "the erection of memorial halls, monuments, statues, gates or archways, celebrations, the publication of town histories, parks, roads leading to points of fine natural scenery, decorations upon public buildings, or other public ornaments or embellishments, designed merely to promote the general welfare either by providing for fresh air or recreation, or by educating the public taste, or by inspiring sentiments of patriotism or of respect for the memory of worthy individuals" (8). The power of eminent domain may be given to any enterprise that discharges public functions, like railway, canal, telegraph and telephone, water, gas, or electric companies; perhaps subject to the proviso that the proper discharge of its public duties requires the ownership of property so located that it might not be readily bought by private agreement. A hotel, for instance, must serve the public, but ordinarily could not be given the power of eminent domain, probably because there is so great a choice of convenient locations that private agreement will afford it a proper site.

It will be seen, from comparing this discussion of a public use for the purpose of eminent domain with the discussion of what is a public purpose for taxation, that probably the public objects that may be assisted by taxation are somewhat more limited than those that may exercise the power of eminent domain. This difference is due to the greater likelihood of abuse in the former case. Compensation must be made for what is taken by eminent domain, but taxes are exacted without any definite return for them.

---

(8) Kingman v. Brockton, 153 Mass., p. 256.

§ **211. Same: Esthetic purposes.** There has been some
difference of opinion as to whether the power of eminent
domain may be used for purely esthetic purposes (8a).
The earlier decisions inclined to deny this. In Connecticut
it was held that harbor lines could not be adjusted by
this power so as to preserve a fine view of a beautiful
public structure (9). Some years later it was held in
Massachusetts that the state might forbid the erection
of buildings beyond a certain height about one of the
city squares, in order to preserve its architectural sym-
metry for the benefit of the public, upon making compensation to the land owner whose rights were thus
abridged (10).

§ **212. Legislative discretion.** Whenever property is
taken by the state for a purpose that really is public, the
necessity and convenience of doing it are considerations
wholly for the legislature. There is no rule limiting the
exercise of this power to cases of necessity. Similarly,
if the purpose be really public, the amount of property
to be taken, and the estate in it to be condemned are also
legislative questions only. If property is taken for a
park, for instance, the legislature may take ten acres or
one thousand acres, providing it be all taken in good
faith for park purposes. If land is condemned for a
street the legislature may take a mere right of way for
the street, or it may take the entire fee in the land. Where
the power is delegated to some corporation or municipality and nothing is expressly stated about the estate to

---

(8a)　See §155 of this volume.

(9)　Farist Steel Co. v. Bridgeport, 60 Conn., 278.

(10)　Attorney General v. Williams, 174 Mass., 476.

be taken, the power is usually strictly construed so that only such an estate may be taken as is necessary for the purposes intended, but this is entirely a matter of construction and not of constitutional power (11). Some states have express constitutional restrictions of their own limiting the above rules.

§ 213. **What kind of property may be taken?** It is believed that any kind of property really needed for a public purpose may be taken under the power of eminent domain. Contracts may be so taken, as where a water company whose property is taken by eminent domain has contracts to supply water to individuals and municipalities. These contracts may be taken by the state, and if taken must be paid for (12). The franchises of a corporation may be taken. A corporation was chartered by Pennsylvania to build locks in a river, with a franchise to charge tolls for their use. It was held that when the United States appropriated these locks under its commercial powers, it must pay for the franchise to take tolls (13). Where a city has granted an exclusive franchise for a term of years, making thereby a contract which the Constitution forbids it to impair, it may yet take this corporate charter by its power of eminent domain, upon the payment of compensation therefor. It has been suggested that the state could not take corporate franchises from one corporation, merely to confer them upon another similar corporation, though both were exercising public functions. However this may be,

(11) Fairchild v. St. Paul, 46 Minn., 540.
(12) Long Island Water Co. v. Brooklyn, 166 U. S., 685.
(13) Monongahela Co. v. United States, 148 U. S., 312.

the state may take the franchise from a corporation by
eminent domain and exercise the functions of the corporation itself, as where a water works property is condemned and the business conducted thereafter by the
public (14).

§ 214. **What amounts to a taking of property?** Suppose A owns a piece of land on a river bank in a city.
On one side of his land is a street and on the other side
he has a right of way across the adjoining land of X.
Each of the following cases raises questions whether A
property has been taken so that the public must com-
pensate him:

(a) The entire estate in part of the land is taken for a
public building.

(b) A right of way is taken across the land for a new
street.

(c) X's adjoining land is taken for a public building,
which destroys A's right of way across it.

(d) A's access to the river is cut off by the abutments
of a new bridge.

(e) The river is widened so that it flows over part of
A's land.

(f) The river is dammed so that the water backs up
on A's land, but he is at liberty to build embankments and
keep it off.

(g) A steam railroad crosses the adjoining land and
the noises and smoke of its operation greatly diminish the
value of A's land.

---

(14) Long Island Water Co. v. Brooklyn, 166 U. S., 685, 694.

(h)   A's access to the navigable channel of the river is cut off by a pier placed in the river to improve navigation.

(i)   The street in front of A's land is graded up so as to make access to it very difficult.

(j)   An elevated street railroad is put in the street, which interferes with A's access, light, and air.

(k)   A steam railroad for through traffic is laid in the street, which likewise interferes with A's access, light, and air.

§ 215. **Physical occupation of property.** As regards cases (a), (b), and (c) (§214) there can be no doubt property is taken, the only difference being in the quality of the interest taken. A right of way is a recognized subject of property, as much as an estate in fee, and compensation must be made for both. Another recognized incident of property is a riparian owner's right of access to the stream. When the public takes this from him, as in (d), above, his property is taken. In case (e), the public has taken from A the right to occupy part of his land permanently with the water of the river which has been widened. Such a right as this in the land of another, called an easement, is also a well-recognized separable property right by the common law and so A must be paid for it. In all of these cases it will be noticed that A's rights have been taken from him in such a fashion that he cannot legally avail himself of them in any way. Rights he once had to the occupation or use of his property are now being enjoyed by the public. Up to this point there is no controversy about the matter.

§ 216. **Substantial intrusion of tangible material.** Cases (f) and (g) (§214) are somewhat different. No right is claimed by the public to keep water on A's land, if A chooses to dike it off; or to make noises or cast soot on A's land, if A can erect some barrier that will prevent these effects. All that is claimed is a right to be free from suit for injuring A's land as incidental to acts done elsewhere. The crude earlier conceptions of the common law undoubtedly regarded these acts as injuries to property, rather than as taking it, and hence they fell outside the constitutional prohibition. In the leading case of Pumpelly v. Green Bay Company (15), decided in 1871, it was held that a substantial flooding of land by water amounted to a taking of it for which compensation must be made. The court said: "Where real estate is actually invaded by superinduced additions of water, earth, sand or other material, or by having any artificial structure placed on it, so as to effectually destroy or impair its usefulness, it is a taking, within the meaning of the Constitution." This case has been generally followed since in this country. Another case decided about the same time that had much effect in settling the law was one where a railroad had cut through a ridge of land which had protected the plaintiff's land from the freshets of a neighboring stream. Afterwards, water came through this cut at flood-time, depositing gravel upon plaintiff's farm and washing away his soil. This was held to amount to a taking of the plaintiff's property, his natural right to be free from such a change in the surface of the earth, and compensation was required (16).

§ 217. **Noise and pollution of atmosphere.** On the other hand, it is generally held that noise and the pollution of

---

(15)　13 Wall., 166.

(16)　Eaton v. Boston, etc. Railroad, 51 N. H., 504.

the atmosphere, as by the operation of a railroad, do not constitute a taking of property for which compensation must be made (17). The ringing of a bell, which has been previously enjoined as a nuisance, may be legalized by the legislature, without compensation, though it causes much discomfort to property owners in the vicinity (18). In these cases, there being no gross physical invasion of the area of the plaintiff's property, it has not been treated as a taking, although it may be shown that under a scientific classification of property rights damage done by noise or smoke is essentially similar to that done by water.

However, property may be taken without physical occupation. In U.S. v. Causby, 328 U.S. 256, it was held that where the noise and glaring lights at night of aircraft making low altitude flights over owner's chicken farm when landing at or leaving a neighboring airport resulted in frightening the chickens, causing them to fly into the wall and kill themselves or stop producing, there was a sufficient interference with the normal use of the chicken farm to amount to a taking entitling the owner to compensation. The court in the Causby case said that although air space is a public highway, if the owner is to have full enjoyment of the land, he must have exclusive control over the immediate reaches of the enveloping atmosphere, otherwise buildings could not be erected, trees could not be planted and even fences could not be run. The landowner owns at least as much of the space above ground as he can occupy or use in connection with the land. The fact that he does not occupy it physically by

(17)   Beseman v. Pennsylvania Railroad, 50 N. J. L., 235.
(18)   Sawyer v. Davis, 136 Mass., 239.

the erection of buildings and the like, is not material. Generally flights over land are not a taking but when they are so low and frequent (skim the surface without touching it) as to amount to a direct and immediate interference with the enjoyment and use of the land, it is an appropriation of the land which is entitled to compensation.

§ 218. **Improvement of navigation.** In case (h) (§214) A's right of access to the stream has been interfered with, but only for the purpose of improving the river for purposes of navigation. Riparian rights are held subject to the paramount right of the public in the navigability of streams, and must yield to improvements in the exercise of this public right. So, in a case where Congress improved a navigable river by building in it, on submerged land in front of plaintiff's shore line, a pier that wholly cut plaintiff off from access to the channel of the river, it was held he could claim no compensation on the theory that his property was taken (19).

§ 219. **Changes in public streets.** Cases (i), (j), (k), (§214) involve the difficult question of what property rights an abutting owner has in a public street. It was early decided that any change of grade of a public street, whether by raising it or lowering it, did not amount to a taking of abutting property, no matter how much the latter might be damaged as a result. The streets were intended for public traffic, and anything that improved them for this purpose, without actually invading the boundaries of abutting property was within the rights of the public, just like improvements upon navigable rivers (§ 218). About 1880 there began in New York a

---

(19) Scranton v. Wheeler, 179 U. S., 141.

remarkable litigation over the construction of the first elevated street railroads. These structures in the streets of New York city diminished the light and air of abutting property, interfered with access to it, and also diminished its value by the noise and dirt of the trains. Abutting property owners attempted to compel the elevated companies to pay for the damage thus done upon the theory that they had some property rights in the streets that were taken by the erection of the elevated structure. The New York courts finally decided that the abutters had such property rights for the taking of which they were entitled to compensation. The theory of these rights has been thus stated by the New York court:

"It has now been decided that, although the land itself was not taken, yet the abutting owner, by reason of his situation, had a kind of property in the public street for the purpose of giving to such land facilities of light, of air, and of access from such street. These rights of obtaining for the adjacent lands facilities of light, etc., were called easements, and were held to be appurtenant to the land which fronted on the public street. These easements were decided to be property, and protected by the constitution from being taken without just compensation. It was held that the defendants, by the erection of their structure and the operation of their trains, interfered with the beneficial enjoyment of these easements by the adjacent land-owner, and in law took a portion of them. By this mode of reasoning, the difficulty of regarding the whole damage done to the adjacent owner as consequential only (because none of his property was taken), and, therefore, not collectible from the defendants, was overcome. The interference with these easements became a taking of them pro tanto, and their value was to be paid for, and in addition the damage done the remaining and adjoining land by reason of the taking was also to be paid for, and this damage was in reality the one great injury which owners sustained from the building and operation of the defendant's road" (20).

These so-called easements of light, air, and access, are wholly subject to the right of the public to improve the street for the purpose of legitimate street traffic. For instance, if a city had erected a public viaduct in the street, to carry it up to a higher grade, and the injury to abutting owners had been just as great as in the case of the elevated railway, the abutters would have had no remedy (21). A striking illustration of this occurred in Buffalo, N. Y. A railroad was authorized to build an embankment six feet high in the middle of a street, which was held to take the abutting owners' easement of access, so that they must be paid for it. The streets crossing this one had to be graded up to the top of the embankment to get across, and the abutters on these streets were not allowed to recover because this grading was done to change the level of the street for street purposes, while the first one was not (22).

§ 220. What are legitimate public uses of streets? Evidently the New York elevated railroad cases depend upon the proposition that the occupation of the street by an elevated street railroad is not a legitimate use of

---

(20)   Bohm v. Metropolitan Railway Co., 129 N. Y., 576, 587-88.
(21)   Sauer v. New York, 206 U. S., 536.
(22)   Reining v. Railroad, 128 N. Y., 157; Rauenstein v. Railroad, 136 N. Y., 528.

a street for the purposes of public street traffic. This view has been disputed in some states on the ground that if the public needs require such a road to accommodate local traffic in a city, it is as much a proper use of a street as are surface street car lines, which are usually permitted without making compensation (23).

As regards the use of streets for various common incidental purposes, like drains, gas and water pipes, lamp posts, telegraph and telephone posts, street railways, and steam railways, the test commonly applied is whether the use is one fairly incidental to local traffic or not. Where telegraph or telephone poles, or steam railways, actually interfere with the use of a street by an abutter it is commonly held that compensation must be made; for the other purposes mentioned above the contrary is usually held. Where the abutting owner has conveyed to the public only an easement for street purposes, but has retained the fee, a number of states hold that he must be compensated for the occupation of the street by telegraph or telephone poles or by a steam railroad, whether his use of the street is affected or not, on the ground that these structures are impairments of the abutter's reserved interest. Upon all these points there are many minor differences of opinion (24).

§ 221. **Compensation in money.** In the case where a tract of land or other piece of property is taken, compensation must be made in money at the fair market value of the property. The money need not be paid at the

---

(23) Garrett v. Elevated Railway, 79 Md., 277.

(24) Randolph, Eminent Domain, §§ 395-416.

time possession is taken of the property, if a certain method of obtaining it within a reasonable time thereafter is provided. In deciding what is a fair market value of property, not only its present use is to be considered but its adaptability to other uses that may reasonably be made of it. Thus, a site on a river advantageously located for a log boom, or land naturally adapted to the purposes of a reservoir site should be valued with reference to these possible uses, if there is a reasonable prospect of realizing them (25).

§ 222. **Compensation in benefits.** Although it is usually said that an owner may not be required to accept anything but money as compensation for property taken, yet by the operation of a rule commonly applied in ascertaining the amount of compensation, he may virtually be required to take part or all of his compensation in the shape of benefits to his remaining property, if part only of a single tract be taken. A concrete case will illustrate the operation of this rule. Suppose a railroad crosses A's farm. The value of the farm before the crossing was $5,000, and the land taken is fairly worth $500. If the severance of the part taken by the railroad, or the construction or the operation of the railroad will still further diminish the value of what is left by $500, the owner is entitled to be paid a full $1,000 as the total injury done. On the other hand, if the existence or construction or operation of the railroad there has, by improving access to the market or draining a swamp, in-

(25) Boom Company v. Patterson, 98 U. S., 403; San Diego Co. v. Neale, 78 Cal., 63.

creased the value of the remainder to the owner by $500 this may be deducted from the value of the land taken, so that nothing need be paid (26). Some states, by statute or constitution, provide that the part actually taken must be paid for in money without deduction for benefits; and that benefits to the remainder can be set off only against injuries to the remainder; but the United State Constitution does not require this. The result is that if an owner has two separate tracts of land, not united in a single use, and one of them is taken by the public to the consequential injury of the other tract, the owner can recover nothing for this latter injury. If, however, the two tracts were united in some common use, so that they formed for business purposes a single property, the owner could recover the value of what was taken, plus the injury to what was left, minus the benefits to what was left (27).

§ 223. **Preliminary surveys before compensation.** To justify an entry upon land to be taken by eminent domain proceedings, a statute must be in existence at the time providing that compensation shall be made without unreasonable delay. If such a statute is in force, it is justifiable to enter the land for the purpose of preliminary surveys before compensation is made, and even before actual proceedings have been begun to condemn the land. If actual damage is done to the property in the course of these surveys the owner has the ordinary right of action therefor, but the mere technical trespass for which an ac-

---

(26)   Bauman v. Ross, 167 U. S., 548.
(27)   White v. Elevated Railway, 154 Ill., 620.

tion could ordinarily be ·brought without showing damage is justified in the course of such proceedings taken in good faith.

§ 224. **Liability for damaging property.** As has been seen above (§§217, 219), the constitutional requirements of compensation for property taken do not include property that is merely damaged. The injustice frequently done where property is legally only damaged has led nearly one-half of our states to add to their constitutions a clause requiring compensation for property damaged as well as taken. Under this provision the state and its agents are liable for any physical injury to property which would be actionable if done by a private individual in the position of the state or its agents. For instance, a private land owner cannot legally maintain a nuisance upon his premises, and the public must likewise refrain from doing this upon its streets or other property, unless it makes compensation therefor. It cannot interfere with an abutter's easement of light, air, and access upon a public street, without compensation, any more than could the owner of land over which there was a private right of way with similar easements. On the other hand, just as a private owner is not liable to his neighbor for putting up an unsightly building that diminishes the value of his neighbor's land, so the public is not liable for damage caused to neighboring property by the building of a jail or police station, or for obstructing the light of windows that do not open on a public way (28).

---

(28) Rigney v. Chicago, 102 Ill., 64; Chicago v. Taylor, 125 U. S. 161.

§ 225. **Condemnation proceedings.** The exercise of the power of eminent domain must be authorized by the legislature before any proceedings to condemn land are taken, and when the statutory proceedings are substantially followed the land owner is usually confined to the remedy provided in these proceedings. Where attempts are made to use the land without taking such proceedings, the owner may ordinarily secure an injunction against further disturbance, until proper proceedings are taken, if the work is not very far advanced; or, where the work is so far advanced that it would be a hardship on the public to stop it at this point, an injunction may be awarded unless the aggressor will pay at once what the court finds to be a fair value of the property (29).

Proceedings to condemn land, being neither criminal cases nor suits at law or in equity, within the meaning of the provisions for jury trial in our constitutions, need not be conducted before a jury nor even under the direction of a court (30). They are administrative suits, as explained in §138, above, and all that is required is a fair hearing before some honest tribunal upon the questions involved.

---

(29)   Galway v. Elevated Railway, 128 N. Y., 132.
(30)   Bauman v. Ross, 167 U. S., 548.

CHAPTER XI.

LAWS IMPAIRING OBLIGATIONS OF CONTRACTS.

§ **226.** **Constitutional prohibitions.** During the disorders consequent upon the Revolution and the exhausted state of public and private credit during the years immediately after, a number of states had passed laws altering or discharging private contracts, greatly to the disturbance of commerce and credit. With very little discussion, therefore, the Philadelphia convention inserted in the proposed Constitution the clause: "No state shall pass any law impairing the obligation of contracts" (1). A proposal that a similar prohibition should be placed upon the United States government was not even seconded in the convention. Probably the framers of the Constitution thought that the national government, subject to the possible hazards and burdens of war, could not be as safely fettered in this respect as might the local state governments relieved of the duty of meeting supreme emergencies. That the United States is not forbidden to impair the obligations of contracts does not mean, however, that it may abrogate at pleasure such as are subject to its jurisdiction. Contracts are property (2), and the Fifth Amendment forbids the United States to take property without due process of law. Any act of

---

(1) Art. I, Sec. 10, § 1.

(2) Long Island Water Co. v. Brooklyn, 166 U. S., 685, 690-91.

sheer confiscation, or of unreasonable abrogation of contracts would doubtless fall within this guaranty.

§ 227. **What acts of impairment are forbidden?** A state may affect the obligation of contracts in a variety of ways. A state court may erroneously interpret a contract in such a way as to deprive one of the parties of a right flowing from it that he should properly have. The Constitution does not forbid this (3). A state court may lay down the law in a certain manner, and upon the faith of this contracts may be made, and then the same court may reverse its former decision and lay down a rule of law so different that the former contracts are seriously impaired or even rendered altogether invalid. This is not forbidden (4). A contract may be unenforceable, and hence impaired, on account of the acts of some administrative officer, or of some private individual, but there is no redress for this under the contract clause of the Constitution.

"In order to come within the provision of the Constitution of the United States which declares that no state shall pass any law impairing the obligation of contracts, not only must the obligation of a contract have been impaired, but it must have been impaired by a law of the state. The prohibition is aimed at the legislative power of the state, and not at the decisions of its courts, or the acts of administrative or executive boards or officers, or the doings of corporations or individuals" (5).

---

(3) Railway Co. v. Rock, 4 Wall., 177.

(4) National Loan Asso. v. Brahan, 193 U. S., 635.

(5) New Orleans Waterworks Co. v. Louisiana Sugar Co., 125 U. S., 18.

The words "pass a law" in the Constitution evidently refer only to legislative law-making, not such incidental law-making as results from the decisions of courts, or the acts of executive officers.

On the other hand legislative enactments against which the prohibition is directed, are not confined to acts of the state legislature. "Any enactment, from whatever source originating, to which a state gives the force of law, is a statute of the state" (6). "The by-laws or ordinances of a municipal corporation may be such an exercise of legislative power delegated by the legislature to the corporation as a political subdivision of the state, having all the force of law within the limits of the municipality, that it may properly be considered as a law, within the meaning of this clause of the Constitution" (note 5, above). A state constitution adopted directly by the people of the state is a "law."

§ 228. **What is a contract?** The contracts protected by the Constitution are those to the terms of which the parties have assented. Obligations imposed by law irrespective of the consent of the parties are not meant, although they may for some purposes be classified as contracts. For instance, A owes X $100, on which A has agreed to pay 6% interest. The legislature could not reduce the rate of interest to 5% on this contract, because this would impair the rights X had arising out of the original contract under the law as it stood when the contract was made. But, if X sues A and obtains a judgment for the $100 and interest, the contract between

(6)   Williams v. Bruffy, 96 U. S., p. 183.

X and A is now destroyed, and its place has been taken by an order of court, in the form of a judgment that A pay its amount or his property will be seized in satisfaction. When the judgment was obtained the law may have entitled X to 6% interest upon the judgment as damages so long as it remained unpaid, but the state may reduce the rate of interest on a judgment at any time. "He has no contract whatever on the subject with the defendant in the judgment, but his right is to receive, and the defendant's obligation is to pay, just what the state chooses to prescribe" (7).

A state may authorize divorces for causes that were not grounds for a divorce when the marriage was entered into; and, where the state constitution does not forbid, the legislature itself may pass an act divorcing parties within the state. The relation resulting from the marriage contract is treated as a status and not merely as a contract, and it is within the legislative power of the state to alter this status in the interest of the public welfare (8).

§ 229. Same: Grants. The first case that came before the United States Supreme Court, requiring an interpretation of the contract clause of the Constitution was the famous case of Fletcher v. Peck. The state of Georgia by an act of its legislature granted land to one Gunn, who sold to various other parties. After Gunn had thus disposed of the land, Georgia passed a statute rescinding the legislative grant previously made to Gunn and

---

(7)   Morley v. Lake Shore Railway Co., 146 U. S., 162.

(8)   Maynard v. Hill, 125 U. S., 190.

asserting the title of the state to the land it contained,
upon the ground of his alleged fraud in obtaining the
grant. The question arose whether this last Georgia
statute could affect the title of persons who had previously bought the land from Gunn in ignorance of the
alleged fraud. It was claimed that the act by which
Georgia purported to do this impaired the obligation of
the state's contract with Gunn and hence was unconstitutional. The Federal Supreme Court upheld this contention. Chief Justice Marshall said:

"Is a grant a contract? A contract is a compact between two or more parties, and is either executory or
executed. An executory contract is one in which a party
binds himself to do, or not to do, a particular thing; such
was the law under which the conveyance was made by the
governor. A contract executed is one in which the object
of contract is performed; and this, says Blackstone, dif-
fers in nothing from a grant. A contract executed, as
well as one which is executory, contains obligations binding on the parties. A grant, in its own nature, amounts
to an extinguishment of the right of the grantor, and
implies a contract not to reassert that right. A party is,
therefore, always estopped by his own grant" (9).

One of the judges in this case doubted whether there
could be said to be any obligations remaining to a contract that had been wholly performed on both sides, and
so whether this act of Georgia could impair any obligation of an executed contract. The ruling of the majority,

(9)   6 Cranch, 87, 136-37.

however, has never been altered by the court, and executed grants are treated as contracts which cannot be
repudiated.

§ 230. **Same: Corporation charters.** The question
whether a corporate charter is a contract protected by
the Constitution, or not, was elaborately discussed in
one of the most famous decisions of the United States
Supreme Court, Dartmouth College v. Woodward (10).
Dartmouth College in New Hampshire had a charter
granted by the English crown in 1769, by which twelve
persons were incorporated as trustees and granted appropriate privileges and powers to conduct the affairs
of the college, with authority to fill all vacancies in their
own body. In 1816 the New Hampshire legislature attempted to alter this charter by increasing the number
of trustees, the additional members to be appointed by
the governor, and placed the more important acts of the
trustees under the control of a board of overseers. The
original trustees contested this legislation and the United
States Supreme Court declared the original charter to
be a contract, perpetually continuing, which the New
Hampshire legislation unconstitutionally impaired. In
a corporate charter, as in a conveyance of land, the court
found a contract that the grant should not be revoked.
Subsequent cases extended the doctrine to all corporate charters, including those of ordinary business
corporations.

A doctrine fraught with consequences so important as
this one has not passed unchallenged, and the Dartmouth

(10)   4 Wheat. 518.

College case has received much criticism. It has been forcibly urged that the grant of a corporate charter is nothing but an ordinary act of legislation, permitting that which without legislative action could not be done. Without legislative authorization, men may not form themselves into that artificial entity called a corporation, but must do business subject to individual liability. For the public convenience, the legislature may authorize men to form such organizations, but this no more constitutes a contract on the part of the state never to repeal the law, than does a sugar bounty or a game law. Such is the opposing argument. Where corporations are chartered, as today, chiefly under general laws that may be taken advantage of by any persons who fulfill certain specified requirements, it is difficult to see in corporate charters any contract on the part of the state; but when each charter required a separate act of the legislature it was manifestly easier to interpret these grants as contracts. The doctrine of the Dartmouth College case is firmly established, whatever may be thought of its grounds.

§ 231. **What is the obligation of a contract.** A brief analysis of the nature of a contract will be helpful in understanding what is meant by the "obligation of a contract." A may promise B to give him a horse. If A does not choose to keep his promise, B can secure redress against A in a court of justice only in case the law applicable to the parties when the promise was made imposed upon A an obligation to perform it. If it be the law applicable to the situation that gratuitous promises are unenforceable, A incurs no legal obligation to B in consequence of this promise. This happens to be the law in all American states. A's contract, if such it can be called, is without obligation, because it is gratuitous or without consideration. Again, suppose A orally agrees to buy B's land, for $100 and B orally agrees to sell the land to A for this sum. Here the promises are not gratuitous, each being the consideration for the other, but still the law of our American states attaches no obligation to the words and intentions of A and B, because agreements for the sale of land must be in writing to be legally enforceable. If one of the parties is a married woman the law of the state may require not only consideration and a writing, but an examination before some public officer to make certain that what she does is unaffected by marital coercion. On some agreements, like those in restraint of marriage, the law may impose no obligation whatever, on account of their bad social tendencies. It is thus clear that the obligation of a contract consists of the duties which the existing law applicable to the situation imposes upon one party in consequence of the form and content of his agreement, and of the correlative rights which the other party has to enforce these duties.

Any state law, therefore, that impairs the duties lawfully arising from a prior contract violates the constitutional prohibition. Of this character is a state bankruptcy law, if made applicable to contracts already in force. A has agreed, for instance, to repay to B on a certain date $100 borrowed from B. A state law declaring that A need not make payment to B, but may discharge himself from this obligation upon surrendering all of his property for distribution among his creditors, impairs the obligation imposed upon A by the prior law, and hence is invalid (11).

The same principles apply to existing laws that affect the validity or construction of a contract at the time it is made. ''A statute of frauds embracing a pre-existing parol contract not before required to be in writing would affect its validity. A statute declaring that the word 'ton' should thereafter be held, in prior as well as subsequent contracts, to mean one-half or double the weight before prescribed, would affect its construction'' (12).

§ 232. **Impairment of remedies for breach of contract.** When a party to a contract inexcusably fails to perform any of the duties that the law imposes upon him in consequence of his agreement, a new right arises to the other party to the contract—a right of suit upon the contract to obtain redress. This right may be to compel the defendant to act or to refrain from acting precisely as he agreed, commonly called a right to specific performance; or it may be to compel the defendant to make compensation for his breach of the contract, called a right to damages. The right to recover specific property at law by replevin or ejectment may be treated for the purposes of this discussion as a right to specific performance. If the plaintiff pursues his right to damages and obtains a judgment against the defendant, then additional rights accrue to him. He may seize the defendant's property

(11)   Sturges v. Crowninshield, 4 Wheat., 117.
(12)   Von Hoffman v. Quincy, 4 Wall., 535, 552.

with certain formalities, and sell it to satisfy his claim for damages.

In earlier decisions under the contract clause it was not clearly intimated to what extent auxiliary rights to the application of remedies were a part of the "obligation" of a contract protected by the Constitution. It was frequently admitted that the remedy might be modified, provided the defendant's duty was not altered, but it was perhaps not clearly perceived what an intimate connection there was between the two. During the hard times consequent upon the panic of 1837 various states passed "stay laws," by which the collection of debts by creditors was postponed or impeded by conditions designed to operate in favor of the debtor. Several of these cases came to the United States Supreme Court, and were held unconstitutional wherever they substantially interfered with the collection of the debt.

In a case from Illinois, where a statute subsequent to the creation of a mortgage provided that the property should not be sold for less than two-thirds of its appraised value and that the mortgagor should have one year in which to redeem it from the sale, the court held that these provisions so seriously affected the previous remedy that they amounted to an impairment of the obligation of the original mortgage contract. The court said:

"It is manifest that the obligation of the contract, and the rights of a party under it, may, in effect, be destroyed by denying a remedy altogether; or may be seriously impaired by burdening the proceedings with new condi-

tions and restrictions, so as to make the remedy hardly
worth pursuing. . . . When this contract was made,
no statute had been passed by the state changing the
rules of law or equity in relation to a contract of this
kind; and it must, therefore, be governed, and the rights
of the parties under it measured, by the rules above
stated. They were the laws of Illinois at the time. . . .
They were annexed to the contract at the time it was
made, and formed a part of it; and any subsequent law,
impairing the rights thus acquired, impairs the obligations which the contact imposed" (13). And a later case:

"Without the remedy the contract may, indeed, in the
sense of the law, be said not to exist, and its obligation
to fall within the class of those moral and social duties
which depend for their fulfillment wholly upon the will
of the individual. The ideas of validity and remedy are
inseparable, and both are parts of the obligation, which
is guaranteed by the Constitution against invasion. The
obligation of a contract 'is the law which binds the parties to perform their agreement.' . . . A right without
a remedy is as if it were not. For every beneficial purpose it may be said not to exist" (14).

But in a still later case the court upheld a state law
granting relief to debtors from foreclosure of valid mort-
gages during the period of an economic emergency (14a).

§ 233. Same: Municipal bond cases. The extent to
which the right to the remedy existing when the contract

---

(13)   Bronson v. Kinzie, 1 How., 311, 319.
(14)   Von Hoffman v. Quincy, 4 Wall., 535, 552, 554.
(14a) Home Building and Loan Association v. Blaisdell, 290 U. S. 398.

was made becomes a part of the obligation of the contract has been most carefully discussed and most fully illustrated in suits upon municipal bonds. When a municipality, whether city, village, county, or other subdivision of the state, borrows money and issues bonds therefor, it acts under some state law, special or general, enabling it to issue the bonds and to levy taxes to pay the interest and principal as it falls due. A suit against a municipal corporation by which a general judgment is obtained against it may not secure payment, because the municipality may have little or no property not used for strictly governmental purposes and it is generally held that property of the latter character cannot be sold upon execution to pay debts, unless specifically mortgaged for this purpose. Practically the only effective remedy of municipal creditors is the exercise of the power of municipal taxation to discharge debts. It has been held, therefore, that existing laws, authorizing municipal taxation the proceeds of which are applicable to municipal debts, become a part of the obligation of contracts by which such debts are incurred. The subsequent abolition or reduction of the municipal taxing power applicable to such debts is invalid if it leaves the municipality unable to discharge its obligations (15).

§ 233a. **Same: No taxing officers.** When a state legislature is willing to connive with one of its municipalities to aid it in repudiating its debts, more difficult problems are presented. Taxes are levied by certain municipal officers. If these refuse to do their duty they may be

---

(15)   Von Hoffman v. Quincy, 4 Wall., 535.

compelled to act by a mandamus issued from either a state or Federal court. Suppose that all of the appropriate municipal officers resign, or that none are elected. If the state legislature acquiesces in this and the state law has provided no remedy for such an emergency the bondholders are for the time being helpless. In one such case they made application to a Federal court to levy the taxes itself and direct a marshal to make up the assessment rolls and collect the taxes required by the obligation of their contract. The Federal court refused to do this, and in a later case gave its reason as follows:

"The power we are here asked to exercise is the very delicate one of taxation. . . . The power must be derived from the legislature of the state. So far as the present case is concerned, the state has delegated the power to the levee commissioners. If that body has ceased to exist, the remedy is in the legislature either to assess the tax by special statute or to vest the power in some other tribunal. It certainly is not vested in any Federal court. . . . It is not only not one of the inherent powers of the court to levy and collect taxes, but it is an invasion by the judiciary of the Federal government of the legislative functions of the state government" (16).

§ 234. Same: Abolition of indebted municipality. Even a repudiating municipality finds it inconvenient to continue permanently without the services of officers authorized to levy taxes, so that other methods of evading its creditors have been sought. Sometimes the state leg-

---

(16) Heine v. Levee Commissioners, 19 Wall., 655, 660-61.

islature has repealed the charter of the indebted municipality, seeking to destroy its corporate existence. Usually when this has been done one or more new municipal corporations have been formed from the territory of the original municipality, or its territory has been annexed to other municipalities. In such cases it has been held that the municipalities that succeeded to the territory, property, and jurisdiction of the old one, also acquired its existing tax laws and became liable to enforce them over the old territory of the former municipality just as the latter could have been compelled to do (17).

If a municipality were abolished and its government, or the taxing power thereof, were assumed directly by the legislature, probably the bondholders could not get relief from the courts, as it would not be possible for the latter to order the legislature to levy the necessary taxes as they could order the appropriate municipal officers to do (18).

§ 235. **Valid changes in remedies.** While what will constitute the complete performance of a contract by the party bound may not be altered at all by a subsequent law, the remedy provided by the state for non-performance may be altered to any extent, provided only that it be substantially as efficacious as was the original one. Courts, process, forms of action may be changed, new rules of evidence or practice may be used, new modes of execution may be substituted, or the time necessary to bar the suit under the statute of limitations may be

---

(17)   Mobile v. Watson, 116 U. S., 289.

(18)   Meriwether v. Garrett, 102 U. S., 472.

altered; in short, any change of procedure or remedy is valid if it is as adequate as the old one.

In what respects a new remedy may be held less efficacious than an old one is well illustrated by a case from Virginia. The state had issued certain bonds, the coupons of which, due semi-annually, were made receivable for state taxes. Direct repudiation of the bonds being impossible on account of this latter provision, Virginia passed a number of laws designed to hamper the use of the coupons for taxes. Expert evidence of the genuineness of the coupons was forbidden to be received; no coupon could be used for taxes unless the bond from which it was cut was produced with proof that it was cut therefrom; and all coupons were required to be used for taxes, if at all, within one year from their maturity. All these provisions were held substantially to impair the coupon holders' remedies and therefore to be invalid. Regarding the shortening of the period for the limitations of actions, the court said:

"The passage of a new statute of limitations, giving a shorter time for the bringing of actions than existed before, even as applied to actions which had accrued, does not necessarily affect the remedy to such an extent as to impair the obligation of the contract within the meaning of the Constitution, provided a reasonable time is given for the bringing of such actions" (19).

§ 236. **Special charter privileges as contracts.** Corporate charters sometimes contain special privileges or exemptions other than merely that of capacity for corpo-

---

(19)   McGahey v. Virginia, 135 U. S., 662.

rate existence. A charter may contain an exemption from taxation, or from state regulation of rates, or from certain kinds of competition. If any of these privileges are placed in a corporate charter, are they also irrepealable? In a long series of cases such privileges have also been declared by the United States Supreme Court to be contracts that cannot be impaired by subsequent state legislatures. As regards a charter exemption from taxation, this was held in 1853 in the case of State Bank of Ohio v. Knoop (20). A charter grant of an exclusive right to bridge a river within a distance of two miles upon either side of the proposed bridge was upheld in 1865, against a later authorization of a competing bridge within the prohibited distance; so also exclusive rights to supply gas and water to cities have been upheld (21). Likewise charter agreements that particular rates may be charged by public service corporations, without subsequent reduction by the state, have been enforced (22).

§ 237. **Qualifications of this doctrine.** Manifestly, if the state or a municipality acting under state authority could thus deprive itself by contract of such important governmental powers as those of taxation, rate regulation, and the encouragement of competition, the door was open for great abuses in a country where municipal

---

(20)   16 How., 369.

(21)   The Binghamton Bridge, 3 Wall., 51; New Orleans Gas Co. v. Louisiana Light Co., 115 U. S., 650; New Orleans Waterworks Co. v. Rivers, 115 U. S., 674.

(22)   Los Angeles v. Los Angeles Water Co., 177 U. S., 558 (water rates); Detroit v. Detroit Street Railway Co., 184 U. S., 368 (street car fares).

and legislative bodies are so commonly improvident and not infrequently corrupt as in America. Side by side with this doctrine of charter contracts have grown up two other doctrines that have greatly qualified the other and greatly limited the likelihood of its abuse. The first of these is that the terms of every special privilege granted by the state must be strictly construed, so that the grantee takes nothing in derogation of public rights unless so clearly expressed that no other interpretation is reasonably possible. The second qualification is that, in respect to certain very important governmental powers, the legislature cannot even by express contract tie its hands for the future. In short, a government cannot by contract abrogate its power of governing.

§ 238. **Strict construction of special privileges.** The great case of Charles River Bridge v. Warren Bridge (23) has always been regarded as the leading case upon the strict construction of corporate charters. In 1785 Massachusetts chartered a company to build a toll bridge over the Charles River, the charter being extended for a period of seventy years, when the bridge was to belong to the state. In 1828 Massachusetts incorporated another company to build a second toll bridge across the Charles a few rods from the former bridge, with a provision that it should become a free bridge in six years. The original bridge company asked an injunction against its rival upon the ground that the grant of a charter to build a bridge and collect tolls included an implied contract that the state should not thereafter make

---

(23) 11 Peters, 420.

the collection of tolls impossible by authorizing a free bridge practically alongside the toll bridge. By a divided vote the Supreme Court denied this contention, saying that any ambiguity in the terms of a public contract must be construed in favor of the public, and that the abandonment of any state legislative power was not to be presumed in the case where a deliberate purpose to abandon it did not appear. The express grant of the power to build a toll bridge carried no implied contract that the state would not subsequently charter a competing bridge.

This doctrine of strict construction of corporate powers has been constantly exemplified since, and is in full force today. A few typical instances of such construction may be given. A newly incorporated railroad company was authorized to construct a railway in Mississippi, and the road was to be exempt from taxation for ten years after the completion of the road. It was held that this tax exemption did not begin until the road was completed, although the greatest need for such exemption would exist during its construction and before it was in full operation (24). In another case a company was chartered to supply a town with water for thirty years, with a provision that "said company shall charge the following rates" during this time. It was held that "shall" was a command to the company not to exceed these rates, and not a contract that the state would not reduce them (25). Another striking case arose in Chi-

---

(24)	Vicksburg Railroad Co. v. Dennis, 116 U. S., 665.
(25)	Rogers Park Water Co. v. Fergus, 180 U. S., 624.

cago. A corporation chartered for twenty-five years was granted by the city of Chicago the right to operate street railways in the city for the period of twenty-five years. A few years later the Illinois legislature extended the existence of this corporation to ninety-nine years, and provided that all contracts, stipulations, licenses, and undertakings entered into between Chicago and the corporation respecting the regulation and use of street railways in the city should be continued in force "during the life hereof." This act was opposed by many citizens of Chicago on the ground that it extended the street railway franchise for ninety-nine years, without the consent of the city, and it was vetoed by the governor of Illinois on this ground. The legislature passed it over the veto, and forty years later it came before the United States Supreme Court for construction. A majority of the court held that the corporate existence was extended for ninety-nine years, but that the right to run a street railway in Chicago was not extended at all, the words "during the life hereof" referring to the life of the original grant from the city, and not the newly extended life of the corporation itself (26).

§ 239. **Special privileges construed non-transferable.** Another phase of the doctrine of strict construction is the rule that any special privilege, even though clearly granted, is to be construed as strictly personal to the grantee and not transferable to anyone else, unless the privilege is made transferable in clear, express terms.

---

(26)   Blair v. Chicago, 201 U. S., 400.

For instance, if the state authorizes the transfer by one corporation of all its property, franchises, and privileges to another corporation, this will not include a tax exemption possessed by the first company. ''The same considerations which call for clear and unambiguous language to justify the conclusion that immunity from taxation has been granted in any instance must require similar distinctness of expression before the immunity will be extended to others than the original grantee. It will not pass merely by a conveyance of the property and franchises of a railroad company, although such company may hold its property exempt from taxation'' (27). Even when two corporations, each of which has a tax exemption, consolidate and form a new corporation, the new one does not become the owner of either of the old tax exemptions (28).

§ 240. **Certain legislative powers unrestrainable by contract. Regulation of public morals.** At various periods during the development of the doctrine that the state might contract away some of its powers in corporate grants, dissenting judges had protested that no legislative body could barter away its powers of legislation in this way. In 1879 an unusual case came to the court. In 1867 Mississippi had chartered a corporation expressly authorized to carry on a lottery for twenty-five years, in return for a certain annual sum and a percentage of the lottery receipts. Two years later Mississippi forbade lotteries, and the lottery company resisted this pro-

---

(27)   Picard v. East Tennessee Railway Co., 130 U. S., 637.
(28)   Yazoo & Mississippi R. R. Co. v. Adams, 180 U. S., 1.

hibition on the ground of its charter contract. When the case reached the United States Supreme Court the subsequent state legislation was upheld. The court said:

"The question is therefore directly presented, whether, in view of these facts, the legislature of a state can, by the charter of a lottery company, defeat the will of the people, authoritatively expressed, in relation to the further continuance of such business in their midst. We think it cannot. No legislature can bargain away the public health or the public morals. The people themselves cannot do it, much less their servants. The supervision of both these subjects of governmental power is continuing in its nature, and they are to be dealt with as the special exigencies of the moment may require. Government is organized with a view to their preservation, and cannot divest itself of the power to provide for them. For this purpose the largest legislative discretion is allowed, and the discretion cannot be parted with any more than the power itself. . . .

"We have held, not, however, without strong opposition at times, that this clause protected a corporation in its charter exemptions from taxation. While taxation is in general necessary for the support of government, it is not part of the government itself. Government was not organized for the purposes of taxation, but taxation may be necessary for the purposes of government. As such, taxation becomes an incident to the exercise of the legitimate functions of government, but nothing more. No government dependent on taxation for support can bargain away its whole power of taxation, for that would be substantially abdication. All that has been determined thus far is, that for a consideration it may, in the exercise of a reasonable discretion, and for the public good, surrender a part of its powers in this particular.

"But the power of governing is a trust committed by the people to the government, no part of which can be granted away. The people, in their sovereign capacity, have established their agencies for the preservation of the public health and the public morals, and the protection of public and private rights. These several agencies can govern according to their discretion, if within the scope of their general authority, while in power; but they cannot give away nor sell the discretion of those that are to come after them, in respect to matters the government of which, from the very nature of things, must 'vary with varying circumstances.' They may create corporations, and give them, so to speak, a limited citizenship; but as citizens, limited in their privileges, or otherwise, these creatures of the government creation are subject to such rules and regulations as may from time to time be ordained and established for the preservation of health and morality" (29).

§ 241. **Same: Public health and safety.** A few years later this doctrine was reaffirmed in a case that was treated by the court as concerning the public health. In 1869 Louisiana granted to a corporation the exclusive right to conduct slaughter houses in New Orleans, and in 1881 the legislature violated this exclusive privilege. The Supreme Court denied that the first contract could

---

(29) Stone v. Mississippi, 101 U. S., 814, 819-20.

be made irrevocable by the legislature. It said: "The denial of this power, in the present instance, rests upon the ground that the power of the legislature intended to be suspended is one so indispensable to the public welfare that it cannot be bargained away by contract. It is that well-known but undefined power called the public power. . . . While we are not prepared to say that the legislature can make valid contracts on no subject embraced in the largest definition of the police power, we think that, in regard to two subjects so embraced, it cannot, by any contract, limit the exercise of those powers to the prejudice of the general welfare. These are the public health and public morals" (30).

In later cases the public safety has been said to be another subject concerning which the state cannot contract away its power to legislate. "Rights and privileges arising from contracts with the state are subject to regulations for the protection of the public health, public morals, and public safety, in the same sense, and to the same extent as are all contracts, or all property, whether owned by natural persons or corporations" (31).

§ 242. Same: Important administrative and economic interests. In other cases the doctrine has been extended to governmental powers other than those exercised to protect the public health, morals, or safety. In Newton v. Commissioners (32) it was said that a state

---

(30)   Butchers Union Co. v. Crescent City Co., 111 U. S., 746, 750-51.
(31)   New Orleans Gas Co. v. Louisiana Light Co., 115 U. S., 650, 672.
(32)   100 U. S., 548.

could not make an irrepealable contract with the donors
of public buildings and lands that a county seat for the
holding of court should be established and kept in perpe-
tuity at the place where the donors had given property
for this purpose. In Illinois Central Railway Co. v. Illinois (33) it was held that the Illinois legislature could
not irrevocably convey to a railroad company the land
under the harbor of Chicago. The legislative duty to
act freely for the public good in respect to so important
a matter could not be relinquished by any grant or contract transferring such property. It has also been suggested that a legislature could not irrevocably empower
a railroad to make consolidations with competing lines,
so that a subsequent legislature could not forbid future
consolidations of that character; that a charter contract
empowering a bank to issue non-taxable stock could be
revoked at any time as to future stock issues; and that
even the power to regulate rates could not be given up
by contract for a term grossly unreasonable in point of
time (34).

From these decisions and dicta it appears that the
subjects concerning which a state may not irrevocably
contract away its governmental powers are considerably
more extensive than the public health, morals, and safety.
Probably the doctrine is or will come to be that no state
may make an irrevocable contract substantially impair-

---

(33)   146 U. S., 387.

(34)   Louisville & Nashville R. R. Co. v. Kentucky, 161 U. S., 677;
Bank of Commerce v. Tennessee, 163 U. S., 416; Home Telephone Co.
v. Los Angeles, 211 U. S., 265, 273.

ing its governmental powers in respect to any matter seriously affecting the public welfare.

§ 243. **Private contracts that affect the public.** However it may be with contracts to which the public is a party, represented by the state or some part of it, there is no doubt that *private individuals* cannot by contract prevent the legislature from regulating their future relations to the public. For instance, if A contracts with B to sell liquor in Iowa for ten years, this will not affect Iowa's right to prohibit the sale of liquor in the state. If two street railroad companies validly agree that each will charge ten cent fares, this cannot prevent the legislature from reducing the rates to five cents (35). If A and B, owners of land on a certain creek, contract not to obstruct the creek, this will not prevent the legislature from authorizing A to erect a dam at the place for public purposes (36). The difference between the cases just mentioned and a case where the legislature might try to reduce the interest on a loan already made, is that in the latter case the rate of interest paid on a debt affects primarily the parties to the contract, and the interests of the general public are not substantially concerned with it   Where it is the law, at the time the private contract is made, that the debtor may be imprisoned for non-payment, or that absolutely all of his property may be sold to satisfy the debt, the legislature may still abolish imprisonment for debt, and exempt from execution such

---

(35)   Buffalo East Side R. R. Co. v. Buffalo Street R. R. Co., 111 N. Y., 132.

(36)   Manigault v. Springs, 199 U. S., 473.

tools and necessary property as may prevent the debtor from becoming a charge upon the community (37). This is because the public has an interest in human freedom and in preventing pauperism. It has no such substantial interest in the terms of pecuniary compensation for a loan.

§ 244. **Reserved power of states to repeal corporate charters.** After the Dartmouth College case the American states began by constitutions and statute to forbid the grant to corporations of irrevocable charters or tax exemptions. This has been continued until today such grants are forbidden by the constitutions of almost all American states. This reserved power to alter or repeal the corporate charter is of course a part of the obligation of the original charter contract, if indeed that can be called a contract which may be revoked by one of the parties at pleasure. Where this reserved power of revocation has been exercised, the courts have been required to pass upon its effect. In one case Massachusetts incorporated a street railroad and empowered it to haul freight through the streets of Boston. Afterwards, in the exercise of the state's reserved power, its charter was repealed and a new company was incorporated to do its business. The effect of this repeal was stated by the Supreme Court as follows:

"One obvious effect of the repeal of a statute is that it no longer exists. Its life is at an end. Whatever force the law may give to transactions into which the corporation entered and which were authorized by the charter

---

(37) Von Hoffman v. Quincy, 4 Wall., 535, 553.

while in force, it can originate no new transactions dependent on the power conferred by the charter. . . .
If the essence of the grant of the charter be to operate a railroad, and to use the streets of the city for that purpose, it can no longer so use the streets of the city. In short, whatever power is dependent solely upon the grant of the charter, and which could not be exercised by unincorporated private persons under the general laws of the state, is abrogated by the repeal of the law which granted these special rights.

"Personal and real property acquired by the corporation during its lawful existence, rights of contract, or choses in action so acquired, and which do not in their nature depend upon the general powers conferred by the charter, are not destroyed by such a repeal; and the courts may, if the legislature does not provide some special remedy, enforce such rights by the means within their power. The rights of the share-holders of such a corporation, to their interest in its property, are not annihilated by such a repeal, and there must remain in the courts the power to protect those rights" (38).

§ 245. **Protection of property acquired before repeal.** A striking instance of the above doctrine, which protects property acquired by the use of corporate powers even after the corporate powers themselves are repealed, occurred in New York. The legislature granted a repealable charter to a corporation which was given power to acquire a street railway franchise from New York city,

---

(38)   Greenwood v. Marginal Freight Co., 105 U. S., 13, 18-19, 21.

if one could be obtained from that municipality. This franchise, under the New York constitution, could be acquired only from the city, and no state law made such a franchise repealable. By gross bribery the corporation acquired the Broadway street railway franchise from New York city. Upon the discovery of the facts the charter of the corporation was revoked by the legislature, and several of the participants in the bribery were sent to the penitentiary. Most of the corporate stock at this time was in the hands of innocent stockholders, and it was held that the Broadway franchise, an irrepealable contract of great value, was part of the property of the defunct corporation that survived for the benefit of its stockholders. The powers of the corporation ceased upon its repeal, but the Broadway franchise, not being a power granted to the corporation by the state, was not revoked and could not be under the Federal Constitution (39). It may thus readily happen that a corporation with a repealable charter may own as property an irrepealable franchise. State constitutions that forbid all irrepealable grants to corporations by the state, have never gone so far as to forbid all such grants by municipalities, though such grants are commonly limited to terms of years.

§ 246. **Effect of state bankruptcy laws.** It was early admitted that if a state bankruptcy law was in force when a contract was made in that state, the provisions of the bankruptcy law became a part of the obligation of the contract, so that the latter was not impaired by the

---

(39)   People v. O'Brien, 111 N. Y. 1.

discharge of the debtor in bankruptcy according to the provisions of this law (40). Where both the debtor and creditor were citizens of the state having the bankruptcy law and in which the contract was made, the matter was free from difficulty. A serious controversy arose over cases where the parties were citizens of different states. Suppose the contract were made in New York between a creditor living in Kentucky and a New York debtor, the New York bankruptcy law being then in force. If the Kentuckian leaves New York and the New Yorker then is discharged from his debt by a New York proceeding in bankruptcy to which the Kentuckian is not a party, does this discharge bind the Kentuckian? The Federal courts finally held it did not, probably not because the discharge impaired the obligation of a contract, which it could hardly do because not being a subsequent *law;* but because jurisdiction over the Kentuckian is necessary in such a proceeding (41) to affect his property, the debt due him.

As regards state bankruptcy laws, then, the result of the decisions is this: A state bankruptcy law can discharge only contracts made in the state, between citizens of that state, and subsequent to the bankruptcy law. Citizens of other states can only be affected by a discharge in bankruptcy when they become parties thereto.

§ 246a. **Foreign suit on contract.** As regards contracts made in one state, but sued upon and enforced

---

(40) Ogden v. Saunders, 12 Wheat., 213.

(41) Ogden v. Saunders, 12 Wheat., 213; Baldwin v. Hale, 1 Wall., 223.

in another state, it seems clear that the creditor cannot demand that the latter state give him the same remedies that he would have been entitled to in the state where the contract was made. Anyone who chooses or is compelled to bring suit outside of his own jurisdiction must expect such remedies only as are afforded by the law of the place where he sues. This law was never a part of the obligation of the contract made elsewhere, and so the creditor from another jurisdiction must take the domestic law and remedies as he finds them (42).

§ 247. **Foreign contracts.** The contract clause of the Constitution does not apply to contracts made in a foreign country with corporations of that country, even though suit may be brought upon such contracts in the United States. Legislation of the foreign government, impairing the obligation of the contract, will be respected here (43).

§ 248. **Laws increasing the obligation of contracts.** State legislation that provides a better remedy upon a contract, or a more certain enforcement, or which validates a void contract does not violate this clause of the Constitution (44). Such laws certainly do not *impair* the obligations of contracts, though they may perhaps be arbitrary or unjust, and may violate other constitutional provisions, such as the prohibition against taking property without due process of law.

---

(42) Bank of United States v. Donnally, 8 Pet., 361.
(43) Canada Southern Railway Co. v. Gebhard, 109 U. S., 527.
(44) Satterlee v. Mathewson, 2 Pet., 380.

PART III.

THE FEDERAL GOVERNMENT.

CHAPTER XII.

FEDERAL POWERS AND THEIR EXERCISE.

§ 249. **General principles of construction: Strict versus liberal.** As has already been said (§§ 27, 28) the two great principles of construction applicable to the powers of the United States are, first, that it can exercise no powers except those expressly or by fair implication granted to it in the Constitution; and second, that over such granted powers it has absolute control, and its legislation thereunder is paramount to all conflicting state laws. The importance of these principles demands some further discussion.

Political parties in this country have long divided upon the question of interpreting the Constitution strictly or liberally. These distinctions are political in their nature. The duty of the judicial branch of the government is shown by the following quotation from Chief Justice Marshall:

"This instrument contains an enumeration of powers expressly granted by the people to their government. It has been said that these powers ought to be construed strictly. But why ought they to be so construed? Is

there one sentence in the Constitution which gives coun-
tenance to this rule? In the last of the enumerated powers, that which grants, expressly, the means for carrying
all others into execution, Congress is authorized 'to make
all laws which shall be necessary and proper' for the
purpose. But this limitation on the means which may be
used, is not extended to the powers which are conferred;
nor is there one sentence in the Constitution, which has
been pointed out by the gentlemen of the bar, or which we
have been able to discern, that prescribes this rule. We do
not, therefore, think ourselves justified in adopting it.
What do gentlemen mean by a strict construction? If
they contend only against that enlarged construction
which would extend words beyond their natural and
obvious import, we might question the application of the
term, but should not controvert the principle. If they
contend for that narrow construction which, in support
of some theory not to be found in the Constitution, would
deny to the government those powers which the words of
the grant, as usually understood, import, and which are
consistent with the general views and objects of the instrument; for that narrow construction, which would
cripple the government, and render it unequal to the objects for which it is declared to be instituted, and to which
the powers given, as fairly understood, render it competent; then we cannot perceive the propriety of this
strict construction, nor adopt it as the rule by which the
Constitution is to be expounded. . . . As men whose in-
tentions require no concealment, generally employ the
words which most directly and aptly express the ideas

they intend to convey, the enlightened patriots who framed our Constitution, and the people who adopted it, must be understood to have employed words in their natural sense, and to have intended what they have said. If, from the imperfection of human language, there should be serious doubts respecting the extent of any given power, it is a well-settled rule that the objects for which it was given, especially when those objects are expressed in the instrument itself, should have great influence in the construction. . . . We know of no rule for construing the extent of such powers, other than is given by the language of the instrument which confers them, taken in connection with the purposes for which they were conferred'' (1).

§ 250. Implied powers. In McCulloch v. Maryland (2) the question arose whether Congress could charter a national bank. Congress has express power to collect taxes and borrow money. Was the power to create a banking corporation fairly inferable from these? Chief Justice Marshall said:

''Among the enumerated powers, we do not find that of establishing a bank or creating a corporation. But there is no phrase in the instrument which, like the Articles of Confederation excludes incidental or implied powers; and which requires that everything granted shall be expressly and minutely described. . . . A constitution, to contain an accurate detail of all the subdivisions of which its great powers will admit and of all the means

---

(1) Gibbons v. Ogden, 9 Wheaton, 1, 187-9.
(2) 4 Wheat., 316.

by which they may be carried into execution, would partake of the prolixity of a legal code, and could scarcely be embraced by the human mind. It would probably never be understood by the public. Its nature, therefore, requires that only its great outlines should be marked, its important objects designated, and the minor ingredients which compose those objects be deduced from the nature of the objects themselves. . . . In considering this question, then, we must never forget that it is a constitution we are expounding. . . .

'The power of creating a corporation is never used for its own sake, but for the purpose of effecting something else. No sufficient reason is, therefore, perceived, why it may not pass as incidental to those powers which are expressly given, if it be a direct mode of executing them. . . . [It is urged] Congress is not empowered to make all laws, which may have relation to the powers conferred on the government, but such only as may be 'necessary and proper' (3) for carrying them into execution [and], that it excludes choice of means and leaves to Congress, in each case, that one choice most direct and simple. . . . Is it true, that this is the sense in which the word 'necessary' is always used? Does it always import an absolute physical necessity, so strong that one thing, to which another may be termed necessary, cannot exist without that other? We think it does not. If reference be had to its use in the common affairs of the world, or in approved authors, we find that it frequently

---

(3)   Const., Art. I, sec. 8, § 18.

imports no more than that one thing is convenient, or useful, or essential to another. To employ the means necessary to an end is generally understood as employing any means calculated to produce the end, and not as being confined to those single means, without which the end would be entirely unattainable. . . . We think the sound construction of the Constitution must allow to the national legislature that discretion, with respect to the means by which the powers it confers are to be carried into execution, which will enable that body to perform the high duties assigned to it in the manner most beneficial to the people. Let the end be legitimate, let it be within the scope of the Constitution, and all means which are appropriate, which are plainly adapted to that end, which are not prohibited, but consist with the letter and spirit of the Constitution, are constitutional.''

The creation of a national bank was thus upheld. Similarly, although the United States is nowhere expressly given the power of eminent domain, yet it may exercise it in the execution of other express powers (4).

§ 251. **Powers implied from groups of other powers.** ''It is not indispensable to the existence of any power claimed for the Federal government that it can be found specified in the words of the Constitution, or clearly and directly traceable to some one of the specified powers. Its existence may be deduced fairly from more than one of the substantive powers expressly defined, or from them all combined. It is allowable to group together any number of them and infer from them all that the power claimed has been conferred'' (5).

---

(4) Kohl v. United States, 91 U. S. 367. The Preamble to the Constitution confers no power upon the United States, Jacobson v. Mass., 197 U. S. 11, 22.

(5) Legal Tender Cases, 12 Wall., 457, 534.

Thus, the Constitution gives the United States express power to punish only four crimes, counterfeiting, felonies committed on the high seas, offenses against the law of nations, and treason; but Congress has of course implied power to punish the breaking of any Federal law, and to protect prisoners in its custody (6). A very strong instance of implied Federal powers are the various acts making paper a legal tender money. See §§ 310, 311, below. Instances of other implied powers will be found in the sections upon various Federal powers following this.

§ 252. **Exclusive and concurrent powers.** When a power is granted to the United States in the Constitution is it therefore denied to the states (exclusive power), or may they also exercise it so long as their laws are not inconsistent with Federal laws on the subject (concurrent power)? The accepted rule has been judicially stated as follows: "The states may exercise concurrent or independent power in all cases but three: 1. Where the power is lodged exclusively in the Federal Constitution. 2. Where it is given to the United States and prohibited to the states. 3. Where, from the nature and subjects of the power, it must necessarily be exercised by the Federal government exclusively" (7).

An instance of the first case is the power to borrow money on the credit of the United States. The states never had such a power, it being lodged exclusively in the Constitution. An instance of the second case is the power to tax imports. The states originally had this, but the Constitution gives it to Congress and prohibits the states to exercise it. An instance of the third class is the

(6)   Logan v. United States, 144 U. S., 263.
(7)   Gilman v. Philadelphia, 3 Wall., 713.

power of naturalization, which the states once had, which is given to Congress, but is not expressly prohibited to the states. The nature of the power is such that Congress alone may exercise it. See § 88, above.

Instances of powers that are concurrent because not falling within any of these classes are the power to pass bankruptcy laws (8), to tax, and to make certain regulations of commerce (see § 284, below).

§ 253. **Purposes for which Federal powers may be exercised.** When it is said that Congress has complete control over all powers granted to it, does this mean that Congress may exercise such powers for any purpose, or to secure any result that it pleases; or can even the granted powers be exercised only for some purposes within the scope of the Federal powers? An illustration will show how important is this question. Congress is given by the Constitution no power directly to regulate lotteries in a state. If a state charters a lottery and makes it a part of its revenue system, it is acting wholly within its reserved powers, and Congress cannot directly interfere. Now Congress has control of the post-office. May Congress exercise its postal powers to exclude lottery matter from the mails—not for the sake of the post-office, nor in the exercise of any other Federal power, like that of regulating commerce or passing bankruptcy laws, but solely in order to hamper lotteries in a state? It has been held that this may be done (9). Likewise it has been held that Congress may forbid the carriage from state to state of lottery tickets under its power to regulate interstate commerce, even though this power be here exercised

---

(8)   Sturges v. Crowninshield, 4 Wheat., 117.

(9)   In re Rapier, 143 U. S., 110.

for no strictly commercial purpose, but solely to prevent the moral and economic evils of lotteries in the state. "The power of Congress to regulate commerce among the states is plenary, is complete in itself, and is subject to no limitations except such as may be found in the Constitution" (10).

A far-reaching application of this principle, one that goes too far, as appears from § 255, is found in McCray v. United States (11), where Congress imposed a tax upon the manufacture of artificially colored oleomargarine so high (as was assumed in argument) as to prevent its manufacture. The Supreme Court said that the Constitution gave Congress power to lay taxes and that the purpose for which they were laid could not be investigated by the court, that being solely in the discretion of Congress. Under the operation of this principle there would be almost no business or occupation (except perhaps managing land) which could not be effectively regulated by Congress. The power to exclude from the postoffice and from interstate commerce, and to tax out of existence would enable Congress virtually to prohibit in a state matters of the most local and domestic nature, provided that a majority of Congress wished to prevent them in the country at large.

§ 254. **Prohibitions upon the exercise of Federal powers.** In various parts of the Constitution, notably in Article I, section 9, and in the amendments there are various general prohibitions upon the Federal government. These prohibitions limit the exercise of all powers to which they are applicable. Thus, while the United States has, as against the states, full power over the post-

---

(10) Lottery Case, 188 U. S., 321, 356.
(11) 195 U. S., 27. See also Ellis v. U. S., 206 U. S. 246, 255-56.

office and interstate commerce, yet these powers must be
so exercised as not to violate these general prohibitions,
like those forbidding unreasonable searches and seizures
and the taking of property without due process of law
in the Fourth and Fifth Amendments. The scope of
these general prohibitions or guarantees is fully considered in Chapters V to X, above.

§ 255. **Reserved powers of the states.** ''The powers
not delegated to the United States by the Constitution,
nor prohibited by it to the states, are reserved to the
states respectively or to the people'' (12).

From the nature of the Federal government, being
one of delegated powers, it is not likely that this provision places any additional constitutional limitation upon
Federal action. Some authority, express or implied,
must be found in the Constitution for all Federal activities. In a considerable number of instances acts of Congress have been held invalid because not falling fairly
within any grant of the Constitution.

Thus Congress has no power to forbid the sale in a
state of dangerous illuminating oil; or to forbid the
wrongful use, in the internal commerce of a state, of
registered trade-marks; or to regulate the liability of
railroad employees for accidents occurring in the internal
commerce of a state; or to forbid persons in a state from
harboring alien prostitutes, when not done in connection
with their coming into the United States (13). In none
of these cases was there anything to be found in the

---

(12) Const., Amend. X.
(13) United States v. DeWitt, 9 Wall., 41; Trade Mark Cases, 100
U. S., 25; Howard v. Illinois Central Railroad, 207 U. S., 463; Keller
v. United States, 213 U. S., 138.

Constitution expressly or impliedly authorizing Congress to deal with the subject matter in question.

It thus appears that acts of Congress may be invalid either (a) because, although in the exercise of a granted power, they exercise it in a forbidden way; or (b) because they are not in the exercise of any granted power.

Further illustrations of these principles are found in the child labor cases. In the first of these, Hammer v. Dagenhart (14), Congress passed a law excluding from interstate commerce any article or commodity which was the product of child labor. This law was held invalid. The court pointed out that the grant of power to Congress over the subject of interstate commerce was to enable it to regulate such commerce and not to give it authority to control the states in their exercise of the police power over local trade and manufacture. For a similar reason, among others, the National Industrial Recovery Act of 1933 was declared invalid. The Act, though purporting to be an exercise of the power to regulate interstate commerce, undertook, through the enforcement of "codes of fair competition" in various businesses and industries, to regulate the details of local as well as interstate business. The chief reason, perhaps, for declaring the Act invalid was that it was an unwarranted delegation of legislative power, but of almost equal weight was "the attempted regulation of intrastate transactions which affect interstate commerce only indirectly (15).

In the second child labor case, Bailey v. Drexel Furniture Company (16), it was held that Congress could not

---

(14)   247 U. S. 251; overruled by U.S. v. Darby, 312 U.S. 100.

(15)   Schechter v. U. S., 295 U. S. 495.

(16)   259 U. S. 20.

use its taxing power to control the employment of child labor within the states. The tax imposed was more of the nature of a penalty than a tax. A similar holding is found in United States v. Butler (17) invalidating the Agricultural Adjustment Act of 1933. The court held that the processing tax imposed by the Act was not a true tax. It was not imposed to raise funds to support the Government, but was a mere incident to the main purpose of regulating agricultural production. Congress has power to lay and collect taxes, but it cannot, by the exercise of that power, invade the rights of the states. The court said, "The Act invades the reserved rights of the states. It is a statutory plan to regulate and control agricultural production, a matter beyond the powers delegated to the Federal Government.

"The tax, the appropriation of the funds raised, and the direction for their disbursement are but parts of the plan. They are but means to an unconstitutional end.

. . . It is an established principle that the attainment of a prohibited end may not be accomplished under the pretext of the exertion of powers which are granted. . . . The power of taxation, which is expressly granted, may, of course, be adopted as a means to carry into operation another power also expressly granted. But resort to the taxing power to effectuate an end which is not legitimate, nor within the scope of the Constitution, is obviously inadmissible" (18).

---

(17)   297 U. S. 1, 102 A.L.R. 914.

(18)   Section revised by publisher's editorial staff.

CHAPTER XIII.
TERRITORIES, DEPENDENCIES, AND NEW STATES.

§ 256. **Cession of western lands to United States.**
When the Constitution was adopted there had already
been ceded to the United States a great expanse of territory between the Mississippi river and the western boundary of the thirteen original states. This territory had
been previously claimed, to a various extent, by several
of the states, and its cession to the general government
was required as a condition to the accession of the smaller
states to the Confederation. They felt that such great
additions to the bulk of their larger neighbors would
make relations between them upon anything like equal
terms impossible; hence their insistence, particularly
that of Maryland, that the larger states cede their claims
to the western land to Congress.

Article IV, section 3, of the Constitution contains provisions concerning this territory and the mode in which
new states may be admitted to the Union. These provisions are quoted below in their proper places.

§ 257. **Implied powers to annex territory.** The Constitution contains no express grant of power to Congress
to annex new territory to the country, and when the great
Louisiana purchase was so suddenly made in 1803 there
was much discussion of its constitutionality. Whatever

doubts were then felt have long since disappeared, and whenever our courts have referred to the matter they have declared that the power of the United States to make war and to make treaties included the power to acquire territory in either of these ways (1). The right of the United States to acquire territory by discovery and occupation has also been judicially affirmed (2). This is to be implied from the complete control over our external relations given to Congress by the Constitution. The power over these relations is denied to the states and now rests in the United States, except in so far as the exercise of particular powers may be expressly prohibited.

Moreover, it is for the political departments of the government, the legislative and executive, to determine who is the sovereign of any territory whatever, and their decision is binding upon the courts. If these departments recognize certain territory as under the jurisdiction of the United States, the political rights of the United States there can not be discussed in American courts. The same is true if some other nation is thus recognized as entitled to jurisdiction. Decisions illustrating this have been rendered concerning the Panama Canal Zone and the Isle of Pines (3).

§ 258. **Federal sovereignty in territories.** The Constitution, Article IV, section 3, §2, provides:

---

(1)   American Insurance Co. v. Canter, 1 Pet., 511, 542.

(2)   Jones v. United States, 137 U. S., 202.

(3)   Wilson v. Shaw, 204 U. S., 24; Pearcy v. Stranahan, 205 U. S., 257.

"The Congress shall have power to dispose of and make all needful rules and regulations respecting the territory or other property belonging to the United States; and nothing in this Constitution shall be so construed as to prejudice any claims of the United States, or of any particular state."

It was early held that the United States had full governmental power over the territories, implied from the power to acquire the territory itself, as well as expressly conferred in the clause above quoted (4). In the states, the national government is sovereign only in regard to subjects committed to it by the Constitution. On all other matters the state governments are sovereign. In the territories the United States unites the powers of both national and state governments. Congress may govern the territories by its own direct legislation, or it may delegate all or part of this legislative power to territorial legislatures, commissions, or even executives and judges (5).

§ 259. **Application in territories of constitutional prohibitions.** The only serious questions concerning Federal power over the territories have been as to the applicability there of certain constitutional limitations upon the powers of the United States. In various parts of the Constitution, particularly in the first ten amendments,

---

(4)   American Insurance Co. v. Canter, 1 Pet. 511; Mormon Church v. United States, 136 U. S., 1.

(5)   Dorr v. United States, 195 U. S., 138. A full history of the government of United States territories before 1871 is given in Clinton v. Englebrecht, 13 Wall., 434.

there are a variety of prohibitions upon the actions of the United States government.

(a) By the express language of some of these prohibitions they limit the power of the government only in respect to the states. Such instances are "no tax or duty shall be laid on articles exported from any state," and "no preference shall be given by any regulation of commerce or revenue to the ports of one state over those of another" (6).

(b) The express language of at least one prohibition limits the power of the Federal government everywhere within its jurisdiction. "Neither slavery nor involuntary servitude . . . shall exist within the United States or any place subject to their jurisdiction" (7).

(c) Some prohibitions expressly apply only within the "United States." For instance, "All duties, imposts, and excises shall be uniform throughout the United States" (8). The guarantee of citizenship by birth is in similar language; "All persons born . . . in the United States . . . are citizens of the United States" (9).

(d) The great majority of the prohibitions upon the United States government do not expressly state or clearly show to what territory they are applicable. This includes all of the first nine amendments which constitute the Federal bill of rights.

---

(6)   Art. I, sec. 9, §§ 5 and 6.
(7)   Amend. XIII.
(8)   Art. I, sec. 8, § 1
(9)   Amend. XIV, sec. 1.

§ 260. Spanish cessions of 1898. Power to acquire "unincorporated" territory. The earlier acquisitions of territory by the United States formed a contiguous body of territory, all situated within latitudes readily inhabitable by the white race, and all held with the ultimate prospect of its being admitted to the Union as states, as each local division of it might become thus qualified in property and population. Alaska alone, acquired in 1867, was an exception to this statement, but its geographical location and sparseness of population prevented its presenting any important political problems.

By the treaty of peace that closed the Spanish war of 1898 the United States became the sovereign of an Asiatic archipelago containing several million inhabitants of an alien race, unused to our customs and laws, and apparently unfitted for a full measure of local self-government. This novel situation has compelled a careful inquiry into the constitutional status of territory acquired by the United States.

Before the Spanish war no serious questions had arisen regarding the status of territory acquired by the United States and not yet admitted to statehood. No decision had ever turned upon the question whether annexed territory became an integral part of the United States, or was merely held as a dependency, like, for instance, an English colony. In 1820 Chief Justice Marshall had uttered a dictum to the effect that the United States was the name of our great republic, composed of states and territories, and that the District of Columbia and the territory west of the Missouri was not less within the

United States than Maryland or Pennsylvania (9a); but the matter received no thorough consideration until after the Spanish war.

Puerto Rico and the Philippines were acquired by treaty from Spain with the proviso that "the civil rights and political status of the native inhabitants. . . . shall be determined by Congress." Shortly thereafter Congress passed an act taxing goods passing from Puerto Rico into the continental parts of the United States. This was challenged on the ground that Puerto Rico became by annexation a part of the United States, and that the Constitution (Art. I, sec. 8, §1) required duties to be uniform throughout the United States. A majority of the Supreme Court held that while Puerto Rico ceased to be a foreign country upon annexation (10), it did not thereby become at once a part of the United States. The power to acquire territory implied also the power to prescribe the terms upon which it shall be held. By treaty and act of Congress annexed territory may be at once incorporated into the United States and be as much a part of this country as is one of the states; but, if the political departments of the government so desire, annexed territory may be held and governed outside of the United States, virtually as a colony or dependency. Such territory is in the position of a British colony, which is neither foreign to Great Britain nor yet a part of the latter. It was held that the territory acquired from Spain, under the terms of the Spanish treaty and in

---

(9a)	Loughborough v. Blake, 5 Wheat., 317.
(10)	De Lima v. Bidwell. 182 U. S., 1.

view of Congressional legislation, occupied this position, and, not being a part of the United States, Puerto Rican duties need not be uniform with those in the United States (11).

§ 261. **Territorial classification of Federal jurisdiction.** It thus appears that territory within which the United States may exercise authority falls into at least five different classes:

(a) The states of the Union. Example: Massachusetts.

(b) Annexed territory incorporated into the United States, but not yet admitted to statehood. Example: Alaska, before it was admitted into the Union as a state.

(c) Annexed territory not yet incorporated into the United States, but governed as a dependency. Example: Puerto Rico.

(d) Territory temporarily occupied by the United States, for military or other purposes, but without annexation. Example: Cuba after the Spanish war until the withdrawal of the United States.

(e) Territory within the limits of an organized foreign country, over which the latter permits the United States to exercise some jurisdiction. Example: The jurisdiction formerly exercised by the American consular courts over American citizens in certain undeveloped countries like China.

In each one of these five classes of territory, the question may be raised how far constitutional prohibitions upon governmental actions are applicable. An interest-

---

(11) Downes v. Bidwell, 182 U. S., 244.

ing series of cases, most of them decided since the Spanish war, has furnished the material for answers.

§ 262. Prohibitions applicable in states and incorporated territories. (a) All constitutional prohibitions upon the action of the Federal government apply in the states. This was the principal object in placing them in the Constitution.

(b) In the incorporated territories all constitutional prohibitions apply to the Federal government, except those meant to be applicable to the states only. Prior to statehood, the question had arisen in Alaska whether persons could be tried for a crime in Alaska without a jury (of twelve men) required by the Sixth Amendment of the Constitution. It was held that the terms of the treaty by which Alaska was acquired and the subsequent legislation of Congress had the effect of incorporating Alaska into the United States, and that the Sixth Amendment therefore applied, even though it concerned merely a matter of judicial procedure (12). A similar decision has been made regarding the District of Columbia, which is at least in as favorable a situation as incorporated territory, inasmuch as it once formed a part of the state of Maryland and was then certainly a part of the United States (13).

§ 263. Judiciary article applies in states only. One important part of the Constitution, though not made expressly applicable to the states alone, has been held not

---

(12)   Rassmussen v. United States, 197 U. S., 516.

(13)   Callan v. Wilson, 127 U. S., 540; Downes v. Bidwell, 182 U. S., 244, 261.

to apply to incorporated territory. This is the first clause of the judiciary article: "The judicial power of the United States shall be vested in one Supreme Court, and in such inferior courts as the Congress may from time to time ordain and establish. The judges, both of the Supreme and inferior courts, shall hold their offices during good behavior, and shall, at stated times, receive for their services a compensation which shall not be diminished during their continuance in office" (14). This clause has always been interpreted as applying only to United States courts in the states. In the incorporated territories Congress has habitually created courts whose judges hold office for short terms of years instead of during good behavior (15). These territorial courts exercise a local territorial jurisdiction which is derived from the power of Congress to govern the territories, not from the specific grant of judicial power to the United States in the judiciary article. The latter was designed only to regulate the exercise of Federal judicial power in the states which already had judicial systems of their own. As soon as a territory is admitted to the Union as a state its former territorial courts lose all jurisdiction whatever, and cannot even dispose of pending cases (16).

§ 264. **Unincorporated territory.** (c) Unincorporated territory, not being a part of the United States, is of course not entitled to the benefit of such prohibitions upon Federal action as apply to that action merely in

---

(14) Art. III, sec. 1.

(15) American Insurance Co. v. Canter, 1 Pet., 511.

(16) Benner v. Porter, 9 How., 235.

the United States. Federal taxes and bankruptcy laws, for instance, must be uniform throughout the United States, but unincorporated territory may be treated differently. Similarly, the provision that all persons born in the United States shall be citizens would seem not to apply to unincorporated territory.

In Downes v. Bidwell it was urged by counsel that if the United States could annex territory without making it a part of the United States, then it would not be bound by any of the prohibitions of the Constitution and could govern such unincorporated territory in any arbitrary manner it saw fit. These general prohibitions upon the Federal government are contained mainly in Article I, section 9, and Amendments I to X, XIII, and XV. They are not specifically confined to actions of the United States within the United States, but are general prohibitions, as for instance that Congress shall make no law prohibiting the free exercise of religion; that no one shall be deprived of life, liberty, or property without due process of law; that all criminal trials shall be by jury; and the like.

On the other hand it was urged that if all of these prohibitions applied to the United States in the Philippines, for instance, it would be very embarrassing, as the people there were quite unaccustomed to jury trials as a part of civil and criminal procedure. Upon this point Mr. Justice Brown said:

"We suggest, without intending to decide, that there may be a distinction between certain natural rights, enforced in the Constitution by prohibitions against interference with them, and what may be termed artificial or remedial rights, which are peculiar to our own system of jurisprudence. Of the former class are the rights to one's own religious opinions and to a public expression of them, or, as sometimes said, to worship God according to the dictates of one's own conscience; the right to personal liberty and individual property; to freedom of speech and of the press; to free access to courts of justice, to due process of law, and to an equal protection of the laws; to immunities from unreasonable searches and seizures, as well as cruel and unusual punishments; and to such other immunities as are indispensable to a free government. Of the latter class are the rights of citizenship, to suffrage, and to the particular methods of procedure pointed out in the Constitution which are peculiar to Anglo-Saxon jurisprudence, and some of which have already been held by the states to be unnecessary to the proper protection of individuals.

"Whatever may be finally decided by the American people as to the status of these islands and their inhabitants—whether they shall be introduced into the sisterhood of states or be permitted to form independent governments—it does not follow that, in the meantime, awaiting that decision, the people are in the matter of personal rights unprotected by the provisions of our Constitution, and subject to the merely arbitrary control of Congress. Even if regarded as aliens, they are entitled under the principles of the Constitution to be protected in life, liberty, and property. . . . We do not desire, however, to anticipate the difficulties which would naturally arise in this connection, but merely to disclaim any intention to hold that the inhabitants of these territories are subject to an unrestrained power on the part of Congress to deal with them upon the theory that they have no rights which it is bound to respect'' (17).

These important suggestions have been applied in two other cases, in which it was held that the requirement of grand and trial juries for the prosecution of criminals did not bind the United States government in Hawaii (18), or in the Philippines (19).

§ 265. **Foreign territory temporarily occupied.** (d) As regards territory temporarily occupied by this country, though not annexed, probably the Constitution does not apply at all. During the American occupation of Cuba after the Spanish war, the entire government was administered under American control. An American citizen who was alleged to have committed a crime in Cuba was arrested in this country to be sent back there for trial. The contention of the defendant and the answer of the court appear in the following quotation:

"It is contended that the act of June 6, 1900, is unconstitutional and void in that it does not secure to the accused, when surrendered to a foreign country for trial in its tribunals, all of the rights, privileges, and immunities that are guaranteed by the Constitution to persons charged with the commission in this country of crime against the United States. Allusion is here made to the

---

(17) Downes v. Bidwell, 182 U. S., 244, 282-3.
(18) Hawaii v. Mankichi, 190 U. S., 197.
(19) Dorr v. United States, 195 U. S., 138.

provisions of the Federal Constitution relating to the writ of habeas corpus, bills of attainder, ex post facto laws, trial by jury for crime, and generally to the fundamental guarantees of life, liberty, and property embodied in that instrument. The answer to this suggestion is that those provisions have no relation to crimes committed without the jurisdiction of the United States against the laws of a foreign country'' (20).

§ 266. **Foreign consular jurisdiction.** (e) It seems also that the Constitution of the United States does not apply to any actions of our government that may be authorized within foreign countries by the law there. If the Japanese government permits American consuls to conduct trials in Japan in the consular courts, no jury need be provided. ''The Constitution can have no operation in another country. When therefore the representatives or officers of our government are permitted to exercise authority of any kind in another country, it must be on such conditions as the two countries may agree, the laws of neither one being obligatory upon the other'' (21).

§ 267. **Admission of new states into the Union.** The Constitution provides, Article IV, section 3, § 1: ''New states may be admitted by the Congress into this Union; but no new states shall be formed or erected within the jurisdiction of any other state; nor any state be formed by the junction of two or more states, or parts of states, without the consent of the legislatures of the states concerned as well as of the Congress.''

---

(20)   Neely v. Henkel, 180 U. S., 109, 122.

(21)   In re Ross, 140 U. S., 453, 464.

It was contemplated that new states, formed out of
the territory owned by the United States, should be admitted to the Union from time to time, as the various
organized territories became fitted for this. The first
new state admitted under this clause was Vermont in
1791, and the number has increased until, with the admission of Alaska and Hawaii in 1960, it reached thirty-
seven in addition to the original thirteen. It is generally
admitted today that the admission of a state to the Union
is irrevocable, and that the state can neither withdraw
nor be excluded.

"The Constitution, in all its provisions, looks to an
indestructible Union, composed of indestructible states.
When, therefore, Texas became one of the United States,
she entered into an indissoluble relation. All the obligations of perpetual union and all the guarantees of republican government in the Union, attached at once to the
state. The act which consummated her admission into
the Union was something more than a compact; it was
the incorporation of a new member into the political body.
And it was final. . . . There was no place for reconsideration, or revocation, except through revolution, or through
consent of the states. . . . Texas continued to be a state,
and a state of the Union, notwithstanding the transactions [secession and Civil war] to which we have referred" (22).

§ 268. Can new states be admitted with powers less
than those of other states? A state can only be admitted
upon the same footing as the other states and any attempt

---

(22)   Texas v. White, 7 Wall., 700.

by Congress in the terms of admission, either to increase its own powers or diminish those of the new state as compared with its neighbors, are invalid (23). Congress has at various times purported to limit in certain particulars the legislative powers of states newly admitted, like Utah, or "reconstructed," like Mississippi, the former in respect to the future legalization of polygamy, and the latter in respect to the restrictions upon suffrage. These attempts are doubtless invalid (24).

A distinction has been made, however, between terms of admission limiting the political rights of new states, and those limiting their rights with respect to property. Thus, provisions qualifying the right of Minnesota to deal with the public lands of the United States in the hands of the latter or its transferees have been upheld as an agreement respecting property made by the new state upon its admission (25).

---

(23) Coyle v. Smith, 221 U. S. 559.
(24) Sproule v. Fredericks, 69 Miss. 898.
(25) Stearns v. Minnesota, 179 U. S., 223.

CHAPTER XIV.

REGULATION OF COMMERCE.

§ 269. **Historical outline.** Commercial difficulties arising from the divergent legislation of the original states, and the discriminatory regulations of foreign countries to which America could oppose no united resistance, created perhaps the strongest single influence that led to the adoption of the Constitution. In the convention the southern delegates wished to forbid the United States from taxing exports or from prohibiting the slave trade; and to restrict the national power to regulate commerce and to pass navigation laws. The interests of the northern commercial states were opposed to all these views, and a compromise was finally agreed upon. The United States was forbidden to tax exports or to prohibit the slave trade for twenty years. On the other hand Congress was given unrestricted power "to regulate commerce with foreign nations, and among the several states, and with the Indian tribes." Tonnage taxes and duties on imports were denied to the states. All of these provisions having a commercial purpose may conveniently be discussed together.

SECTION 1. DUTIES ON IMPORTS, EXPORTS, AND TONNAGE.

§ 270. **State duties on imports prohibited.** "No state shall, without the consent of the Congress, lay any im-

274

posts or duties on imports or exports, except what may
be absolutely necessary for executing its inspection laws;
and the net produce of all duties and imposts, laid by
any state on imports or exports, shall be for the use of the
treasury of the United States; and all such laws shall be
subject to the revision and control of the Congress'' (1).

At the time the Constitution was adopted most of the
imports to the United States from foreign countries entered the country through the ports of the two or three
states having good harbors, notably New York and Rhode
Island. These states, by levying duties upon imports,
not only reserved this valuable source of revenue to themselves, but were enabled to levy tribute upon all of the
other states using imported goods. The impost duties
levied by New York simply added that much to the price
of the imported articles afterwards shipped from New
York to other states, and the citizens of the non-importing states got no benefit from the taxes finally borne by
them. It was at once recognized in the Philadelphia convention that the power to levy import duties should be
placed in the hands of Congress, and that the revenue
therefrom should belong to the national government.
There was little objection, therefore, to the adoption of
the clause quoted above.

§ 271. **What is an import?** The first question that naturally presents itself is whether this prohibition extends
to goods imported from other states or only to those imported from foreign countries. The question was not
directly presented to the Supreme Court until 1869, when

------

(1) Const., Art. I, sec. 10, § 2.

it was decided, after a careful consideration of the historical meaning of the words used, that imports referred only to goods coming from foreign countries (2). Obviously the term applies only to property, not to free persons entering the country.

§ 272. **What is a tax on imports?** Of course many imports remain physically intact for a long time after importation and so it may be asked for how long after importation does the exemption from state taxation continue? This was the question presented to the Supreme Court in the important case of Brown v. Maryland (3) which was decided in 1827. A law of Maryland, requiring a license fee from all importers who sold imported goods, was resisted. The view might have been taken that a tax upon imports was a tax imposed only on account of or upon the occasion of the importation of property; and that a tax upon all property alike, domestic and foreign, after it had reached its destination in the state, was not a tax upon imports at all. This would effectively have prevented a state from raising a revenue from a tax levied specifically upon imports, or discriminating against them, and doubtless would have satisfied the purposes of the framers of the Constitution. Chief Justice Marshall, however, went further, and interpreted the clause to forbid a state's taxing imports at all, even by a general property tax, so long as the import had not been used, sold, or taken out of the original package in which it was imported. He also decided that a tax upon

---

(2) Woodruff v. Parham, 8 Wall., 123.

(3) 12 Wheaton, 419.

the selling of an article was substantially a tax upon the article itself and fell within the prohibition upon the latter.

The principal reason for this decision was that otherwise it was impossible to prevent the importing states with good seaports from exacting tribute from the necessities of users of imported goods in other states. When the importations were not made directly by persons in the state where they were used, it would be necessary to buy them from the original importer, and, if his state taxed them, even under a general tax, their price would be increased to the next purchaser. Therefore they were allowed to be sold once before being subject to any state taxation whatever. If not sold, but used or taken out of the original package by the importer, the necessity for an exemption for the above purpose of course ceased, and they could be taxed. Such was the origin and purpose of the now famous "original package" doctrine.

§ 273. **Development of the "original package" doctrine.** The result of the decision in Brown v. Maryland is that stocks of imported goods, no matter how large, are exempt from all state or municipal taxation so long as they remain unsold in the original packages. Curiously enough, the question what constituted the original package did not come before the Supreme Court for over 110 years after the adoption of the Constitution. Then it arose in a case from New Orleans. An importer of dry goods in the city would order from Europe 500 dozen towels. The towels would be wrapped by the foreign manufacturer in small packages of several dozen towels

each, and 100 of these small separately wrapped packages
would then be shipped to New Orleans in a large wooden
packing case. The importer there would open the case
and offer for sale the separately wrapped packages.
These latter packages were never broken. Did the small
parcels constitute the "original package" protected by
the importing clause, or was the large wooden case the
original package? The court decided that the latter was
the true meaning, and that opening the large case and
offering the small parcels for sale separately deprived
them of their immunity from taxation (4).

§ 274. Same: How large must an "original package"
be? Immediately after this decision, the court was
called upon to settle how large a package must be in order
to be an "original package," even if actually imported
separately. Suppose cigarettes are imported in single
boxes of ten each and beer in separate bottles, are these
exempted from taxation until sold, not to the retailer, but
to the consumer? Under the commerce clause of the Constitution goods shipped from one state into another are
free from certain kinds of state regulation so long as
they remain unsold in the original package. This is fully
discussed in §§ 296-98, below. A state prohibiting the
sale of liquor or cigarettes within it might find its policy
entirely defeated, by the importation into it of small
separate packages of spirits or tobacco of a size adapted
to the retail trade, through its inability to regulate the
sale of interstate and foreign goods in the original package. This phase of the matter was actually presented

---

(4) May v. New Orleans, 178 U. S., 496.

in Austin v. Tennessee. In 1900, single packages of cigarettes shipped into Tennessee separately were offered for sale as original packages in defiance of the laws of Tennessee to the contrary. The court said:

"The real question in this case is whether the size of the package in which the importation is actually made is to govern; or, the size of the package in which bona fide transactions are carried on between the manufacturer and the wholesale dealer residing in different states. We hold to the latter view. The whole theory of the exemption of the original package from the operation of state laws is based upon the idea that the property is imported in the ordinary form in which, from time immemorial, foreign goods have been brought into the country. These have gone at once into the hands of the wholesale dealers, who have been in the habit of breaking and distributing their contents among the several retail dealers throughout the state. It was with reference to this method of doing business that the doctrine of the exemption of the original package grew up. By taking the words 'original package' in their literal sense, a number of so-called original package manufactories have been started through the country, whose business it is to manufacture goods for the express purpose of sending their products into other states in minute packages, that may at once go into the hands of the retail dealers and con- sumers, and thus bid defiance to the laws of the state against their importation and sale. . . . Without undertaking to determine what is the proper size of an original package in each case, evidently the doctrine has no application where the manufacturer puts up the package with the express intent of evading the laws of another state, and is enabled to carry out his purpose by the facile agency of an express company and the connivance of his consignee'' (5).

So far as the constitutional prohibition upon taxing imports is concerned, this interpretation is precisely in the spirit of the original interpretation that exempted ''original packages.'' It was designed to enable non-importing states to purchase goods from importers resident in the importing states without having to pay taxes to the governments of the latter. This result is amply secured by protecting the wholesale trade in imports.

§ 275. **State and Federal duties on exports forbidden.** The Constitution, Article I, section 9, § 5 provides: ''No tax or duty shall be laid on articles exported from any state.'' This is a prohibition on the Federal government, and, with the one on the states already quoted (§ 270, above), forbids any tax whatever on exports in the United States.

The word export in this clause applies only to goods exported to a foreign country. It does not apply to goods passing between the United States and territorial dependencies like Porto Rico (6).

§ 276. **What is a tax on exports?** The general excise tax levied by the United States upon all property of a certain class alike, such as tobacco or cheese, is not a tax upon exports simply because some of these goods are

---

(5)   Austin v. Tennessee, 179 U. S., 343, 359-60.
(6)   Dooley v. U. S., 183 U. S., 151.

afterwards actually exported, or even when they are manufactured under a contract for export. It is only when goods are taxed by reason of or upon the occasion of their exportation that it is a tax upon exports (7).

The stamp tax imposed on bills of lading for any goods exported from the United States amounts to a tax on exports. Commercial usage almost necessarily requires that bills of lading be issued upon the occasion of exporting, and a tax upon a necessary incident of export amounts to a tax upon the goods exported (8).

§ 277. **State inspection laws.** "We feel quite safe in saying that neither at the time of the formation of the Constitution nor since has any inspection law included anything but personal property as a subject of its operation. . . . What is an inspection? Something which can be accomplished by looking at or weighing or meas uring the thing to be inspected, or applying to it at once some crucial test. When testimony or evidence is to be taken and examined, it is not inspection in any sense whatever." Therefore the Supreme Court held invalid a law of New York requiring foreign immigrants to pay so-called inspection fees for ascertaining whether they were criminals, paupers, or orphans (9).

"Recognized elements of inspection laws have always been quality of the article, form, capacity, dimensions, and weight of package, mode of putting up, and marking and branding of various kinds, all these matters being

---

(7)   Cornell v. Coyne, 192 U. S., 418.

(8)   Fairbanks v. U. S., 181 U. S., 283.

(9)   People v. Comp. Gen. Transatlantique, 107 U. S., pp. 61, 62.

supervised by a public officer having authority to pass or not pass the article as lawful merchandise, as it did or did not answer the prescribed requirements" (10).

The Constitution permits states, at least in the absence of Congressional prohibition, to lay duties on imports and exports sufficient to execute their inspection laws (§ 270, above). If the duties laid for this purpose are not too high for the law to be regarded as a bona fide inspection law the duties imposed are valid, apparently even though the court may think them somewhat excessive for their purpose. The Supreme Court has suggested that under the wording of this clause Congress is the proper tribunal to decide whether a fee, really for inspection, is excessive; and that the court cannot interfere (11). Where the alleged inspection fee is too high to have been intended in good faith solely for this purpose, the courts may pronounce it invalid as really not an inspection law at all but designed for other purposes (12).

§ 278. State tonnage duties forbidden. The Constitution, Article I, section 10, § 3, provides: "No state shall, without the consent of Congress, lay any duty of tonnage."

This does not prevent a state in which a vessel has a situs for taxation (§§ 173, 288) from taxing it upon its assessed property value, or even from imposing on it a fixed license fee for its employment in navigation, but it

---

(10)   Turner v. Maryland, 107 U. S., p. 55.

(11)   Patapsco Guano Co. v. No. Carolina, 171 U. S., p. 355.

(12)   Brimmer v. Rebman, 138 U. S., 78.

apparently prevents a tax *proportioned* to tonnage, as $1 a ton, and so forth (13). When the imposition is not really a tax, but is compensation for the benefit of specific improvements or services, like improved waterways, wharves, or quarantine inspection, the charge may be according to tonnage (14). Compare § 290, below.

SECTION 2. INTERSTATE COMMERCE. GENERAL CONCEPTIONS.

§ 279. **Commerce clause.** The Constitution, Article I, section 8, § 3, gives Congress power "to regulate commerce with foreign nations, and among the several states, and with the Indian tribes."

The early decisions upon this clause were largely devoted to determining whether the power to regulate interstate and foreign commerce was exclusively with the United States, or was a concurrent power. Later the litigation was chiefly over the line to be drawn between the exclusive and concurrent parts of the power; and more recently the important decisions have concerned the extent to which Congress may regulate matters incidental to commerce. It will be convenient to consider the subject roughly in this order.

§ 280. **What is commerce?** In the earliest great case upon the subject, Gibbons v. Ogden (15), it was said by Chief Justice Marshall that commerce was intercourse—commercial intercourse in all its branches, including navigation and the carriage of passengers as well as goods.

---

(13)   State Tonnage Tax Cases, 12 Wall., 204.

(14)   Huse v. Glover, 119 U. S., 543.

(15)   9 Wheaton, 1.

Fifty years later it was said "commerce is a term of the largest import. It comprehends intercourse for the purposes of trade in any and all of its forms,·including the transportation, purchase, sale, and exchange of commodities." The court in later cases extended the definition of the term "commerce" to include the taking of liquor into a dry state for personal consumption (16); driving a stolen car across a state line (16a); crossing an interstate bridge by pleasure automobile (16b); transmission of information by telephone or telegraph (16c); the operation of a correspondence school (16d); radio broadcasting, the transmission of electricity and gas, and the insurance business (16e).

It has several times been decided that where intercourse is not involved in the transaction it is not commerce. Manufacturing, for instance, is not commerce; nor is agriculture, nor mining, nor fishing. An early prosecution under the Federal anti-trust act, which forbade combinations in restraint of commerce among the states, failed when directed against a combination to manufacture sugar. "Commerce succeeds to manufacture, and is not a part of it." The combination to manufacture was not subject to Federal control, although a combination in selling the manufactured article would be (16f). Although the cases so holding have not all been overruled, the courts have since said that "Whether the

---

(16)   U.S. v. Simpson, 252 U.S. 465.

(16a)   Brooks v. U.S., 267 U.S. 432.

(16b)   Kelly v. U.S., 277 F. 405.

(16c)   Pensacola Teleg. Co. v. Western Union Teleg. Co., 96 U.S. 1.

(16d)   International Textbook Co. v. Pigg (217 U.S. 91).

(16e)   U.S. v. Southeastern Underwriters, 322 U.S. 533.

(16f)   United States v. Knight Co., 156 U.S. 1.

subject of the regulation in question was production, consumption, or marketing, is . . . not material for purposes of deciding the question of Federal power." The test is the effect on interstate commerce (16g).

§ 280a. **Interstate commerce.** The phrase "interstate commerce" encompasses all trading and movements across state lines, whether of tangible commodities or of intangibles such as documentary material, radio waves or information. It includes commercial interstate movements such as the shipment of cattle across state lines (16h) and such noncommercial interstate movements as those of kidnappers (17), polygamist's brides (17a) and fleeing witnesses (17b). It includes those parts of an interstate journey which take place solely within one state (17c) and it extends from the moment the journey has begun (17d) until the final destination, where the goods become an inseparable part of the mass of products within a state (17e).

It includes all those services connected with the receipt, handling and delivery of property transported, such as the furnishing of cars (17f), fares and freight charges for interstate commerce (17g), loading and unloading of cargo (18), the sale of goods in interstate commerce and

(16g) Wickard v. Filburn, 317 U.S. 111.

(16h) Thornton v. U.S., 271 U.S. 414.

(17) Gooch v. U.S., 297 U.S. 124.

(17a) Cleveland v. U.S., 329 U.S. 14.

(17b) Hemans v. U.S., 163 F2d 228.

(17c) The Daniel Ball 10 Wall. 557.

(17d) Coe v. Errol, 116 U.S. 517.

(17e) Walling v. Jacksonville Paper Co., 317 U.S. 564.

(17f) Pletcher v. Chicago, R. I. and Ry Co., 177 P. 1, 103 Kan. 834.

(17g) Neubert v. Chicago, R. I. and G. Ry Co., 248 S.W. 141.

(18) 63 P 2d 537, 189 Wash. 131.

the terms of such sales (18a). It embraces all . . . "activities which are so closely related to interstate transportation as to in practice and legal relation be a part thereof" (18b).

§ 281. Distinction between intrastate and interstate commerce. The term "intrastate commerce" generally refers to that commerce which both begins and ends and at all times takes place within a single state. The term "interstate commerce" embraces two concepts: (a) Those acts which involve the crossing of state boundaries and (b) those activities which are so closely related to or have such a substantial economic effect on interstate commerce that they will be considered within the scope of the commerce clause and subject to Federal regulation.

In Wickard v. Filburn (19), the Supreme Court of the United States found that the growing of wheat by an Ohio farmer in excess of his marketing quota was an act affecting interstate commerce and was subject to congressional regulation, even though all transactions were local in nature. In that case, the appellee had for many years operated a small farm in Ohio, maintaining a herd of dairy cattle, selling milk, raising poultry, and selling poultry and eggs. He raised a small amount of winter wheat, part of which he sold, part of which he used to feed the poultry and livestock, part of which he used to make flour, and the rest of which he kept for seeding the following year. The court said that whether the activity was local and whether it was regarded as commerce or not . . . "it may be (regulated) by Congress if it exerts

(18a) Dahnke-Walker Co. v. Bondurant, 257 U.S. 282.
(18b) McLeod v. Treshhold, 319 U.S. 491.
(19)   317 U.S. 111.

a substantial economic effect on interstate commerce."
The consumption of wheat is the most variable factor
in the disappearance of the wheat crop. Even though the
appellee's contribution to the demand for wheat may be
trivial by itself, that is not enough to remove him from
the field of Federal regulation. His contribution, together with others in similar circumstances, had a substantial influence on price and market conditions.

An act which is essentially intrastate will not be considered as affecting interstate commerce merely because
of the necessity to regulate certain industries in their
entireties; nor does the mere fact that a local transaction
may cause a movement in interstate commerce make the
transaction interstate commerce; nor is the entire business of a corporation having both interstate and intrastate operations either directly interstate or intrastate
. . . the character of the commerce will be determined
by the transactions involved. The Federal courts have
enunciated three tests for determining whether a transaction having both interstate and intrastate features is
interstate commerce:

(1) Was the transaction primarily interstate in nature
rather than intrastate?

(2) Was there a substantial relation to interstate commerce, rather than an isolated contact?

(3) Was the intrastate feature relevant to the interstate transaction, and is its control an appropriate means
to the end of regulating interstate commerce?

§ 282. Beginning and ending of commercial transit.

The question of when goods enter commerce is not determined by the mere intention of the parties, nor by making preliminary movements for the purpose of making proper arrangements for their journey, nor assembling them at the point where the real journey is to begin. The point of time at which commerce begins may be when the subject of it is actually started on a continuous journey to another state, or is delivered to a carrier for such transportation, or when the shipper has called for and had a car delivered to him for loading (since transportation includes the furnishing of cars).

Interstate commerce generally ends when the parties intend it to end—that is, when the product moved arrives at its destination. Thus interstate commerce ceases when the products come to rest at a definite place, as when they arrive at destination and are held for final disposition or when they are kept at an intermediate point between the place of shipment and ultimate destination for the benefit and use of the owner, such as a sale, or to await further orders (20).

However, the interstate character of the journey isn't destroyed when the movement of goods is temporarily halted for purposes incidental to making the journey. Consequently, stoppage of transit in order to make railroad connections, care for fruit and animals, wait for high water to continue the flotation of logs (21), and

---

(20)   Coe v. Errol, 116 U.S. 517.
(21)   General Oil Co. v. Crain, 209 U.S. 211.

delivery of goods to the consignee at the terminal point and unloading them, unless the car is to be used for indefinite storage or as a distributing point for local sale, have not been held to stop the interstate transfer. Thus in Boyd v. U.S., the placing of a car containing an interstate shipment, under an order bill of lading, on the side track of the consignee was not a delivery which took the shipment out of interstate commerce (22); nor is placing goods on a pier for delivery to consignee, where the consignee has not taken possession of or paid the freight charge for the goods, and the 48-hour period during which the consignee has to remove the goods has not expired (23).

§ 283. **Transit across state border is not an essential part of transaction.** It is no longer significant that nothing which is the subject of congressional legislation crosses state borders so far as the "commerce clause" is concerned. All that need be shown to bring the clause into operation is that similar action by all those in the position of the one whose conduct is in issue would have a substantial effect on interstate commerce (24).

§ 284. **Is Federal power to regulate commerce exclusive?** For many years after the adoption of the Constitu-

---

(22)   275 F 16.

(23)   Jones v. Missouri Pac. R. Co., 48 S.W. 2d 123.

(24)   Lee Wickard v. Filborn, 317 U.S. 111.

tion the members of the Supreme Court were much divided over the question whether the grant of commercial power to Congress was wholly exclusive, or whether it could also be exercised by the states until Congress acted inconsistently therewith. This conflict was finally brought to an end in 1851 by an opinion of Mr. Justice Curtis in the case of Cooley v. Board of Wardens (24), concerning a pilotage law of the port of Philadelphia. He said:

"The diversities of opinion, therefore, which have existed on this subject have arisen from the different views taken of the nature of this power. But when the nature of a power like this is spoken of, when it is said that the nature of the power requires that it should be exercised exclusively by Congress, it must be intended to refer to the subjects of that power, and to say they are of such a nature as to require exclusive legislation by Congress. Now, the power to regulate commerce embraces a vast field, containing not only many but exceedingly various subjects quite unlike in their nature; some imperatively demanding a single uniform rule, operating equally on the commerce of the United States in every port; and some, like the subject now in question, as imperatively demanding that diversity which alone can meet the local necessities of navigation.

"Either absolutely to affirm or deny that the nature of this power requires exclusive legislation by Congress, is to lose sight of the nature of the subjects of this power, and to assert concerning all of them what is really appli-

---

(24)   12 How., 299.

cable but to a part. Whatever subjects of this power are in their nature national, or admit only of one uniform system, or plan of regulation, may justly be said to be of such a nature as to require exclusive legislation by Congress.''

Since then this rule has always been accepted, but naturally there has been some difference of opinion as to what commercial subjects are in their nature national and what are local. For the next fifty years the work of the Supreme Court in interpreting the commercial clause consisted chiefly in deciding where this division line lay in a number of classes of cases. This will be discussed below.

SECTION 3. STATE LEGISLATION DISCRIMINATING AGAINST INTERSTATE COMMERCE.

§ 285. **Discriminatory legislation prohibited.** The principal legislative powers by which interstate or foreign commerce may be affected are the powers of taxation and of regulation (including prohibition). It was early settled that any state legislation discriminating against interstate or foreign commerce in favor of domestic commerce was invalid. The securing of virtual free trade between the states was one of the prime objects of the Constitution, and hence all discriminatory legislation affects the subject in a national respect and thus is beyond the power of the states under the rule laid down in the Cooley case. This is so whether the discrimination takes the form of taxation or regulation. No state can require a discriminatory license fee for the sale of goods produced outside of it (25). It cannot require the inspection of interstate goods when offered for sale, if it does not require a like inspection of domestic goods; nor can it forbid the sale of imported liquor in the state if it permits domestic liquor to be thus sold (26).

SECTION 4. STATE TAXATION AFFECTING INTERSTATE COMMERCE WITHOUT DISCRIMINATION.

§ 286. **Taxes upon transportation.** The transportation of goods into or out of a state—an activity which is the very essence of interstate commerce—cannot be taxed by a state at all, even without discrimination. This was first clearly decided in a case where Pennsylvania had attempted to levy a small tax upon every ton of freight carried in the state. As regards interstate transportation the Supreme Court held that such a tax was a restraint upon the right to have the subjects of commerce pass freely from one state to another, and that this was a matter national in its nature and so unfit for local regulation (27). Later it was decided that a percentage tax upon gross receipts from transportation was equally bad as to the receipts from interstate transportation, on the ground that these were so closely connected with the transportation that it was in substance the same as taxing the transportation. License taxes for the privilege of engaging in interstate transportation are likewise invalid; and so are taxes upon the business of soliciting

---

(25)   Welton v. Missouri, 91 U. S., 275.

(26)   Scott v. Donald, 165 U. S., 58.

(27)   State Freight Tax, 15 Wall., 232.

interstate transportation, as was held in a case where California attempted to tax a railroad agency in San Francisco for soliciting passengers going east to take a particular line between Chicago and New York (28). The same principles have been applied to the transmission of intelligence, by telegraph, telephone, and radio.

§ 287. **Taxes upon sales.** A state tax upon the sale of goods in the state at the time is valid, even though the goods have been brought from outside and are offered for sale in the original packages (29). If, however, the goods to be sold are outside of the state, and the business done in the state consists in selling or soliciting the sale of goods afterwards to be shipped in to fill the order, the state cannot tax this selling or soliciting (30). The principle seems to be that a state may place no impediments upon the transfer of goods from one state to another. But where a state imposes a tax on local sales it may, at the same time, impose a compensating "use or storage" tax on goods ordered from outside the state to prevent evasion of the local sales tax (30a). On the other hand, when the goods have arrived at their destination, they may be taxed as property or dealings with them may be taxed to provide revenue for the government, in return for the protection it affords to the property or to the business done with it. Such taxation affects interstate commerce too slightly to be a national matter. This principle seems to be the one upon which rests the well-

---

(28)   McCall v. California, 136 U. S., 104.
(29)   Woodruff v. Parham, 8 Wall., 123.
(30)   Robbins v. Shelby County Taxing District, 120 U. S., 489.
(30a) Nelson v. Sears, Roebuck & Co., 312 U. S. 359, decided in 1941; State Tax Com. v. General Trading Co. 233 Iowa 877, 10 N. W. 2nd, 659, affirmed by U. S. Sup. Ct. in 1944, 64 S. Ct. 1028.

known distinction between a state's power to tax a pedler selling interstate goods and a drummer selling them. The pedler has his goods with him and may be taxed; the drummer is taking orders for goods to be shipped into the state, and may not be taxed.

Some refinements arising out of the administration of sales and related tax laws were brought out in a case involving the Illinois Retailers Occupation Tax Act. The tax imposed by this act is, in effect, a sales tax, though imposed on persons engaged in the business of selling tangible personal property at retail in the state. The law states expressly that the tax is not imposed upon the privilege of engaging in any business in interstate commerce.

The Norton Company was engaged in the manufacturing business in the State of Massachusetts. It obtained a license to do business in Illinois. It established a branch office and warehouse in Illinois from which it conducted an extensive business. The State of Illinois collected from it the Illinois Occupation Tax on the basis of its entire gross income from sales to inhabitants of Illinois. The company paid the tax under protest and brought suit to recover a part of the amount paid, contending that much of its business was interstate and hence not subject to the tax. The Illinois Courts upheld the States right to collect the tax, and the case was taken to the Supreme Court of the United States.

In Norton Company v. Department of Revenue of the State of Illinois (30b), the Supreme Court upheld the right of the State of Illinois to collect the tax on all

_____
(30b)   340 U. S. 534.

Illinois business of the Company except that derived from orders sent direct to the home office in Massachusetts by the customers and filled by shipment from the home office direct to the customers. With respect to the remainder of the Company's Illinois business the Court said:

"This Corporation has so mingled taxable business with that which it contends is not taxable that it requires administrative and judicial judgment to separate the two. We conclude that, in the light of all evidence, the judgment attributing to the Chicago branch income from all the sales that utilized it either in receiving the order or distributing the goods was within the realm of permissible judgment. Petitioner has not established that such services as were rendered by the Chicago office were not decisive factors in establishing and holding this market. On this record, no other source of the customer relation ship is shown.

"This corporation could have approached the Illinois market through solicitors only and it would have been entitled to the immunity of interstate commerce. But, from a competitive point of view, that system has disadvantages. The trade may view the seller as remote and inaccessible. He cannot be reached with process of local courts for breach of contract, or for services if the goods are defective or in need of replacement. Petitioner elected to localize itself in the Illinois market with the advantages of a retail outlet in the State, to keep close to the trade, to supply locally many items and take orders for others, and to reduce freight costs to local consumers. Although the concern does not by engaging in business within the State lose its right to do interstate business with tax immunity (30c), it cannot channel business through a local outlet to gain the advantage of a local business and also hold the immunities of an interstate business.''

§ 288. **Taxes upon property engaged in interstate commerce.** While goods shipped from one state to another are actually in transit they are probably not taxable by any state (31), but as soon as they reach their destination they are taxable in that state, even though they are still in the "original package" (32). The prohibition against state taxation of imports extends only to goods from foreign countries. Goods from other states are not imports (§ 271, above). The fact that goods have been brought into the state for sale and that such sales are being solicited will not prevent the goods being taxed by the state as property, without discrimination.

The instruments by which commerce is carried on, like cars and ships, may be also taxed as property in any state where they have a situs for taxation. See § 173, above.

§ 289. **Taxes as conditions precedent to engaging in interstate commerce.** State taxes upon property or upon business, otherwise valid, may be imposed in such a manner as to be an unconstitutional interference with interstate commerce. Suppose, for instance, that a telegraph company is taxed upon its capital in the state, with a proviso that if it does not pay the tax it may thereafter

---

(30c) Cooney v. Mountain States Telegraph Co., 294 U. S. 384.
(31) Coe v. Errol, 116 U. S., 517.
(32) Brown v. Houston, 114 U. S., 622.

do no business within the state. This manner of collecting the tax is unconstitutional, as forbidding the exercise of a right protected by the United States Constitution from state interference—the right to do interstate commerce. The tax may be collected by seizing and selling the company's property, or in any other way that does not impose upon it a legislative prohibition to exercise a Federal right (33). Similarly, it would not be doubted that a state statute was invalid that attempted to deprive persons of the right to use the post-office, for non-compliance with some state regulation.

§ 290. **Tolls for the use of improvements.** Suppose a state improves the condition of a waterway or road over which interstate commerce is conducted, and charges toll for the use of the improvement. A bona fide and reasonable toll for such a purpose is valid. It is distinguished from a tax upon interstate transportation, upon the ground that it is a reasonable compensation for the use of a definite improvement made under state authority, while a tax is simply a measure for revenue irrespective of any specific benefit obtained therefrom (34). Upon a similar principle are justified wharfage fees, bridge tolls, and quarantine and inspection charges, all of which are fairly proportional to services rendered or facilities afforded. Compare § 278, above.

§ 291. **Taxes upon franchises, and compensation for their grant.** As has been explained elsewhere in this

---

(33) Western Union Telegraph Co. v. Massachusetts, 125 U. S., 530.
(34) Huse v. Glover, 119 U. S., 543.

article (§ 180, above), a franchise is a privilege grant-
able by the government at its pleasure, which cannot be
exercised without such a grant. The government that
grants a franchise may, in the absence of a contract to
the contrary, tax it as property at its fair value; or may
impose upon it an excise tax measured in any reasonable
manner; or, if the franchise be revocable, it may tax it
quite arbitrarily as the price of not revoking it (35). A
tax upon a corporate franchise, therefore, is not subject
to the same limitations as taxes upon property and business. If a state measures the tax upon a corporate franchise by the gross receipts from the business done, this
is valid, even though the receipts are from interstate
commerce. It is not a tax upon the commerce, but upon
the franchise which the state created at pleasure, and
which it may therefore tax (36). In so far as a corporate franchise consists merely of the power to do interstate commerce, a state cannot tax it if it has been
granted by another state or by the United States, for
this would be the taxation, not of a particular privilege
created by itself, but of a privilege created by another
sovereignty and used only in the exercise of a Federal
right.

As a state is not obliged to grant a franchise at all, it
may make such pecuniary conditions as it pleases when
the grant is made, including an exaction of a large percentage (20%) of the receipts from transportation, even

---

(35)   California v Central Pacific Railroad Co., 127 U. S., 1, 40-42.
(36)   Maine v. Grand Trunk Railroad Co., 142 U. S., 217.

though these are largely derived from interstate commerce (37).

§ 292. **Taxes indirectly affecting commerce.** Of course any tax on property or business must be paid ultimately out of the capital or receipts of the business, and if any part of the business is interstate commerce this ultimately bears its share of the tax, no matter upon what it is directly imposed. Such indirect effect of taxation, however, does not regulate interstate commerce in any national aspect, and so is within the concurrent power of the states. For instance, Georgia imposed a tax upon the business of conducting an employment agency to hire laborers to be employed beyond the limits of the state. Of course the laborers who were hired went out of the state, thus engaging in or becoming the subject of interstate commerce, but the tax upon the business of securing laborers to work elsewhere was so incidentally connected with the actual transportation that it was not invalid (38).

SECTION 5. STATE REGULATION AFFECTING INTERSTATE COMMERCE WITHOUT DISCRIMINATION.

§ 293. **Regulation of transportation: Rates.** The increasing importance to the public of transportation has in recent years enormously increased the amount of legislative regulation, state and Federal, which it has received. Some of the most important cases ever decided under the commerce clause have dealt with the question

(37) Railroad Co. v. Maryland, 21 Wall., 456.
(38) Williams v. Fears, 179 U. S., 270.

of the respective fields of the state and Federal governments in regulating transportation. The great case upon state regulation of interstate railroad rates is that of the Wabash Railway Company, decided in 1886 (39). An Illinois statute forbade any railroad to charge as much for hauling freight or passengers any distance within the state as it at the same time charged for the same service over a greater distance upon the same road. This being interpreted by the Illinois courts to include interstate traffic, the law was held unconstitutional by the United States Supreme Court. The entire interstate journey must be treated as a unit, and to permit one state to prescribe the rate for services to be performed partly in other states, and in the price of which citizens of other states have an equal interest, would be for a state to interfere with interstate commerce in one of its national aspects. This decision was at once followed by the establishment of the Federal Interstate Commerce Commission, by which interstate rates are now regulated.

The principle of this decision has been extended to all cases where any part of the through journey from point to point passes outside of a single state, even though both ends of the journey are in one state. Thus, New York may not regulate rates between New York and Buffalo, when the goods pass through Pennsylvania on the way; nor may California regulate ocean rates between California points, where the vessel goes upon the high seas (40). Nor may a state require that a purely

(39)   118 U. S., 557,

(40)   Hanley v. Kansas City, etc., Railway Co., 187 U. S., 617.

internal rate be not higher than an interstate rate for the same distance, as this puts an effective pressure upon the amount of interstate rates. When a state regulates its internal rates it must do so with reference only to the earnings and expenses of internal traffic. Interstate receipts and expenses must be disregarded (41). See p. 307.

§ 294. **Same: Services.** As regards state regulation requiring certain kinds of service from transportation companies, these are upheld unless they substantially hamper the carrier in conducting its interstate business. Instances of the latter are: Compelling through interstate trains to make an unreasonable number of local stops, making unreasonable rules about furnishing cars for interstate shipments, regulating the delivery of telegraph messages in other states, and requiring separate coaches for whites and negroes in interstate travel.

§ 295. **Same: Instruments, agents, liability, etc.** These phases of interstate transportation may usually be regulated by the states without involving any matter of national importance. The speed of interstate trains in the state may be regulated, their engineers may be required to be examined for color blindness, the heating of passenger trains by stoves may be forbidden, contracts exempting railways from liability for negligence may be forbidden, and freight trains may not be permitted to run on Sunday except with perishable freight (42).

§ 296. **Conditions precedent and prohibitions upon engaging in interstate commerce.** Just as a state may not

---

(41)   Smythe v. Ames, 169 U. S., 466, 540 ff.

(42)   Most of the cases upon the subject are cited in C. C. C. & St. Louis Railway v. Illinois, 177 U. S., 514.

make the payment of a tax a condition precedent to exercising the Federal right of engaging in interstate commerce, neither may it make a compliance with any state regulation a like condition precedent. Thus, though a state may require that persons engaged in foreign commerce shall report various particulars about persons brought into the country, a similar report of certain facts about the vessel may not be required as a condition precedent to engaging in interstate commerce; nor can an express company be required to have a certain actual capital in order to do interstate business in a state (43). From this it would seem clear that state legislation absolutely forbidding interstate commerce would ordinarily be invalid. Even foreign corporations may not be forbidden to do interstate business in a state, either absolutely or upon conditions (44), though of course a corporation may be made to submit to conditions as the price of a corporate charter from a state, which it could not otherwise obtain (45). Compare § 291, above.

§ 297. **Same: Liquor prohibition cases.** Certain decisions in which the Supreme Court dealt with this question excited extraordinary interest on account of the important social and economic factors involved. An Iowa statute forbade the manufacture, sale, or transportation into the state of any intoxicating liquors, with certain unimportant exceptions. The prohibition upon

---

(43) Sinnot v. Davenport, 22 How., 227; Crutcher v. Ky., 141 U. S., 47.

(44) Pembina Co. v. Pennsylvania, 125 U. S., 181, 190; Crutcher v. Kentucky, 141 U. S., 47, 57.

(45) Ashley v. Ryan, 153 U. S., 436, 440-41.

manufacture was upheld as preceding commerce, under the principle discussed in § 280, above (46). The provision against transporting liquors into the state was held unconstitutional as affecting in a national aspect a legiti mate article of commerce in the interstate transportation of which other states than Iowa were interested (47). Then followed the great case of Leisy v. Hardin (48) in 1890, involving the remainder of the statute. In favor of the prohibition of the sale in Iowa of liquor brought from other states, it was urged that the admitted social and economic effects of liquor selling made its regulation in each state a local rather than a national matter. If the public policy of a single state were opposed to liquor selling this was primarily a matter of local self-protection rather than a matter for national consideration, and so the law should be upheld. On the other side it was argued that Iowa could no more compel the rest of the country to cease interstate commerce with Iowa in liquor than in any other commodity, so long as liquor was generally regarded as a legitimate subject of commerce. It was admitted that states might exclude articles in bad condition, like infected rags or diseased meat, but not articles irrespective of condition or quality. The Supreme Court took the latter view and declared the statute unconstitutional, holding that the Federal right to engage in interstate commerce continued after the goods had been transported into the state until they had been

---

(46)   Kidd v. Pearson, 128 U. S., 1.
(47)   Bowman v. C. & N. Railway Co., 125 U. S., 465.
(48)   135 U. S., 100.

sold in their original package, or the package broken, or
the contents used, applying the "original package" doctrine explained in § 272, above. Immediately after this
decision Congress passed a law (the Wilson act) providing that liquors transported into any state should, upon
arrival there, be subject to the operation of state laws
(see § 301, below). The word "arrival" in this statute
has been interpreted to mean delivery to the consignee
at the ultimate destination, not merely arrival within the
borders of a state (49), so that a state still could not forbid the shipment into it of intoxicating liquor. But it
might tax and probably forbid the soliciting in it of sales
of liquor to be shipped into the state (50). Section 2 of
the twenty-first amendment now gives the states power to
forbid transportation into them of intoxicating liquors.

§ 298. Same: Later cases. Some years after the Leisy
case the court passed upon a Massachusetts statute forbidding the sale in the state of oleomargarine colored to
look like butter, even though healthful and properly
labelled. This was upheld, even as applied to interstate
oleomargarine, on the ground that it was a reasonable
means of preventing fraud (51). More recently a New
York statute forbade any one to possess dead game in
the state during the season when its killing was forbidden.
This was held by the Supreme Court validly to forbid
the possession in the state of game lawfully killed elsewhere and shipped into New York, on account of the

----

(49) Rhodes v. Iowa, 170 U. S., 412.
(50) Delamater v. South Dakota, 205 U. S., 93.
(51) Plumley v. Massachusetts, 155 U. S., 461.

ease with which the statute could otherwise be avoided
(52). It is difficult to see why the enforcement of its
prohibition laws is not as good a local purpose as the enforcement of a state game law, and if interstate commerce may be forbidden to enforce the latter, it would
seem at least as reasonable to do so for the former. The
reasoning in Leisy v. Hardin has not met with general
acceptance.

Diseased animals, or those likely to convey disease,
may be excluded from a state for a period of time reasonably necessary to prevent danger from contagion (53).

§ 299. **Regulations indirectly affecting interstate commerce.** State regulations that affect interstate commerce
only indirectly are generally valid. For instance, a state
may obstruct navigable waters (at least where the head
of navigation is in the state) by bridges or dams in making local internal improvements, although interstate
commerce by water is thus physically impeded (54); it
may enact quarantine, pilotage, and inspection laws; it
may regulate grain elevator rates, even though part of
the grain passing through the elevator is in interstate
commerce; it may protect its game, by forbidding it to be
killed for shipment out of the state (55); rules of evidence may be enacted for interstate transactions; and
corporations doing business in the state may be required
to submit to many regulations, even though they are doing some interstate commerce. And a city may constitutionally apply its Smoke Abatement Code to shipping in

(52) Silz v. Hesterberg, 211 U. S., 31.
(53) Smith v. St. Louis & S. W. Ry., 181 U. S., 248.
(54) Willamette Bridge Co. v. Hatch, 125 U. S., 1.
(55) Geer v Connecticut, 161 U. S., 519.

its harbor, even though the ships are operated in interstate commerce and costly structural alterations would be required in order to comply with the Code, as long as it doesn't amount to a material burden on interstate commerce (55a).

SECTION 6. POWER OF CONGRESS OVER INTERSTATE AND FOREIGN COMMERCE.

§ 300. Power of Congress complete and paramount. It has been said repeatedly by the Supreme Court that, whatever may be the concurrent powers of the states in the absence of Congressional action, when Congress chooses to act it has complete and paramount control over the entire subject, and all of its incidents. Congress has never chosen to enter a great part of this possible field of legislation, but what it has already done gives a fair idea of the extent of its powers. As regards interstate transportation, Congress has authorized the construction of interstate railways and bridges, and has regulated interstate railway rates throughout the country; it has forbidden combinations of railroads to maintain interstate rates, and more recently has even forbidden the formation of a single corporation to own the stock of two competing railways (56); it has absolutely forbidden the transportation of lottery tickets from one state to another (§ 253, above); it has condemned locks and dams for public use in interstate commerce, and may presumably do the same with railroads and telegraph lines. As regards the instruments and agencies of transportation Congress has regulated pilots, lighthouses, and

---

(55a) Huron Portland Cement Co. v. City of Detroit, 326 U.S. 440.
(56) Northern Securities Co. v. United States, 193 U. S., 197.

quarantines; it has enlarged or obstructed rivers and harbors; it has compelled railways to use safety appliances and air-brakes on interstate freight trains; it has established qualifications for marine officers, and has regulated the rights, duties, and liabilities of ships, seamen, passengers, and shippers engaged in commerce by water; and a law regulating the liability of interstate railroads to their employees has been upheld in principle, though declared invalid for including internal as well as interstate commerce (57). It has since been repassed by Congress, confined to interstate commerce. On the other hand, it has been said that an employee's membership in a labor union is not closely enough related to interstate commerce to enable Congress to forbid a railroad to discharge an employee solely on account of such membership (58).

As regards the buying and selling of interstate goods, the United States has enacted the meat inspection and pure food laws, designed to exclude from interstate traffic unhealthful or adulterated food products; it has forbidden combinations of capital in restraint of interstate trade, and also combinations of employees or labor unions to boycott interstate goods (59).

The decision of the Supreme Court in upholding the National Labor Relations Act of 1935 (59a), suggests that Congress may exercise a much greater control over what seem to be purely local or intrastate matters than students of the Constitution have generally considered

(57) Howard v. Illinois Central Railway Co., 207 U. S., 463.

(58) Adair v. United States, 208 U. S., 161.

(59) Addyston Pipe Co. v. United States, 175 U. S., 211; Loewe v. Lawlor, 208 U. S., 274.

(59a) 29 U. S. Code, § 151 and following.

possible. This Act guarantees to employees the rights of self-organization and collective bargaining, and declares to be unfair labor practices such acts as interfering with or coercing employees in the exercise of these rights, discriminating in regard to hiring or discharging or conditions of employment for the purpose of encouraging or discouraging membership in labor organizations, and refusing to bargain collectively with the representatives of employees; and it creates the National Labor Relations Board with extensive powers to prevent such unfair practices as they affect interstate commerce.

In upholding the Act as applied in the manufacture and distribution of steel, the Court did not enlarge the meaning of interstate commerce. The employer was admitted to be engaged in interstate commerce. The Court rather recognized that Congress, under present conditions, may exercise broader powers in regulating local matters affecting interstate commerce than was formerly considered within the constitutional grant. The workers in the steel mills involved in the case were engaged in the manufacturing department of the business, and manufacturing has generally been considered not to be commerce, but to be a purely local matter beyond the powers of the Federal Government to regulate (§ 255 and 280 above). The reasoning of the Court appears in the following taken from the opinion of the Court delivered by Chief Justice Hughes:

"The Congressional authority to protect interstate commerce from burdens and obstructions is not limited to transactions which can be deemed to be an essential part of a 'flow' of interstate or foreign commerce. Burdens and obstructions may be due to injurious action springing from other sources. The fundamental principle is that power to regulate commerce is the power to enact 'all appropriate legislation' for 'its protection and advancement,' to adopt measures 'to promote its growth and insure its safety,' 'to foster, protect, control, and restrain.' That power is plenary and may be exerted to protect interstate commerce 'no matter what the source of the dangers which threaten it.' Although activities may be intrastate in character when separately considered, if they have such a close and substantial relation to interstate commerce that their control is essential or appropriate to protect that commerce from burdens and obstructions, Congress cannot be denied power to exercise that control. . . . The question is necessarily one of degree. . . . Whatever amounts to more or less constant practice and threatens to obstruct or unduly to burden the freedom of interstate commerce is within the regulatory power of Congress under the commerce clause, and it is primarily for Congress to consider and decide the fact of the danger and meet it (59b)."

So long as Congress regulates matters directly affecting interstate commerce, that is, the transportation of goods from state to state, or the selling of goods to be delivered in interstate trade, or the buying of goods immediately after their arrival from another state, there is no doubt that the power of Congress is complete, subject only to the general prohibitions of the Constitution upon the exercise of all Federal powers, such as the Fifth

---

(59b) N.L.R.B. v. Jones & Laughlin Steel Corporation, 301 U. S. 1, 108 A.L.R. 1352. The quoted expressions are from Supreme Court cases previously decided. § 300 revised by publisher's editorial staff.

Amendment (60). The principal questions upon which courts are likely to differ in the future concern the extent of congressional power to regulate matters that affect interstate commerce only incidentally. If the connection is too remote Congress cannot act, but here is much room for difference of opinion.

§ 301. **Congressional power to enlarge the field of state action.** After the decision in Leisy v. Hardin and the passage of the Wilson act permitting the states to regulate interstate shipments of liquor after their arrival in the state (§ 297, above), the constitutionality of the Wilson act was at once attacked. It was urged with much force that if the Constitution made the regulation of this matter exclusively for Congress, Congress could not delegate its own exclusive powers to the states. The Supreme Court decided that Congress's complete power over the subject enabled it to determine what matters did not require national regulation, and at what point state regulation might begin, and so upheld the act (61). How far Congress might go in making such determinations is unsettled. A possible distinction has been suggested between permitting the states to regulate the sales within their boundaries and permitting them to forbid contracts to ship goods into the state, the latter transaction necessarily taking place in more than one state, and so perhaps not even permissible to a state by act of Congress (62).

---

(60)   Monongahela Co. v. United States, 148 U. S., 312.

(61)   In re Rahrer, 140 U. S., 545.

(62)   Rhodes v. Iowa, 170 U. S., 412, 424.

Section 7. The Maritime Power.

§ 302. **Extent of jurisdiction.** The Constitution, Article III, section 2, § 1, provides that the Federal judicial power shall extend to all cases of admiralty and maritime jurisdiction. In England the admiralty jurisdiction extended only so far as the tide ebbed and flowed. England being a small island the ebb and flow of the tide fairly measured the limits of navigability of its rivers; but, when it was attempted to apply a similar test to the great interior rivers and lakes of this country, difficulties at once appeared. At first the tidal test was used, with the result of excluding Federal admiralty jurisdiction on the great lakes and over the greater part of our interior rivers. Later, this was overruled and the Federal admiralty jurisdiction now extends over all navigable waters of the United States (63). This does not include, however, all water in the country that is actually navigable. It comprehends only such navigable waters as are accessible by water from a state other than that in which they lie. For instance, Great Salt Lake, being inaccessible by water from any other state than Utah, is not a navigable water of the United States, and is not under the Federal admiralty jurisdiction. Lake Tahoe, on the boundary between California and Nevada, is a Federal water, because each part of it is accessible by water from another state. The great lakes and most navigable rivers in this country are Federal waters, but a part of a river may be so obstructed by falls or dams

(63) The Daniel Ball, 10 Wall., 557.

that it is inaccessible by water from other states. In
such a case it is a state water only (64).

§ 303. **Artificial waters.** The Federal jurisdiction extends over artificial waters, like canals, as well as natural ones, provided only that the artificial water be connected with other navigable waters leading out of the
state. The Erie canal is thus subject to Federal jurisdiction (65).

§ 304. **Maritime jurisdiction distinct from commercial
power.** The early cases confused the maritime jurisdiction of the United States with its jurisdiction over interstate commerce, and refused to permit a Federal jurisdiction over the purely internal navigation of a state.
The later decisions have now established that the two
subjects are distinct, although to considerable extent
governing the same subject matter. Matters connected
with the navigation of navigable waters of the United
States are within the maritime jurisdiction, even though
the commerce concerned is purely internal. On the other
hand, if the commerce is interstate or foreign the Federal
jurisdiction governs traffic by land as well as water (66).

§ 305. **Federal jurisdiction is legislative as well as
judicial.** The clause in the Constitution quoted at the
beginning of this section is in the judiciary article, and
purports to concern only the jurisdiction of the Federal
courts. Other clauses of the same article confer upon
the Federal courts a judicial jurisdiction for which there

---

(64)   Commonwealth v. King, 150 Mass., 221.
(65)   The Robert W. Parsons, 191 U. S., 17.
(66)   In re Garnett, 141 U. S., 1.

is no corresponding legislative power. For instance, the Federal courts may hear controversies between citizens of different states over the title to land in one state, but Congress may not legislate concerning state land titles in such a case. The Federal courts appear to hold that Congress has full legislative power over maritime affairs, in addition to the jurisdiction of the courts (67). The source of this power has never been clearly explained. Perhaps it is incidental to the full control the United States has over our external relations, inasmuch as foreign water-borne traffic may traverse any water navigable from the sea, if local regulations permit it, and in any event much of this traffic is upon the high seas.

§ 293 (continued). [See p. 297.] In the Minnesota Rate Cases, decided in June, 1913, the Federal Supreme Court held that the direct regulation of internal rates by a state was not invalidated, at least without the action of Congress, merely because the competitive effect of such rates virtually compelled carriers to make voluntarily a corresponding alteration of their interstate rates.

---

(67) See 25 A. & E. 863, 58 C. J. 31.

CHAPTER XV.

MONEY AND BANKING.

§ 306. Constitutional provisions. The clauses of the United States Constitution that somewhat directly concern the state and national powers over money and banking are as follows:

"[The Congress shall have power] to borrow money on the credit of the United States; . . .

"To coin money, regulate the value thereof, and of foreign coin.

"No state shall coin money; emit bills of credit; [or] make anything but gold and silver coin a tender in payment of debts" (1).

These provisions were agreed to in the Philadelphia convention without serious controversy. The various experiments with paper money that were tried during the Revolution and just afterwards by a number of the states had produced general conviction upon this point among the commercial classes who exercised the principal influence in favor both of the formation and the adoption of the Constitution.

§ 307. Bills of credit. There being no prohibition against the United States government issuing bills of

---

(1) Art. I, sec. 8, §§ 2 and 5; sec. 10, § 1.

credit it has done this freely upon various occasions. The first was during the war of 1812.

The prohibition upon the issue by states of bills of credit has been liberally interpreted in favor of the borrowing power of the states. In only one instance has the Federal Supreme Court held obligations issued by a state to be void as bills of credit. In 1821 Missouri passed a statute authorizing state loans of sums less than $200 to its citizens on personal securities. The loans were to be made by issuing certificates in denominations between 50c and $10, which were to be receivable for all taxes and for the salaries and fees of state officers. The faith of the state was pledged for the redemption of these certificates, and one-tenth of them were to be retired annually. A majority of the Supreme Court held these certificates to be bills of credit (2).

On the other hand, the bills issued by state banks, which ordinarily circulated freely as currency, are not state bills of credit, even when the state owns all of the stock in the bank (3). Coupons of Virginia bonds, payable to bearer so that they could pass from hand to hand and receivable for all state taxes, were held not to be bills of credit (4). The state of Texas issued state warrants to pay its debts, when there was no money in the treasury, in denominations of $1 and $5, printed on bank note paper of ordinary size, payable to bearer, and by law made receivable by public officers for all taxes and

(2)   Craig v. Missouri, 4 Pet., 410.

(3)   Briscoe v Bank of Kentucky, 11 Pet., 257.

(4)   Poindexter v. Greenhow, 114 U. S., 270.

public dues, and disbursable by the state as money to
public creditors who would receive them at par as money.
Payments due the state school fund from railroads might
also be made in these warrants by any railroad who would
receive them at par for its freight and passenger traffic.
When received by the state they were not to be reissued.
The Supreme Court held these warrants not to be bills
of credit. They were not bills of credit unless they were
"designed to circulate, in the common transactions of
business, as money"; and provisions designed to facili-
tate their receipt by the state for its dues were not sufficient to indicate any improper purpose. The court said:

"The decisions of this court have shown great reluct-
ance, under this provision as to bills of credit, to interfere with or reduce the very important and necessary
power of the states to pay their debts by delivering to
their creditors their written promises to pay them on
demand, and in the meantime to receive the paper as payment of debts due the state for taxes and other like
matters" (5).

§ 308. **Bank notes.** As intimated in the preceding subsection the states may authorize state banks to issue
bills that circulate generally as currency, although not
legal tender. One of the earliest acts of the United
States government was to charter a national bank, which
issued bank notes and conducted a general banking business, as well as aided the government in its fiscal operations. The national power to create such an institution,

---

(5)   Houston & Texas Railroad Co. v. Texas, 177 U. S. 66.

after much discussion, was finally settled in the great case of McCulloch v. Maryland (6) in 1819. The powers of the United States to raise revenue and to disburse it involve, by implication, the power to make such use of its cash surpluses as to supply commercial needs for a stable circulating medium. Other governments having these powers and the power to borrow money find it convenient to exercise them through the medium of national banks, and the United States can do the same.

During the Civil war Congress taxed state bank notes out of existence in order that the field might be fully occupied by its own treasury and national bank notes, and this also was upheld as a further means of exercising these powers (7).

§ 309. **Legal tender.** The power to prescribe what may legally be offered by a debtor to discharge such of his obligations as are payable in money is an important function of government. The location of this power, in the United States, is not specifically prescribed by the Constitution, but it is left to inference. The United States is given the power to "coin money, regulate the value thereof, and of foreign coin"; and the states are forbidden to coin money or make anything but gold and silver coin a tender in payment of debts (§ 306). It appears, therefore, that the states *may* make gold and silver coin a legal tender; but it does not appear expressly whether the United States may make its action in this respect exclusive if it chooses.

---

(6)   4 Wheat. 316.

(7)   Veazie Bank v. Fenno, 8 Wall., 533.

It has always been understood that the United States, having the power to coin money, has all customary incidental powers connected therewith, including that of making such coined money a legal tender (8). Can Congress also declare that nothing shall be legal tender except what it prescribes? During the "free silver" controversy of 1893 a law was proposed in Colorado making Mexican silver a legal tender for Colorado debtors. Before Congress had prescribed what should be legal tender, such legislation would doubtless be valid. After the Revolution, it is said that the scarcity of American coin caused legislation making English and Spanish coins a legal tender for a period. Doubtless Congress may exclude all state regulation of this matter if it chooses, and its present legislation seems designed to cover the whole field.

Some years ago a few states passed laws forbidding the so-called "gold contracts," by which debtors agreed to pay in gold coin only, of a standard weight and fineness. Several judges of the United States Supreme Court have apparently concurred in a dictum that such laws are inconsistent with the act of Congress giving a legal tender quality to gold coin, the reasoning being that if Congress makes gold a legal tender a state cannot forbid it to be thus used, even exclusively, by private contract (9).

§ 310. **Government notes as legal tender.** Prior to the Civil War no attempt was made by the United States

---

(8)   Hepburn v. Griswold, 8 Wall., 603, 615.

(9)   Woodruff v. Mississippi, 162 U. S., 291, 306-9.

government to make its bills of credit a legal tender for private debts. The pressure of the war, however, and the increasing difficulty of borrowing at reasonable rates of interest induced Congress in 1862 to pass an act making United States notes receivable for debts due to or from the United States, except import duties and interest on the public debt; and in addition to make them a legal tender in payment of all debts, public and private, within the United States, except as aforesaid.

The constitutionality of this was much doubted, but the law was upheld in fifteen out of seventeen state courts before which it came before a case finally reached the Federal Supreme Court. Meanwhile it was decided that the ordinary "debts" did not include state taxes, which the states could require to be paid in coin; and that it did not include contracts by their express terms requiring the payment of coin (10). It referred only to obligations payable in money generally.

Finally, in 1867, a case came before the Supreme Court involving the constitutional question at issue. A debtor was sued upon a promissory note given and payable before the legal tender acts were passed. After the passage of the acts the debtor tendered United States notes in payment of his debt, the tender was refused, and the notes were paid into court. The highest court of Kentucky declared the legal tender law unconstitutional, and, after over two years' consideration of the case, the United States Supreme Court affirmed the Kentucky decision by

(10) Lane County v. Oregon, 7 Wall., 71; Bronson v. Rodes, 7 Wall., 229.

a vote of five to three. The argument of the majority was, briefly, first, that Congress had no power to make its bills of credit legal tender at all, especially not to make them legal tender for debts already in existence, because this added very little to the value of the legal tender notes; and second, even if Congress had some power to make its notes a legal tender, it amounted to taking property without due process of law to make them legal tender for previous debts. A promissory note payable in money, given before 1862, was intended by both parties to be payable in what was then money—gold and silver coin, and a creditor could not be compelled to accept paper money of a less value. If Congress could not require all creditors to accept 50c where $1 was due, it equally could not require creditors to accept a 50c paper dollar where a $1 coined one was due (11).

§ 311. Same (continued). Though the decision in Hepburn v. Griswold was, strictly speaking, applicable only to cases like that, where the debt was in existence before the legal tender acts were passed, yet the reasoning of the majority seemed to deny to Congress the power to make United States notes legal tender even for future debts; and great uneasiness and consternation was created in business circles, the vast majority of then (1870) existing debts having been incurred since the legal tender acts and in reliance upon them. It was understood that the question was to be reargued and meanwhile business judgment upon the matter was suspended.

There was one vacancy upon the Supreme Court when

_____

(11) Hepburn v. Griswold, 8 Wall., 603.

Hepburn v. Griswold was decided, and before the decision was announced one of the majority judges resigned,
though it did not take effect until after the announce-
ment of the decision. Two new judges nominated previously by President Grant were confirmed by the Senate
on the day Hepburn v. Griswold was decided. A case
then pending in court involved the question of the validity of the acts as applied to contracts made after their
passage, and by a vote of five to four the acts were declared constitutional on grounds that applied to contracts made before their passage as well as after. The
acts were upheld on the grounds that they were reasonably necessary to carry on the war, and so justified under
the power to make war; and also because the United
States, having the power to issue bills of credit and to
borrow money, might do these things by any means
within the usage of governments generally. This included borrowing by means of legal tender bills of credit.
Governments generally have exercised this power in time
of need, and contracts payable in money are made subject to the power of the government to declare what shall
be money when they are paid (12).

After the war steps were taken for some time to reduce
the United States legal tender notes, the so called "green-
backs"; but in 1878 Congress ceased this policy and
ordered their reissue as fast as the old ones were can-
celled or destroyed. At this date the act could no longer
be justified as a war measure and so its opponents once
more challenged its validity. It was finally upheld in

_____

(12) Legal Tender Cases, 12 Wall., 457.

1884 as the exercise of a power legitimately implied from
the power to borrow money and to issue bills of credit.
Just as the power to coin money gave Congress by implication the power to make it a legal tender, so the
power to issue bills of credit contained a similar implication (13).

§ 312. **Present exclusive Federal control of money.**
The final result of the decisions discussed in this chapter has been to give the United States complete control
over the money of the country, whether in the form of
coin or paper currency, with full power to make such part
of either a legal tender as may please Congress, and with
like power to exclude the states wholly or partly from any
regulation of the subject. Congress has made all coins
and currencies of the United States (including Federal
Reserve Notes and the circulating notes of Federal Reserve Banks and national banking associations) heretofore or hereafter coined or issued, legal tender for all
debts, public and private, public charges, taxes, duties,
and dues. Gold has been withdrawn from circulation entirely. Congress has enacted that provisions in obligations requiring payment in gold or a particular kind of
coin or currency may be discharged on payment, dollar
for dollar, in any coin or currency which at the time of
payment is legal tender for public and private debts (14).
These measures have been held to be within the power of
Congress (15).

---

(13)   Juilliard v. Greenman, 110 U. S. 421.

(14)   U. S. Code, Title 31, §§ 441, 462, 463.

(15)   Perry v. U. S., 294 U. S., 330, 95 A.L.R. 1335; Nortz v. U. S., 294
U. S. 317, 95 A.L.R. 1346; Norman v. B. & O. R. Co., 294 U. S. 240, 95
A.L.R. 1352.

CHAPTER XVI.

VARIOUS FEDERAL POWERS.

§ 313. Scope of chapter. The more complex Federal powers, about the nature and extent of which there has been a considerable amount of litigation, have been treated in separate chapters. The principal remaining powers are dealt with briefly in this chapter.

§ 314. Federal powers of taxation. The Constitution, Article I, section 8, § 1, provides: "Congress shall have power to lay and collect taxes, duties, imposts, and excises, to pay the debts and provide for the common defense and general welfare of the United States; but all duties, imposts, and excises shall be uniform throughout the United States."

Section 9, §§ 4 and 5, provide: "No capitation, or other direct tax shall be laid, unless in proportion to the census or enumeration hereinbefore directed to be taken.

"No tax or duty shall be laid on articles exported from any state."

Besides these express prohibitions, there is an implied restriction upon the United States, growing out of the nature of our dual government, which prevents Congress from taxing the essential governmental functions of a state. "Thus limited, and thus only, the Federal power of taxation reaches every subject and may be exercised at discretion'' (1).

§ 315. Limitations on taxation: Uniformity. Export taxes. It is clear that the uniformity required is a geographical uniformity, not a requirement, for instance, that a tax shall not be progressive as the value of what is taxed increases. Thus, a Federal progressive inheritance tax is valid, which taxes large bequests at a higher rate than small ones, provided that it applies in all of the states alike (2). (As to the meaning of the words ''United States'' in this clause, see § 260, above.)

Exports, under the Constitution, mean only goods going to foreign countries from a state (§ 275, above). The only case where a Federal tax has been held to be on exports is Fairbank v. United States (3), where a Federal stamp tax on bills of lading for exports was held to be virtually a tax upon exports because they were customarily accompanied by bills of lading. An excise tax on goods generally is not invalid merely because some of them may be intended for export later.

§ 316. Same: Direct taxes. The provision that Federal direct taxes must be apportioned among the states according to population was apparently adopted by the convention without any precise understanding of what direct taxes were. Hamilton suggested that the words meant capitation taxes, taxes on land, and general taxes on all of the property of individuals. It was early held

---

(1)   The License Tax Cases, 5 Wall., p. 471.

(2)   Knowlton v. Moore, 178 U. S., 41.

(3)   181 U. S., 283.

that taxes on specific kinds of personal property and on occupations were excise taxes, and not direct. A Federal income tax levied during the Civil war was upheld as an excise tax, without inquiry as to the source of income. In 1894 Congress enacted another income tax, the validity of which was elaborately argued before the Supreme Court. A majority of the court decided that taxes upon real estate or personal property in the mass were direct taxes, and that taxes on the income from such property were within the fair scope of the prohibition (4). In 1909 the Sixteenth Amendment to the Constitution was proposed to the states by Congress, permitting the government to levy an income tax without apportionment, and was adopted in 1913.

A Federal inheritance tax is an excise upon the privilege of succeeding to land or other property and is not a direct tax (5).

§ 317. Same: Taxation of state governmental functions. Just as a state may not tax functions of the Federal government, the Federal government may not tax state functions. The reasons for this are given in § 347, below. Thus, the United States may not tax any steps in state judicial proceedings, nor the property or borrowing power of a state or municipal corporation (including state or municipal bonds) (6).

---

(4) Pollock v. Farmers Loan and Trust Co., 157 U. S., 429; 158 U. S., 601 (all of the previous cases on the subject are here fully discussed).

(5) Knowlton v. Moore, 178 U. S., 41.

(6) Pollock v. Farmers Loan and Trust Co., 157 U. S., 429, 584-6.

But the United States may tax a legacy to a state or city, and may tax the business of selling liquor, even though it is carried on by a state (7). This kind of a governmental function is not sufficiently vital to the state to escape Federal taxation.

§ 318. **Bankruptcy.** The powers of the United States over the subject of bankruptcy are dealt with fully in the article on that subject in Volume X of this work.

§ 319. **Weights and measures.** The Constitution, Article I, section 8, § 5, gives Congress power to "fix the standard of weights and measures."

Congress has never passed any law regarding the use of any particular standards of weights and measures in this country, although it has made the use of the metric system permissible. By common usage English standards have generally been used in this country, except for scientific purposes, where the metric system is ordinarily employed. There has been some question whether, in the absence of Congressional legislation, the states could act upon the matter. Several state courts have intimated that they could and one inferior Federal court has suggested the contrary.

§ 320. **Postal powers.** The plenary power of Congress over the entire subject of the post-office has already been noticed in another connection. See §§ 28, 253, above. The business may be made a government monopoly and private competition made criminal (8). Congress may classify mail matter, apply different rates of postage to

---

(7)   South Carolina v. United States, 199 U. S., 437.

(8)   United States v. Bromley, 12 How., 88; U. S. R. S., §§ 3981-93.

different articles, and prohibit certain classes of matter altogether. It may exclude from the mails matter that is fraudulent or otherwise injurious to the public, and it may refuse to deliver mail to persons who are using the postal service for improper purposes. The reasonable administration of these rules may be delegated to postal officials (9).

§ 321. **Possible extent of postal powers.** Under its power to extend the limits of mailable matter, it would seem competent for Congress to raise the limit of weight so as to include all the parcel business now done by express companies, which is included in the postal service of most European governments. It is quite possible that many articles of freight might also be included. The United States Supreme Court has left open the question whether telegraph lines may not be acquired by Congress as part of its postal business (10). This, too, is a common practice of foreign governments. It seems likely that the United States could construct postroads, including railroads, for its postal service if it saw fit. An early Kentucky case admitted the existence of this Federal power very broadly, and its existence has never been denied by the Federal Supreme Court (11).

§ 322. **Copyright and patents.** The Constitution, Article I, section 8, § 8, gives Congress power "to promote the progress of science and useful arts, by securing

---

(9)   Public Clearing House v. Coyne, 194 U. S., 497.

(10)   Pensacola Telegraph Co. v. Western Union Co., 96 U. S., 1.

(11)   Dickey v. Maysfield Turnpike Co., 7 Dana 113; California v. Pacific Railroad, 127 U. S., 1.

for limited times to authors and inventors the exclusive right to their respective writings and discoveries.''

The principal questions concerning copyright and patents are fully treated in the articles upon these subjects in Volume IV of this work. The patent itself, which is the right to exclude all others from the manufacture, use, or sale of the things patented, is a Federal franchise, and as such cannot be taxed or otherwise interfered with by state law (12). The same is true of copyright (13). The patented article, however, may be taxed or regulated like other property by the states. The patent and the article manufactured thereunder are thus distinct kinds of property, the first one involving a Federal right (14).

§ 323. **Maritime offenses and offenses against the law of nations.** The Constitution, Article I, section 8, § 10, gives Congress power ''to define and punish piracies and felonies committed on the high seas, and offenses against the law of nations.''

The manner in which Congress may define piracies, for instance, is treated in the article on Criminal Law, § 4, in Volume III. The latter part of the Constitutional provision above quoted gives to Congress considerable power that has never been exercised. Under it, Congress apparently might enact laws to protect aliens in this country from violence or other misconduct, which, under the law of nations, might become a ground of com-

---

(12)   In re Sheffield, 64 Fed., 833.

(13)   People v. Roberts, 159 N. Y., 75.

(14)   Webber v. Virginia, 103 U. S., 334.

plaint for foreign powers. Under this clause, it has been held that the United States may punish the counterfeiting in a state of securities of any foreign government, though it could not **punish the** counterfeiting of a state bank-note (15).

§ 324. **Indians.** When the Constitution was adopted there still existed many powerful Indian tribes within the borders of the states, and in the western lands controlled by the United States. These tribes, even when in a state, ordinarily exercised a complete control over their internal affairs, and their relations with the states and the United States were governed by treaties made with formalities similar to those between independent nations. The Constitution gave the power to make treaties to the President and senate, and withdrew it from the states. In consequence, it was early held that the sole external power of governing the Indians lay with the United States (16).

The only legislative power expressly conferred upon Congress by the Constitution in regard to the Indians is the power to regulate commerce with the Indian tribes (17). Prior to 1871 Federal control over the Indians was exercised chiefly by means of treaties, but in that year an act of Congress forbade further dealings with them by the treaty-making power. Later Congress legislated directly for the Indians, though situated in the

---

(15)   United States v. Arjona, 120 U. S., 479; Tennessee v. Davis. 100 U. S., 257, 280.

(16)   Worcester v. Georgia, 6 Pet., 515.

(17)   Const., Art. I, sec. 8, § 3

states, upon a variety of non-commercial subjects, among other things punishing them for crime. These laws were upheld, upon the ground that historically the Federal government had had full control over the Indian tribes through the war and treaty-making powers; but that these were not exclusive methods of dealing with the Indians, and might be supplanted by legislation (18). Only thus, it would seem, could the prohibition of Indian treaties be justified, for Congress doubtless could not forbid the President and senate to make treaties with genuinely independent nations.

When Congress has by statute permitted Indians wholly to leave the tribal relation and to become citizens of the United States, its special powers over the Indian ceases, and he is subject to the Federal jurisdiction only as other citizens are who may reside in the various states. But Congress may retain such partial tribal control as it sees fit (19).

In 1924 Congress declared all non-citizen Indians within the territorial limits of the United States to be citizens.

§ 325. **Aliens.** "It is an accepted maxim of international law, that every sovereign nation has the power, as inherent in sovereignty and essential to self-preservation, to forbid the entrance of foreigners within its dominions, or to admit them only in such cases and upon such conditions as it may see fit to prescribe. In the United States this power is vested in the national government, to which the Constitution has committed the entire control of international relations, in peace as well as in war. It belongs

(18)   United States v. Kagama, 118 U. S. 375.
(19)   Matter of Heff, 197 U.S., 488; Tiger v. Western Co., 221 U. S., 286.

to the political department of the government, and may be exercised either through treaties made by the President and senate, or through statutes enacted by Congress" (20).

"The right of a nation to expel or deport foreigners, who have not been naturalized or taken any steps towards becoming citizens of the country, rests upon the same grounds, and is as absolute and unqualified as the right to prohibit and prevent their entrance into the country" (21).

These quotations correctly state the power of the United States respecting aliens, implied from the government's complete control over our international relations. The alien who has been stopped at our borders, although physically within our boundaries, is to be regarded as if stopped just outside, so that he is not entitled to invoke those constitutional guarantees which apply to persons lawfully within the country, such as free speech and the like (22).

The rigor of the Federal laws excluding or expelling Asiatics are constitutionally based upon these doctrines. The government's right to entrust the administration of these laws entirely to executive tribunals is discussed in § 138, above. The power to exclude or expel without jury trial does not include the power to punish aliens by imprisonment at hard labor for violating the exclusion

---

(20)   Nishimura Ekiu v. United States, 142 U. S., p. 659.

(21)   Fong Yue Ting v. United States, 149 U. S., 698.

(22)   United States v. Williams, 194 U. S., p. 292; United States v. Ju Toy, 198 U. S., 253, 263.

acts. Criminal punishment by the United States is subject to the provisions of the Fifth Amendment (23).

§ 326. **Federal treaty powers.** The Constitution, Article II, section 2, provides with respect to the President: "He shall have power, by and with the advice and consent of the senate, to make treaties, provided two-thirds of the senators present concur."

There are no express limitations upon the power of the United States to make treaties, except those prohibitions, contained chiefly in Article I, section 9, and in the amendments, which limit the exercise of Federal powers of government generally. Doubtless the United States by treaty could not gain the power to tax exports or take property without compensation, these acts being expressly forbidden. The important question which is not yet definitely settled is how far the United States may control, by treaty, matters which Congress could not control by legislation. For instance, Congress is given by the Constitution no power to regulate the holding of land in a state. If the United States, by treaty with France, permits Frenchmen to hold land in the United States, is this valid against a state prohibition of local land ownership by aliens? This has been upheld in several instances.

"That the treaty power of the United States extends to all proper subjects of negotiation between our government and the governments of other nations, is clear. It is also clear that the protection which should be afforded to the citizens of one country owning property in another,

---

(23) Wong Wing v. United States, 163 U. S., 228.

and the manner in which that property may be transferred, devised, or inherited, are fitting subjects for such negotiation and of regulation by mutual stipulations between the two countries. . . . The treaty power, as expressed in the Constitution, is in terms unlimited except by those restraints which are found in that instrument against the government itself and that of the states. It would not be contended that it extends so far as to authorize what the Constitution forbids, or a change in the character of the government or in that of one of the states, or a cession of any portion of the territory of the latter, without its consent. But with these exceptions, it is not perceived that there is any limit to the questions which can be adjusted touching any matter that is properly the subject of negotiation with a foreign country'' (24). Likewise it has been held in Massachusetts that a Federal treaty supersedes state laws regarding the administration of property of deceased aliens, and may limit the jurisdiction of the state courts in suits for alien seamen's wages (25). It has also been said that when any rights are secured to an alien by treaty, Congress may legislate to protect these rights, although but for such treaty aliens would be obliged to rely upon state laws only (26).

§ 327. **Same: Another view.** The view expressed above is perhaps the one commonly held in this country by students of the subject. It has been strongly urged,

(24)   Geofroy v. Riggs, 133 U. S., 258, 266.
(25)   Wyman, Petitioner, 191 Mass., 276.
(26)   Baldwin v. Franks, 120 U. S., 678, 683.

in opposition, that the framers of the Constitution could hardly have intended to reserve a control of local matters in the states as against Congress, only to permit them to be regulated at pleasure by treaties between the United States and foreign nations. To the argument that the power to make such arrangements with foreign nations is too valuable to have been destroyed altogether by the Constitution, and so must be with the Federal government, which alone can make treaties, it is pointed out that another clause of the Constitution permits a state, with the consent of Congress, to make agreements with foreign powers (27). It is suggested that this clause was intended to enable each state, with the consent of Congress, to make agreements with foreign countries respecting the reciprocal rights of their inhabitants (28).

The controversy over the alleged treaty rights of Japanese children in the public schools of California illustrates the interest and importance of the subject. It cannot be considered as yet settled either way by the Federal courts.

§ 328. Federal districts within a state. The Constitution, Article I, section 8, § 17, gives Congress power "to exercise exclusive legislation in all cases whatsoever, over such district (not exceeding ten miles square) as may, by cession of particular states and the acceptance of Congress, become the seat of the government of the United States, and to exercise like authority over all places purchased by the consent of the legislature of

---

(27)   Art. I, sec. 10, § 3.

(28)   William E. Mikell, in 57 American Law Register, 435, 528.

the state in which the same shall be, for the erection of forts, magazines, arsenals, dock-yards, and other needful buildings.''

The cession contemplated by this clause was made by Virginia and Maryland and constitutes the District of Columbia, in which are located the city of Washington and the seat of the Federal government. In 1841 the part of the District south of the Potomac river was ceded back to Virginia by Congress. The casual reading of the latter part of the clause quoted above might create the impression that this was intended to take the place of the acquisition of land by the Federal power of eminent domain. The distinction between the Federal powers over territory acquired in the two ways is this: The United States has exclusive jurisdiction in all particulars over land purchased with the consent of the state legislature. Over land taken by eminent domain the United States has governmental powers for Federal purposes only. Thus, if land for a post office is purchased in Chicago without the consent of Illinois, the state retains such jurisdiction over the property as does not interfere with postal purposes. If Illinois consents to the acquisition, it loses all jurisdiction not expressly retained (29).

§ 329. **Military powers: Constitutional provisions.** The Constitution, Article I, section 8, §§ 11-16, gives Congress power:

"To declare war, grant letters of marque and reprisal, and make rules concerning captures on land and water;

"To raise and support armies, but no appropriation

---

(29) Fort Leavenworth Railroad Co. v. Lowe, 114 U. S., 525.

of money to that use shall be for a longer term than two years;

"To provide and maintain a navy;

"To make rules for the government and regulation of the land and naval forces;

"To provide for calling forth the militia to execute the laws of the Union, suppress insurrections and repel invasions;

"To provide for organizing, arming, and disciplining the militia, and for governing such part of them as may be employed in the service of the United States, reserving to the states respectively the appointment of the officers, and the authority of training the militia according to the discipline prescribed by Congress."

Section 9, § 2, provides: "The privilege of the writ of habeas corpus shall not be suspended, unless when in cases of rebellion or invasion the public safety may require it."

§ 330. Same: During actual hostilities. These provisions give the United States all of the belligerent powers ordinarily exercised by sovereign nations in carrying on war, foreign or domestic. Although Congress alone may declare war, the executive department may recognize its existence in fact, in advance of congressional declaration, and may take appropriate military action to meet the situation. Thus, battles between the American and Mexican troops had taken place before Congress formally declared the existence of the Mexican war; and important armed collisions took place during the Civil war before

any action on the part of Congress. Indeed, the existence of civil war is rarely accompanied by any public
declaration of the fact, the test of its existence being that
the regular course of justice in the courts is interrupted
by the insurrectionary proceedings (30).

When a state of war exists as a fact, the entire territorial area in insurrection may be treated as hostile territory, and property and persons within it may be dealt
with according to the laws of war, although in fact a
considerable number of inhabitants be loyal citizens of
the United States (31). As a part of its belligerent
powers Congress may confiscate the property of residents of the enemy's country, or of hostile territory, as
well as all property so situated as to be of use to the
enemy, no matter where the owner lives. This power
was exercised to a considerable extent by Congress during the Civil war, and it was upheld as justified by the
war power, and not invalid either as an ex post facto law,
a punishment for crime without a jury trial, or a taking
of property without due process of law (32).

The state militia may be called into Federal service for
the purposes specified in the Constitution, whenever the
proper Federal authorities may decide this to be necessary. An act of Congress at present commits the determination of this necessity to the President. The
United States is not dependent upon state militia, but
may raise its own armies by volunteer enlistment or by

---

(30) The Prize Cases, 2 Black, 635.
(31) Ibid.
(32) Miller v. United States, 11 Wallace 268.

draft or conscription, as was largely done during the Civil war (33).

The period of beginning and ending hostilities is fixed by the public acts of the political departments of government, and will be followed by the courts. These periods differed slightly in different southern states during the Civil war (34).

The rules of warfare proper to be observed between belligerents, and the general conduct of hostilities under the rules of war are discussed in the article on International Law in Volume X of this work.

§ **331. Military jurisdiction.** In Ex parte Milligan (35) it was said by one of the judges:

"There are under the Constitution three kinds of military jurisdiction: one to be exercised both in peace and war; another to be exercised in time of foreign war without the boundaries of the United States, or in time of rebellion and civil war within states or districts occupied by rebels treated as belligerents; and a third to be exercised in time of invasion or insurrection within the limits of the United States, or during rebellion within the limits of states maintaining adhesion to the national government, when the public danger requires its exercise. The first of these may be called jurisdiction under military law, and is found in acts of Congress prescribing rules and articles of war, or otherwise providing for the government of the national forces; the second may be

---

(33) Kneedler v. Lane, 45 Pa., pp. 274-323.
(34) The Protector, 12 Wallace 700.
(35) 4 Wall., 2.

distinguished as military government, superseding, as far as may be deemed expedient, the local law, and exercised by the military commander under the direction of the President, with the express or implied sanction of Congress; while the third may be denominated martial law proper, and is called into action by Congress, or temporarily, when the action of Congress cannot be invited, and in the case of justifying or excusing peril, by the President, in times of insurrection or invasion, or of civil or foreign war, within the districts or localities where ordinary law no longer adequately secures public safety and private rights.''

§ 332. Same. Controverted questions. The problem of the jurisdiction of military courts over civilians employed by the Armed Forces overseas was recently brought to the attention of the Supreme Court (35a). It was decided that ''a civilian, entitled as he is, by Art. VI of the Amendments to the Constitution, to trial by jury, cannot legally be made liable to the military law and jurisdiction, in time of peace.'' As regards the third jurisdiction, there was much controversy during the Civil War. The concrete question most frequently presented was whether the President could suspend the writ of habeas corpus as to persons arrested by the government in parts of the country not the scene of insurrection or hostilities, or could try them by martial law. Where Congress has not authorized this, a presidential suspension of the writ is apparently illegal (36); but a contrary practice was common during the Civil war and

_____

(35a) McElroy v. U.S. ex rel. Guagliardo, 361 U.S. 281 (1960).

(36) Ex parte Merryman, Taney, 246.

was subsequently ratified by Congress, or indemnity provided for executive officers. The Supreme Court divided five to four in a dictum against the power of the President or Congress to cause the trial of men by martial law where the courts are open and not subject to hostile interference, but it cannot be said that the question has been definitely settled (37).

§ 333. Quartering soldiers in private houses. "No soldier shall, in time of peace be quartered in any house, without the consent of the owner, nor in time of war, but in a manner to be prescribed by law" (38).

Happily it has not been necessary for the Federal courts to consider this provision in this country. It doubtless does not apply to territory in actual insurrection or at the scene of actual hostilities, as military operations in such places would be governed by the war power. See § 330, above.

---

(37)   Ex parte Milligan, 4 Wall., 2.
(38)   Const., Amend. III.

CHAPTER XVII.

INTERGOVERNMENTAL RELATIONS.

§ 334. **States in many respects treated as foreign to each other.** Except where controlled by some provision of the Constitution, express or implied, the states stand in the same relation to each other as do foreign countries. Particularly is this true with respect to their right to exclude each other's corporations, and with reference to their domestic laws and policies. The principal phases of these are treated in the article on Conflict of Laws, in Volume IX of this work. See §§ 149, 180, above.

SECTION 1. INTERSTATE PRIVILEGES AND IMMUNITIES OF CITIZENS.

§ 335. **Scope of constitutional provision.** The Constitution, Article IV, section 2, § 1, provides: "The citizens of each state shall be entitled to all privileges and immunities of citizens in the several states."

This clause, in substantially the same form, was in the Articles of Confederation that preceded the Constitution. It secured a close community of interest between the people of the several states, and secured them against the disabilities of alienage in all parts of the Union. Of the scope and purpose of the clause, the Supreme Court has said:

335

"The constitutional provision there alluded to did not create those rights, which it called privileges and immunities of citizens of the states. It threw around them in that clause no security for the citizen of the state in which they were claimed or exercised. Nor did it profess to control the power of the state governments over the rights of its own citizens. Its sole purpose was to declare to the several states, that whatever those rights, as you grant or establish them to your own citizens, or as you limit or qualify, or impose restrictions on their exercise, the same, neither more nor less, shall be the measure of the rights of citizens of other states within your jurisdiction" (1).

§ 336. **Enumeration of rights protected.** As to what constitute the principal privileges and immunities of citizens in the several states that are protected against discrimination by this clause of the Constitution, an enumeration made by Mr. Justice Washington in 1825 has been frequently quoted with approval. He said:

"The inquiry is, what are the privileges and immunities of citizens in the several states? We feel no hesitation in confining these expressions to those privileges and immunities which are, in their nature, fundamental; which belong, of right, to the citizens of all free governments; and which have, at all times, been enjoyed by the citizens of the several states which compose this Union, from the time of their becoming free, independent, and sovereign. What these fundamental principles are, it would perhaps be more tedious than difficult to enumerate.

---

(1)   Slaughter House Cases, 16 Wall., 36, 77.

They may, however, be all comprehended under the following general heads: Protection by the government; the enjoyment of life and liberty, with the right to acquire and possess property of every kind, and to pursue and obtain happiness and safety; subject nevertheless to such restraints as the government may justly prescribe for the general good of the whole. The right of a citizen of one state to pass through, or to reside in any other state, for purposes of trade, agriculture, professional pursuits, or otherwise; to claim the benefit of the writ of habeas corpus; to institute and maintain actions of any kind in the courts of the state; to take, hold and dispose of property, either real or personal; and an exemption from higher taxes or impositions than are paid by the other citizens of the state, may be mentioned as some of the particular privileges and immunities of citizens, which are clearly embraced by the general description of privileges deemed to be fundamental; to which may be added, the elective franchise, as regulated and established by the laws or constitution of the state in which it is to be exercised. These, and many others which might be mentioned, are, strictly speaking, privileges and immunities, and the enjoyment of them by the citizens of each state, in every other state, was manifestly calculated (to use the expressions of the preamble of the corresponding provision in the old Articles of Confederation) 'the better to secure and perpetuate mutual friendship and intercourse among the people of the different states of the Union' '' (2).

---

(2) Corfield v. Coryell. 4 Wash. C. C., 371, 380, quoted in Blake v. McClung, 172 U. S. at 248-49

§ 337. **Illustrations of forbidden discriminations.** A few particular instances of invalid discrimination by a state against the citizens of other states in favor of its own citizens may be mentioned. Maryland attempted to require traders, not permanent residents of the state, to take out licenses for the sale of goods. It was held that citizens of other states could not be prevented by this method from selling goods in Maryland upon the same terms as permitted to Maryland citizens (3). Likewise the property of citizens of other states cannot be taxed by a state at a higher rate or in a different manner from that in which it taxes the property of its own citizens (4). If a state permits its own citizens to hold property as trustees, or to take certain property by law, it must extend the same privileges to citizens of other states as to property within its borders (5). Nor may a state give to its own citizens who are creditors a preference over the citizens of other states, who are also creditors, in the distribution of the assets of an insolvent business located within the state limits. All must be permitted to share on the same terms (6).

§ 338. **Valid discriminations: Proprietary rights.** It must not be supposed, however, that absolutely no discrimination may be made by a state in favor of its own citizens. Discriminations based solely upon citizenship are bad, but citizenship or permanent residence in a state may be necessarily accompanied by circumstances,

---

(3)   Ward v. Maryland, 12 Wall., 418.
(4)   Re Stanford's Estate, 126 Cal., 112.
(5)   Roby v. Smith, 131 Ind., 342.
(6)   Blake v. McClung, 172 U. S., 239.

or may give rise to situations, upon which a discrimination may be reasonably and validly based, despite the fact that it is necessarily or usually associated with citizenship or non-citizenship in the state. For instance, the right to fish in the oyster beds of New Jersey, these being the common property of the citizens of the state, was reserved solely to New Jersey citizens by that state. This was upheld, as being but the exercise of ordinary property rights in excluding non-owners from the use of property, although ownership here happened to bé restricted to New Jersey citizens (7). Similar discriminations in regard to fish, wild game, and the running navigable waters of a state have been sustained. Upon similar principles may be justified the practices of most states in charging higher fees to non-citizens than to citizens for admission to their schools and higher educational institutions. The state owns these and administers them in a proprietary as well as in a governmental capacity. The citizens of a state, being the common proprietors, may properly claim some advantages therein that are not equally free to non-proprietors. Doubtless foreign citizens could not be charged a higher fee than domestic citizens for the use of the courts or for the protection of the police, although the court-houses and the weapons of the officers of the law are owned by the state, but this is perhaps because dispensing justice and protecting from injury are historically essential functions of government, while affording an education is not.

§ 339. Same: Procedural rights as affected by dom-

---

(7)   Corfield v. Coryell, 4 Wash. C. C., 371.

icil. Non-residence in a state, though usually associated with non-citizenship in it, may be a just ground for discrimination in a variety of situations besides those involving proprietary rights. Resident defendants may obtain the benefit of the statute of limitations, while non-residents may not, because suit could have been begun against residents at any time during the statutory period, while the absence of the non-residents prevents this. An attachment may be allowed against the property of non-resident defendants, when not allowed against resident defendants, for the non-residents are likely to stay out of the state and leave the plaintiff to follow them as best he can after getting judgment. Moreover, if a non-resident remains out of the state altogether, there is no way in which a resident plaintiff may secure a valid judgment against him in the state, except by attaching his property. The United States Supreme Court has said:

"We must not be understood as saying that a citizen of one state is entitled to enjoy in another state *every* privilege that may be given in the latter to its own citizens. There are privileges that may be accorded by a state to its own people in which citizens of other states may not participate except in conformity to such reasonable regulations as may be established by the state. For instance, a state cannot forbid citizens of other states from suing in its courts, that right being enjoyed by its own people; but it may require a non-resident, although a citizen of another state, to give bonds for costs, although such bond be not required of a resident. Such a regulation of the internal affairs of a state cannot reasonably be characterized as hostile to the fundamental rights of citizens of other states. So, a state may, by a rule uniform in its operation as to citizens of the several states, require residence within its limits for a given time before a citizen of another state, who becomes a resident thereof, shall exercise the right of suffrage or become eligible to office. It has never been supposed that regulations of that character materially interfered with the enjoyment by citizens of each state of the privileges and immunities secured by the Constitution to citizens of the several states. The Constitution forbids only such legislation affecting citizens of the respective states as will substantially or practically put a citizen of one state in a condition of alienage when he is within or when he removes to another state, or when asserting in another state the rights that commonly appertain to those who are part of the political community known as the people of the United States, by and for whom the government of the Union was ordained and established'' (8).

§ 340. **Same: Occupational qualifications as affected by domicil.** Wherever citizenship or residence in a state, or such citizenship or residence for a certain period, may be thought better to qualify a person for some occupation or profession to be followed in the state, this may be required. Lawyers are very commonly required to be citizens of the state in which they practice, as they are officers of the courts. The same requirement is sometimes made of retail liquor dealers, one court saying:

(8) Blake v. McClung, 172 U. S., 239, 256-257.

"It is not an unreasonable requirement that a person who desires to avail himself of a license to retail intoxicating liquors shall submit himself to the jurisdiction of the state, by becoming an inhabitant thereof, to the end that he may be readily apprehended and punished for any violation of the law in connection with his business" (9). In many states a certain number of years' practice in the state is accepted in lieu of an examination for a license to practice medicine. A similar amount of practice outside of a state is not accepted. This discrimination has been sustained on the ground that the local practitioner is likely to have a better knowledge of local diseases, and also proof of his character and experience are more easily obtainable (10). A requirement that barbers be citizens of the state where they pursue their occupation is invalid (11).

Section 2. Other Interstate Relations.

§ 341. **Interstate recognition of public acts, records, and judicial proceedings.** "Full faith and credit shall be given in each state to the public acts, records, and judicial proceedings of every other state, and the Congress may by general laws prescribe the manner in which such acts, records and proceedings shall be proved, and the effect thereof" (12).

The effect of this constitutional provision is discussed

---

(9)   Welsh v. State, 126 Ind., p. 78.

(10) Ex parte Spinney, 10 Nev., 323.

(11) Templar v. Michigan Board of Examiners, 131 Mich., 254.

(12) Const., Art. IV, sec. 1.

in the article on Conflict of Laws in Volume IX of this work.

§ 342. **Interstate extradition and rendition.** "A person charged in any state with treason, felony, or other crime, who shall flee from justice and be found in another state, shall, on demand of the executive authority of the state from which he fled, be delivered up to be removed to the state having jurisdiction of the crime" (13).

This provision is discussed in the article on Criminal Procedure, §§ 35-40, in Volume III of this work.

"No person held to service or labor in one state, under the laws thereof, escaping into another, shall, in consequence of any law or regulation therein, be discharged from such service or labor, but shall be delivered up on claim of the party to whom such service or labor may be due" (14).

This clause referred especially to fugitive slaves, and is now obsolete, unless perhaps it might apply to some form of service like that of a sailor, which may be specifically enforced without violation of the Thirteenth Amendment against slavery. See § 102, above.

§ 343. **Agreements between states.** "No state shall, without the consent of Congress . . . enter into any agreement or compact with another state" (15).

The required consent of Congress to interstate agreements need not be given expressly nor with any particular formalities. It is sufficient if Congress by some

---

(13) Const., Art. IV, sec. 2, § 2.

(14) Const., Art. IV, sec. 2, § 3.

(15) Art. I, sec. 10, § 3.

positive act signify its approval or assent. For instance, the admission by Congress of Kentucky as a state
amounted to an assent to an agreement between Kentucky and Virginia by which the former was detached
from the territory of the latter (16). Recently it has
been decided that this prohibition upon state agreements
applies only to agreements having a substantial tendency
to increase the political power or influence of one or more
of the states affected. It applies to an agreement by
which the territory of one state is substantially increased,
but not to an agreement in good faith to settle a disputed
boundary line (17). Uniform legislation by states respecting railroads or waters connecting them is also valid.

SECTION 3. RELATIONS BETWEEN THE UNITED STATES
AND THE STATES.

§ 344. **Nature of the Union.** "The Constitution, in all
its provisions, looks to an indestructible Union, composed
of indestructible states." This political theory was finally settled by the Civil war. So far as the Supreme
Court has discussed the status of the southern states during that war, it appears that territorially speaking the
insurgent states were never out of the Union, nor were
their Federal obligations and those of their citizens suspended during the struggle. The illegal conduct of the
state governments and of their people suspended their
rights as members and citizens of the Union, and those
rights were later restored by various acts of Congress.

---

(16)   Green v. Biddle, 8 Wheaton, pp. 85-87.
(17)   Virginia v. Tennessee, 148 U. S., 520.

If a state chose to elect no Federal senators and representatives or temporarily to suspend the operations of its state government it would also meanwhile lose its corresponding Federal rights (18).

§ 345. Participation of the states in the Federal government. Certain state action at regular intervals is by the Constitution necessary to the continued existence of the Federal government. Each state prescribes the qualifications for electors of United States senators and of representatives in Congress; and each state chooses, as its legislature directs, its quota of electors to choose the President of the United States (19).

§ 346. State interference with Federal functions: Conflicting laws. "This Constitution, and the laws of the United States which shall be made in pursuance thereof; and all treaties made, or which shall be made, under the authority of the United States, shall be the supreme law of the land; and the judges in every state shall be bound thereby, anything in the Constitution or laws of any state to the contrary notwithstanding" (20).

In view of the nature of the Federal government, probably its laws and treaties would have been superior to conflicting state laws, even without this clause of the Constitution. This provision, however, has placed the matter beyond doubt. Direct conflicts between state and

(18) Texas v. White, 7 Wall., 700.
(19) Const., Art. I, sec. 2, § 1; Amend. XVII; Art. II, sec. 1, § 2.
(20) Art. VI, § 2.

Federal laws are thus readily disposed of in constitutional theory. Indirect interferences by the states with Federal laws or functions offer more difficulty.

§ 347. Same: State taxation of Federal agencies or property. After the establishment of the second United States bank Maryland imposed a tax upon the issue of bank notes by the institution. This was declared invalid by the Supreme Court upon the ground that it interfered with the operation of an agency created by the Federal government in the exercise of its powers (21). Likewise a state may not tax United States bonds owned and kept within its borders. Such a tax directly increases the rate of interest that the United States must pay to purchasers of these bonds, and so means a tax upon the borrowing power of the government (22). Similarly a state may not tax any franchise granted by the Federal government or a patent (23), nor property owned by the Federal government. But, overruling a number of previous decisions, the United States Supreme Court has held that a state may levy a non-discriminatory income tax on the salary of Federal officers (24).

§ 348. Same: Taxation of property of Federal agents. Taxation remotely affecting Federal functions. Property owned by private individuals or corporations may be taxed by the states where it is located, although it is employed in the Federal service, as, for instance, the

---

(21) McCulloch v. Maryland, 4 Wheat., 316.

(22) Weston v. Charleston, 2 Pet., 449.

(23) California v. Central Pacific R. R. Co., 127 U. S., 1; People v. Assessors, 156 N. Y., 417.

(24) Graves v. New York, 306 U. S. 466.

property of a Federal railroad corporation or that of a Federal contractor (25).

If state taxation affects Federal functions remotely instead of substantially it is not invalid, at least unless expressly forbidden by Congress. For instance, a state may tax the transfer of private property at the death of the owner, including Federal bonds and legacies left to the United States (26).

§ 349. State interference with private exercise of Federal rights. A state may not interfere with any private right derived expressly or impliedly from the Federal Constitution, laws or treaties. The principal express prohibitions upon such state interferences, such as those against ex post facto laws, impairing the obligation of contracts, taking property or liberty without due process of law, or denying the equal protection of the laws, have been discussed at length in other parts of this article. Private Federal rights under the commerce clause are discussed in Chapter XIV, §§ 279-99. Implied rights are entitled to the same protection. Thus, the right to inform Federal officers of the commission of a crime against the United States is an implied Federal right of every citizen, and may not be interfered with either by states or individuals (27). The right of a witness to testify in the Federal courts may not be restrained by a state prosecution for alleged perjury therein (28).

---

(25) Railroad Co. v. Peniston, 18 Wallace 5

(26) Plummer v. Coler, 178 U. S., 115.

(27) In re Quarles, 158 U. S., 532.

(28) In re Loney, 134 U. S., 372.

§ 350. **Federal interference with state functions.** The property of the states, and their essential governmental functions are protected from Federal interference to substantially the same extent as Federal functions are protected from state interferences (29). Some illustrations of this as regards Federal taxation are mentioned in § 317, above.

The United States Supreme Court, however, has held that the Federal Government can impose a non-discriminatory income tax on the salaries of state officers and employes. In its opinion, the Court said: ''The effect of the immunity, if allowed, would be to relieve respondents (State employes) of their duty of financial support to the National Government, in order to secure to the state a theoretical advantage so speculative in its character and measurement as to be unsubstantial. A tax immunity desired for protection of the states as governmental entities cannot be pressed so far (30.)''

---

(29)   United States v. Railroad Co., 17 Wallace 322; Collector v. Day, 11 Wallace, 113.

(30)   Helvering v. Gebhardt, 304 U. S. 405.

CHAPTER XVIII.

JURISDICTION OF THE FEDERAL COURTS.

SECTION 1. IN GENERAL.

§ 351. Classification of Federal judicial powers. The Constitution, Article III, section 2, § 1, provides: "The judicial power shall extend to all cases, in law and equity, arising under this Constitution, the laws of the United States, and treaties made, or which shall be made, under their authority; to all cases affecting ambassadors, other public ministers and consuls; to all cases of admiralty and maritime jurisdiction; to controversies to which the United States shall be a party; to controversies between two or more states; between a state and citizens of another state; between citizens of different states; between citizens of the same state claiming lands under grants of different states; and between a state or the citizens thereof, and foreign states, citizens or subjects."

It will be noticed that practically the whole of this grant of judicial power falls into two great classes: (1) cases dependent upon the character of the question litigated; (2) cases dependent upon the character of the parties to the litigation.

The Federal courts are given jurisdiction of all cases involving the following *questions,* no matter who are the parties to the suit: (a) cases in law and equity arising under the Federal Constitution, laws, or treaties; (b) cases of admiralty or maritime jurisdiction.

Likewise, the Federal courts are given jurisdiction of cases having the following *parties,* no matter what the suit may be about: (a) when ambassadors, public ministers, or consuls are parties; (b) when the United States is a party; (c) when two or more states are antagonistic parties; (d) when a state and citizens of another state are antagonistic parties; (e) when citizens of different states are antagonistic parties; (f) when a state or its citizens on one side and foreign states or aliens on the other are antagonistic parties.

§ 352. **Objects of the various judicial powers.** The necessity of securing a uniform and authoritative construction of the Federal Constitution, laws, and treaties was a sufficient reason for giving the Federal courts jurisdiction of questions involving the construction or enforcement of these. Such questions are usually called "Federal questions" and will hereafter be referred to shortly by that name. Obviously, too, suits to which the United States is a party should be in its courts. The national government alone has dealings with foreign nations, and so it is appropriate that its courts should deal with cases affecting the representatives of foreign nations; and, as admiralty matters are largely concerned with international intercourse and with transactions on the high seas, where vessels are under the flag of the nation rather than that of a state, similar considerations made it advisable to give the Federal courts jurisdiction of such matters.

Before the territory west of the Alleghanies was ceded to the United States, there had been conflicting claims to portions of it on behalf of different states, and in some cases bloodshed had occurred between rival groups of settlers claiming the same land under conflicting grants. To secure an impartial tribunal for the settlement of such claims the Federal courts were given jurisdiction of them.

As the states may not go to war or make treaties with each other or with foreign nations, it was necessary that the Federal courts should be given jurisdiction of disputes that might arise between such parties; and to prevent the possibilities of local prejudice in the state courts, the provisions were added which gave the Federal courts jurisdiction of suits between a state or its citizens on one side, and citizens of different states or aliens on the other.

§ 353. **Power of Congress in organization of Federal courts.** The Constitution, Article III, section 1, provides: "The judicial power of the United States, shall be vested in one Supreme Court, and in such inferior courts as the Congress may from time to time ordain and establish. The judges, both of the Supreme and inferior courts, shall hold their offices during good behavior, and shall, at stated times, receive for their services, a compensation, which shall not be diminished during their continuance in office."

The power of Congress over the organization of the Federal courts is very great. While it may not directly abolish the Supreme Court it may increase or diminish the number of its judges at pleasure, subject to the qualification that no sitting supreme court judge can be removed from the court during good behavior. The inferior Federal courts may be established and abrogated at the will of Congress, though it would seem that the judges of such inferior courts would be entitled to their salaries during good behavior, even though their court were abolished. The contrary practice was pursued, however, when a number of newly created Federal courts and judgeships were abolished by the Jeffersonian Republicans in 1801.

§ 354. **Present Federal courts.** The organization of the Federal courts with jurisdiction in the states under the present acts of Congress is as follows:

(a) The United States district courts. Each state is divided into from one to four Federal judicial districts, in each of which there is a district court held by one or more district judges appointed for that district.

(b) United States circuit courts of appeals. The judicial districts of the United States are divided by groups of states into ten circuits, each of which has from three to seven circuit judges and to each is assigned one supreme court justice. In each of the ten circuits there is a court of appeals, composed of three of these judges, which hears appeals from the decisions of the district courts in its respective circuit. District judges may also be assigned to this court when necessary.

(c) Court of claims, court of customs and patent appeals. These courts, composed of five judges each have jurisdiction over special classes of Federal cases.

(d) United States Supreme Court. This is composed

of nine judges, almost all of whose work consists in hearing appeals from the lower Federal courts and from the highest state courts.

§ 355. Original and appellate jurisdiction. The Constitution, Article III, section 2, § 2, provides: "In all cases affecting ambassadors, other public ministers, and consuls, and those in which a state shall be a party, the Supreme Court shall have original jurisdiction. In all the other cases before mentioned, the Supreme Court shall have appellate jurisdiction, both as to law and fact, with such exceptions, and under such regulations as the Congress shall make."

Just as in the organization of the Federal courts, Congress has very extensive powers over their jurisdiction. In only two classes of cases is the Supreme Court given original jurisdiction by the Constitution (original jurisdiction is the jurisdiction of a suit at its beginning; appellate jurisdiction is jurisdiction over it on an appeal from the decision of some other tribunal). Congress cannot enlarge the original jurisdiction of the Supreme Court, but it can give other courts a jurisdiction concurrent with it upon the subjects of its original jurisdiction.

The entire appellate jurisdiction of the Supreme Court being placed under the control of Congress, it can take away that court's appellate jurisdiction in any class of cases even after the appeal has been taken and argued in the Supreme Court (1). Congress may of course pro-

---

(1) Ex parte McCardle, 7 Wall., 506.

vide that certain classes of cases shall be finally decided by Federal courts inferior to the Supreme Court, and in several important classes of cases it has conferred the power of final decision upon the circuit courts of appeal.

§ 356. **Exclusive and concurrent jurisdiction.** The Constitution gives to the Federal courts no exclusive jurisdiction of any matters whatever. For anything that appears in the Constitution the state courts may exercise jurisdiction concurrently over all matters specified in the judiciary article. The regulation of this is entirely in the hands of Congress, which may distribute the subjects of possible Federal jurisdiction as it pleases. Under present statutes Federal courts have exclusive jurisdiction of all Federal crimes, penalties and seizures, of all admiralty, patent right, copyright, and bankruptcy cases, of all suits against the United States, all suits between a state on one side and another state or a foreign nation on the other side (2), and of all suits against Ambassadors, or other public ministers and their domestic servants, or consuls. Most other possible subjects of Federal jurisdiction may be sued upon either in the state or Federal courts as the parties to the suit may prefer (concurrent jurisdiction); but in a few instances Congress has left the jurisdiction wholly with the state courts. For instance, suits between citizens of different states, where no Federal question and less than $3,000 are involved, may not be brought into the Federal courts at all.

§ 357. **Transfer of cases from state to Federal courts: Before trial.** If a suit between A and B, citizens of Illinois, turned in part upon a Federal question within the

---

(2)   U. S. Code, Title 28, § 371.

concurrent jurisdiction of the state and Federal courts, the plaintiff A might at his option bring suit against B in either the state or Federal courts in Illinois. Likewise, if A lives in Indiana and B in Illinois A may sue B in a state or Federal court of Illinois upon the ground of diversity of citizenship, no matter what the question at issue; or, if A can find B in Indiana he may sue him in the Indiana state courts. In the first case above put, if B is sued in the state courts, he may have the case removed, in its entirety, to the Federal courts for trial. The defendant is as much entitled to the benefits of the Federal courts upon Federal questions as is the plaintiff. In the second case put above, if A sues B in the Illinois state courts, B cannot have the case removed to a Federal court. B is being sued in the courts of his own state, and if A is willing to take the chances of local prejudice B cannot complain. If, however, A sues B in the state courts of Indiana, B may have the case removed to the Indiana Federal courts, because he, a citizen of Illinois, is entitled to be protected from the possibility of local prejudice in favor of the Indiana plaintiff in the state courts (2a).

Often more than one question is involved in a case. Suppose there are a dozen questions in a particular case, only one of which is a Federal question, both parties being citizens of New York. Owing to the difficulty and expense of dividing a case for separate trials in different courts, the entire case with all of its questions, state and Federal, is removed to the Federal courts or may be brought there originally, if a single question in it is a

(2a) At present (1951) no suits may be removed from state to Federal courts unless over $3,000 is involved.

Federal question. The Federal court will decide the other questions in the case according to state law as best it can, but the whole case goes to the Federal courts (3).

§ 358. **Same: After trial.** When no Federal question is involved in a case, and both parties permit it to go to trial in a state court, neither can thereafter take the case to a Federal court at any later stage of the proceedings. It being a question of state law only, and neither party having complained of local prejudice, there is no reason for carrying the matter farther. When a case involves a Federal question, however, even though both parties are satisfied to conduct it in the first instance in a state court, yet it is important for the sake of uniformity and for the security of Federal rights that an ultimate authoritative decision be given by a Federal court. The statutes therefore provide that if the highest state court to which the matter can be carried decides *against* some claim of a Federal right set up in the case, it may be carried to the Supreme Court for decision by appeal. No part of the case is carried there except that involving the Federal question, and, if this has been properly decided by the state court, it matters not how poorly the other questions in the case may have been dealt with. If the decision of the state court is in *favor* of the Federal right claimed there is no appeal to the Federal courts, even though the decision be erroneous. But the United States Supreme Court may, by writ of certiorari, have a case sent up from a state court where a Federal question

---

(3)   Tennessee v. Davis, 100 U. S., 257.

is involved whether the decision of the state court is for or against the claim of Federal right (3a).

§ 359. **Federal questions.** A case arising under the Constitution, the laws of the United States, and treaties made under their authority exists, not only when the operation or effect of some written clause of the Constitution, an act of Congress, or a treaty is in controversy, but also when there is a question concerning the existence or exercise of any power, right, or duty arising under the government of the United States. Thus, the right of a citizen unhindered to inform Federal officers of the violation of Federal revenue laws is a right arising under the Constitution and laws of the United States, although there is nothing in the Constitution or any acts of Congress directly bearing upon this (4).

On the other hand a case does not involve a Federal question, so as to give the Federal courts jurisdiction, merely because rights claimed in the case are based upon a Federal law, provided there be no controversy as to the operation or effect of this law. For instance, the title to land may be derived from a United States grant. If, in a suit, the validity of some subsequent deed of this land is in issue, there is no Federal question, although the original Federal grant is part of the alleged title of both parties. If the Federal grant itself was at issue there would be a Federal question (5).

Corporations created by the United States to aid in its governmental functions, like banks or railways, may sue

---

(3a) 28 U. S. Code 344 b; Coleman v. Miller, 308 U. S., 433.

(4) In re Quarles, 158 U. S. 532.

(5) Blackburn v. Portland Mining Co., 175 U. S., 571.

or be sued in the Federal courts, even though the question in controversy does not concern the operation or effect of their corporate charters (6). Perhaps the best reason for this is that the exercise of Federal governmental functions, even by a private corporation, is necessarily the exercise of a power under the United States government, whatever the precise question at issue concerning it.

§ 360. **Habeas corpus proceedings.** The Federal courts are given by statute the right to grant writs of habeas corpus, within their respective jurisdictions, to inquire why any person is restrained of his liberty (7). "Within their jurisdictions" means that the writ can be used by the Federal courts only where the restraint is connected with some subject matter to which the jurisdiction of the Federal courts extends. Thus, a father may not secure from a Federal court a writ of habeas corpus to restore to him his children, detained by citizens of his own state. The relation of father and child is governed by state and not by Federal law and so the application must be made to the state courts (8).

On the other hand, where a Federal marshal was in the custody of state authorities, charged with homicide while acting in defence of a Federal judge, the Federal courts released the marshal absolutely from state custody on the ground that what the marshal had done was in furtherance of a duty owed to the United States. The

---

(6)   Pacific Railroad Removal Cases, 115 U. S., 1.

(7)   U. S. R. S., §§ 751-66.

(8)   In re Burrus, 136 U. S., 586.

Federal courts, however, are reluctant to interfere thus summarily with the administration of justice in the state courts, and state prisoners will not be released before trial by the Federal courts unless it is perfectly clear that important constitutional rights are being violated or that the prisoner's act was justifiably done on behalf of the United States or some foreign nation (9).

§ 361. **Suits between states.** Without its consent, a sovereign state can not be sued, but must be proceeded against by another state, if at all, through diplomatic or military channels. The powers of diplomacy and war being taken from the American states by the Constitution, the settlement of international difficulties between them is consequently relegated to the Federal courts. The jurisdiction has been upheld in a considerable variety of cases, and apparently extends to all matters that would be proper subjects for an international tribunal. Among them may be mentioned boundary disputes (10); the controversy over the right of Illinois to empty the Chicago drainage canal into Missouri waters (11); the dispute between Kansas and Colorado regarding their respective rights to use the Arkansas river for irrigation (12); the suit by South Dakota against North Carolina upon the latter's bonds (13); and the bill in equity brought by Virginia against West Virginia to compel the

---

(9)   Rogers v. Peck, 199 U. S., 425; U. S. R. S., § 753.

(10)   Rhode Island v. Massachusetts, 12 Pet., 657.

(11)   Missouri v. Illinois, 180 U. S., 208.

(12)   Kansas v. Colorado, 185 U. S., 125.

(13)   South Dakota v. North Carolina, 192 U. S., 286.

assumption of a fair share of Virginia's debt before the state was divided (14).

§ 362. **Suits between states and the United States.** The judiciary article expressly provides for suits between states, but there is no express provision for suits between states and the United States. General jurisdiction is given, however, of the cases to which the United States is a party, and this is held to include cases where the United States is a plaintiff and a state an unwilling defendant (15). The United States, being a paramount sovereignty, is not subject to the general rule of public law forbidding one sovereignty to sue another without the latter's consent (§ 368, below). A state as a subordinate sovereignty may not sue the United States without the latter's consent (16).

§ 363. **Diverse citizenship.** The jurisdiction of the Federal courts extends to suits between citizens of different states, and between citizens and aliens. It will be noticed that three considerable classes of persons are wholly omitted from this enumeration: (1) Citizens of the District of Columbia. (2) Citizens of the territories of the United States. (3) All corporations. As regards classes (1) and (2) it was early held that they were outside of this constitutional provision. A citizen of Kentucky who wishes to sue an Ohio defendant may do so in the Ohio Federal courts in order to escape local prejudice; but a citizen of Washington, D. C., or of Alaska, must

(14) Virginia v. West Virginia, 206 U. S., 290.
(15) United States v. Texas, 143 U. S., 621.
(16) Kansas v. United States, 204 U. S., 331.

take what the local state courts will give him when he sues in Ohio or other states.

Class (3) has had a different fate. There were few corporations when the Constitution was adopted and probably they were overlooked or regarded as unimportant when the jurisdictional section was drafted. When cases with corporations as plaintiffs or defendants became more frequent, the Supreme Court first held that, if all the stockholders of a corporation were citizens of the state where it was incorporated, the suit could be treated as virtually a suit by the citizens of that state, and if the other party was a citizen of another state, the necessary diverse citizenship existed to give the Federal courts jurisdiction. Later the court decided that all of the stockholders of a corporation would be conclusively presumed to be citizens of the state in which it was incorporated, for the purposes of Federal jurisdiction (17). This virtually makes a corporation a citizen of the state of its creation, though this is so for the purposes of Federal jurisdiction only.

§ 364. Law applied by Federal courts: No Federal common law. All transactions that occur in the United States, where not governed by some written law (constitution, statute, or treaty), are governed by the unwritten common law. This is not precisely alike in any two of the states, and in a few states it is quite divergent from the ordinary type, due to its basis upon a different system of law (as in Louisiana), or to local peculiarities of climate or custom (as in arid states). When the Con-

(17) Ohio & Mississippi Railroad Co. v. Wheeler, 1 Black, 286.

stitution was adopted, each of the original states had its own body of common law governing its people in all particulars not covered by written law. It might have been held that so much of this common law as concerned subjects delegated to the United States by the Constitution became, upon the adoption of the Constitution, Federal common law, and the rest remained state law. It was early said, however, that this was not so; and the Federal courts have consistently held that the common law of each state, even upon national subjects, is state law until changed by an act of Congress. Thus, although Congress alone can by statute regulate interstate commerce rates, yet, until Congress acts, the common law of each state respecting interstate rates is enforced, requiring, for instance, that they be not unreasonable nor discriminatory (18). For similar reasons, there can be no common law crimes against the United States. They exist against state laws only, while Congress must enact statutes to create Federal crimes (19).

§ 365. **Same: Questions of local common law.** Although there is no Federal common law, the Federal courts must frequently interpret and enforce state common law. A suit between citizens of New York and Indiana regarding land in New York can be brought in the Federal courts on account of the diverse citizenship of the parties, but the only law involved is the local land law of New York. If similar questions have been previously decided by the New York courts, establishing the

---

(18) Western Union Co. v. Call Publishing Co., 181 U. S., 92.

(19) United States v. Hudson, 7 Cranch 32.

New York law upon the point at issue, the Federal courts in New York will follow the decision of the New York courts, whether they think them right or not. It is enough that they appear to establish the law in New York (20). The same will be done with respect to any legal matter that is purely local to New York.

§ 366. **Same: Questions of general or commercial common law.** Suppose instead of being a question of land law it is one of commercial paper. The New York courts, for instance, have decided that the purchaser of a promissory note under certain circumstances cannot enforce it, although in most places outside of New York it would be enforceable. In 1842 an Indiana citizen sued in the Federal courts of New York in such a case; the Federal courts refused to allow the decisions of the New York courts, thinking the New York view wrong and opposed to the rules of commercial law generally (21). This decision established the rule for almost a century, that on matters of general law the Federal Courts were free to exercise an independent judgment. This resulted in there being two different laws on many points in most of the states —one administered between citizens of the state in the state courts, the other between citizens of the state and outsiders in the Federal Courts. The situation was unfortunate. It was difficult to know what questions would be considered general law and what local law. Much learning grew up with respect to the distinction. The soundness of the decision was frequently questioned. It was finally overruled by the United States Supreme Court in Erie Railroad Company v. Tomkins (21a), decided in 1938,

---

(20)   Suydam v. Williamson, 24 How., 427.
(21)   Swift v. Tyson, 16 Pet., 1.
(21a) 304 U. S. 64, decided in 1938.

and Swift v. Tyson, and with it the "General Law" doctrine and its numerous problems ceased to be important (21b).

§ **367. Same: State statutes.** Under the "general law" doctrine every state statute was treated as a local law, and the Federal courts followed the decisions of the state courts in construing state statutes, no matter how unusual the construction might be (22). This they will continue to do.

If conflicting constructions of a statute have been made by a state court the Federal courts will follow the latest decision of the highest state court, subject to the qualification mentioned below.

Suppose a state statute purports to authorize a state to issue bonds. The bonds are issued and in a suit in the state court the statute is held valid and the bonds declared good. Other bonds are bought upon the faith of this decision, but later the state court reverses its former decision, holding the statute invalid and the bonds bad. This involves no Federal question, as it depends wholly upon the construction of a state statute, so citizens of the same state as the city issuing the bonds are remediless. Citizens of other states, however, may sue the city in the Federal courts on the ground of diverse citizenship, and, with respect to contract or property rights acquired on the faith of the first state decision, the Federal courts will follow the first decision and hold the statute valid. As to the contracts made after the second state decision, the Federal courts will follow the second decision (23).

(21b)   § 366 revised by publisher's editorial staff.

(22)   Leffingwell v. Warren, 2 Black, 599.

(23)   Douglass v. Pike County, 101 U. S. 677.

This is the only exception to the rule that the Federal courts will follow the interpretation of state statutes made by state courts. Whether, since the overruling of Swift v. Tyson, this exception will continue, is uncertain.

SEC. 2. SUITS AGAINST STATES. ELEVENTH AMENDMENT.

§ 368. **Political sovereignty not accountable to individuals.** According to the rules of public law it is one of the attributes of sovereignty not to be accountable to individuals against the sovereign's will. The rule has sometimes been expressed in the maxim "The king can do no wrong." Literally, of course, this is far from true, but, inasmuch as the king cannot be sued in his own courts without his consent, the real truth is that he cannot be made responsible for his wrong-doing. Whether the sovereign is an individual ruler, or democracy itself, the rule is the same. Also, by rules of public international law a sovereign may not be sued against his consent in the courts of any other country than his own, unless some statute there in force applicable to the case permits it. A somewhat amusing illustration of this occurred a few years ago in England. The Sultan of Johore, a small independent state in the Malay Peninsula, with which Great Britain was in alliance, came to England and took up a residence there, under the assumed name of Baker. He promised to marry a woman living in England, and later was sued by her in the English courts for breach of promise of marriage. He denied the jurisdiction of the English courts, and it was held that as lawful sovereign of the State of Johore he was entitled to immunity from suit in the courts of other countries, unless he chose to waive this immunity, or it was taken away from him by express statute where he was sued (24).

§ 369. **Chisholm v. Georgia. Eleventh Amendment.** One of the clauses of the judiciary article provides that the judicial power of the United States shall extend "to controversies between a state and citizens of another state." In 1792 a creditor of Georgia living in another state brought suit in the Supreme Court against Georgia for non-payment of the debt. The state argued that the Constitution was to be interpreted in the light of well-known rules of public law, and that therefore this clause applied only to cases where a state should sue a citizen of another state, and not to cases where a state itself was defendant. The court decided by a vote of four to one that the Constitution covered the case of a suit against a state by a citizen of another state (25).

At the first meeting of Congress, thereafter, the Eleventh Amendment to the Constitution was proposed and a few years later became a part of the Constitution in the following language: "The judicial power of the United States shall not be construed to extend to any suit in law or equity, commenced or prosecuted against one of the United States by citizens of another state, or by citizens or subjects of any foreign state."

§ 370. **Repudiation of state debts.** The Eleventh Amendment has enabled a number of American states to repudiate their debts, in whole or in part, at various periods in our history. During the hard times after the

(24)   Mighell v. Sultan of Johore, (1894) 1 Q. B. 149.

(25)   Chisholm v. Georgia, 2 Dall., 419.

panic of 1837 nine or ten middle, western, and southern states defaulted in state debts incurred largely for internal improvements. After the Civil war there was another period of repudiation. Most of the southern states, with much justification, refused to pay debts corruptly or extravagantly incurred by their reconstruction governments, and one or two western states repudiated debts during the "Granger" excitement of the 1870's. Louisiana has repudiated some part of its state debt at four different periods.

Even when a state has expressly consented to be sued and suit has been begun against it and is in process of decision, the state may at any time withdraw its consent to further proceedings, and the Eleventh Amendment at once applies to shield the state (26).

§ 371. **Suits between states upon bond debts.** Decisions interpreting the Eleventh Amendment have been numerous. It was early held that this amendment did not affect suits between states themselves, which the Federal courts are authorized to entertain by another clause of the judiciary article. When Louisiana repudiated her state debt for the last time, the legislature of New Hampshire passed an act permitting its citizens to assign their claims against Louisiana to the state, and directed the attorney-general to sue Louisiana in the name of New Hampshire upon such claims. The assigning creditors were to pay the costs of the suit, and to have the net proceeds of any recovery. Suit was begun against Louisiana under this act by New Hampshire, but

---

(26)   Beers v. Arkansas. 20 How., 527.

was dismissed by the Supreme Court on the ground that the real parties in interest were citizens of the state, not the state itself, and therefore such suits fell within the substance of the Eleventh Amendment (27).

In another case, the owners of some repudiated North Carolina bonds donated them to the state of South Dakota. South Dakota accepted the bonds and at once begun suit against North Carolina upon them in the Supreme Court. Its action was upheld as not within the prohibition of the Eleventh Amendment, inasmuch as South Dakota was the only party having an interest in the subject matter of the suit, so that this action was not a mere cover for other interested individuals, as was true in the New Hampshire case (28). These particular bonds were secured by mortgage on some railroad stock, so that the judgment could be collected merely by selling the stock, without the necessity of a personal judgment against the state. The court admitted that property held by a state for public governmental purposes could not be seized to pay a judgment, and that a court could not compel a state to levy taxes to pay a judgment. This procedure, therefore, is not likely to be effectively used against a defaulting state, save in the exceptional case where some security has been given that may be sold to satisfy a judgment.

See further, respecting suits brought against a state by another state or the United States, §§ 361, 362, above.

§ 372. Suits against municipal corporations. Set-off against state. The Eleventh Amendment applies only to suits brought against the state itself, or where the relief

---

(27)   New Hampshire v. Louisiana, 108 U. S., 76.

(28)   South Dakota v. North Carolina. 192 U. S., 286.

really sought is against the state sovereignty. It does not apply to suits brought against corporations, public or private, created by the state, nor to municipal subdivisions of the state, although created by the latter for governmental purposes (29). It is the state sovereignty itself that is protected, not any lesser creations of the state.

Nor does the prohibition cover the case of a set-off which the state has previously created when used as a defense in a suit brought by the state itself. Virginia issued certain bonds, the interest coupons of which it agreed should be receivable for all taxes and other debts due the state. Virginia repudiated the bonds and refused to receive the interest coupons for taxes. Persons who tendered the coupons for taxes were sued by the state for the amount of their taxes, and their property was seized in satisfaction thereof. It was held that Virginia had contracted to permit these interest coupons to be used as a set-off against taxes due the state, and that making this defense against the state's attempt to collect taxes was not a suit against the state, but merely an answer to the state's suit against individuals (30).

§ 373. **Suits against state by its own citizens.** The Eleventh Amendment in terms forbids only suits brought against a state by citizens of another state, or by aliens. It does not include suits brought against a state by its own citizens. The latter suits have, however, been held

---

(29) Lincoln Co. v. Luning, 133 U. S., 529.

(30) Virginia Coupon Cases, 114 U. S., 269.

to be forbidden by the rule of public law referred to in § 368, above (31).

§ 374. **Suits against state officers: (a) For illegal official act.** When the state is named as a defendant in an action brought by an individual to obtain some relief there is of course no doubt that it is a suit against a state. Suppose, however, that the suit is brought against some state officer, either (a), to obtain redress for some act done for the state in his official capacity; or (b), to prevent his doing some official act for the state; or (c), to compel the doing of some official act for the state. Are any of these suits against a state within the meaning of the Eleventh Amendment?

As regards the first of these classes the matter is clear. For instance, a state, by a law invalid under the United States Constitution, purports to authorize its officers on its behalf, to seize certain property owned by a United States national bank. Acting under this authority, the officers seize the property, and are sued as individual trespassers by the bank. On the one side it is argued that they have acted only for the state, which can act only by human agents, and that therefore the suit is really against the state. On the other side, it is urged that under our law not only the person who authorizes a wrong is liable, but also the agent who carries out the authority and actually commits the wrong; and that in this case the suit against the officers is for the wrong committed by them personally in executing an invalid authority. The officer,

---

(31)   Hans v. Louisiana, 134 U. S., 1

being sued, is liable as an individual unless he can show that his act is protected by a valid governmental authority. Being able to show only an invalid (unconstitutional) authority, he cannot justify his act and hence is personally liable. This reasoning prevailed in an early case upon the facts stated, and it has been universally followed since (32).

§ 375. Same: (b) **To prevent illegal official act.** Of course if a state officer can be personally sued for wrongfully taking private property, even though he purports to act for the state, he can clearly be prevented in advance from doing the illegal act, if it is the kind of an act that courts would prevent if it were threatened by a private individual. This is true even where the unlawful act threatened by state officers is not a physical interference with the person or property of an individual.

The plaintiff had acquired the title to certain land formerly belonging to the state of Oregon. A dispute arose between the plaintiff and the state regarding the land, and a statute was passed requiring the state land commission to cancel plaintiff's title and resell the land. The plaintiff obtained an injunction against the doing of this by the land commissioners, the Supreme Court holding that his suit was against them as individuals to prevent the perpetration of a wrong that would cloud the plaintiff's title to his land. If the state did not really own the land it could not lawfully authorize its officers to sell it, and without lawful authority their acts could

(32) Osborne v. United States Bank, 9 Wheaton, 738, 842-4.

be prevented just like the wrongful acts of any individuals (33).

§ 376. Same: (c) To compel official act. Where the obligation of the state, however, requires affirmative action on the part of an official acting in its behalf, a suit to compel such action cannot be maintained under the Eleventh Amendment.

For instance, Louisiana contracted with its creditors to apply the revenue derived from a certain tax to discharge their claims. Later the state repudiated this and its creditors sued to compel the state officers to apply the funds already collected to the payment of the agreed debts. It was argued for the creditors that this was really a suit against the officers individually to prevent a wrongful omission of their duties, for the second state law, being an impairment of the state's contract with its creditors, was invalid and ought to be disregarded by the state officers. The Supreme Court denied this, pointing out that the relief was really against the state itself, which owed the money, and that the state officers as individuals, apart from their official character, owed no duties to the creditors and hence could not be sued as individuals. "The officers owe duty to the state alone, and have no contract relations with the bondholders. They can only act as the state directs them to act, and hold as the state allows them to hold. . . . They can be moved through the state, but not the state through them" (34).

§ 377. General principle involved. Generally speak-

----

(33)   Pennoyer v. McConnaughy, 140 U. S., 1.
(34)   Louisiana v. Jumel, 107 U. S., 711.

ing, the principle to be gathered from the foregoing de-cisions and others of like tenor appears to be this: If state officers, claiming to act under the authority of the state are doing or threatening acts which if done by pri vate persons would be actionable wrongs, the officers may be made individually liable if the state authority under which they act is really invalid. On the other hand, if state officers owe no duties as individuals which they are violating by action or inaction, a suit to compel the dis charge of purely official duties owed on behalf of the state, is a suit against the state.

§ 378. **Enjoining suit on behalf of state.** One class of cases is not readily explained by the application of the above rule, and has occasioned doubt and uncertainty not yet dispelled. These are cases where a state has passed a law alleged to be invalid, and has by statute authorized certain state officials to enforce the law in the courts or tribunals of the state.

The state of Minnesota, through orders of its railway commission and by statutes, required the railway com-panies in the state to establish certain schedules of rates. The Northern Pacific Railway asked the Federal circuit court to enjoin the railway commission from enforcing these rates as too low to permit a fair profit, and also asked that Young, the state attorney-general, be re-strained from proceeding against the company by man-damus, or by criminal proceedings to enforce the penal-ties of the statute. A temporary injunction was issued against the new rates until a judicial investigation had been made, and Young was also enjoined from taking any

action in the matter meanwhile. He disobeyed the injunction and asked for a mandamus in the state courts to put
into effect the controverted rates. The Federal circuit
court then imprisoned Young for contempt in disobeying
its orders, and the Supreme Court adjudged the imprisonment legal. It was urged that it was a suit against the
state because what the Federal court had enjoined was
not such an action as Young might take as an individual,
but only such action as he might take in behalf of the
state of Minnesota. The court said:

"The act to be enforced is alleged to be unconstitutional, and if it be so, the use of the name of the state to
enforce an unconstitutional act to the injury of com-
plainants is a proceeding without the authority of and
one which does not affect the state in its sovereign or governmental capacity. It is simply an illegal act upon the
part of the state to enforce a legislative enactment which
is void because unconstitutional. If the act which the
state attorney-general seeks to enforce be a violation of
the Federal Constitution, the officer in proceeding under
such enactment comes into conflict with the superior authority of that Constitution, and he is in that case
stripped of his official or representative character and is
subjected in his person to the consequence of his individual conduct" (35).

Mr. Justice Harlan dissented on the ground that where
the very question at issue was the constitutionality of a
statute the attorney-general of a state could not be an
individual wrongdoer in bringing suit on behalf of the

---

(35)   Ex parte Young, 209 U. S., 123, 159-60.

state in its own courts to test the statute. If the decision of the state court should be wrong in the matter it could be finally corrected by carrying the case to the United States Supreme Court. If the attorney-general was doing no individual wrong in bringing suit on behalf of his state, then an attempt to control his purely official acts on behalf of the state was really an effort to prevent the state from acting, that is, to prevent the state from securing a determination of the validity of its own statutes in its own courts in the first instance.

APPENDIX A

CONSTITUTION OF THE UNITED STATES.

We, the people of the United States, in order to form a more perfect union, establish justice, insure domestic tranquillity, provide for the common defense, promote the general welfare, and secure the blessings of liberty to ourselves and our posterity, do ordain and establish this Constitution for the United States of America.

ARTICLE I.

SECTION 1.

All legislative powers herein granted shall be vested in a Congress of the United States, which shall consist of a Senate and House of Representatives.

SECTION 2.

§ 1. The House of Representatives shall be composed of members chosen every second year by the people of the several states, and the electors in each state shall have the qualifications requisite for electors of the most numerous branch of the state legislature.

§ 2. No person shall be a representative who shall not have attained the age of twenty-five years, and been seven years a citizen of the United States, and who shall not, when elected, be an inhabitant of that state in which he shall be chosen.

§ 3. Representatives and direct taxes shall be apportioned among the several states which may be included within this Union, according to their respective numbers, which shall be determined by adding to the whole number of free persons, including those bound to service for a term of years, and excluding Indians not taxed, three-fifths of all other persons. The actual enumeration shall be made within three years after the first meeting of the Congress of the United States, and within every subsequent term of ten years, in such manner as they shall by law direct. The number of representatives shall not exceed one for every thirty thousand, but each state shall have at least one representative; and until such enumeration shall be made, the state of New Hampshire shall be entitled to choose three, Massachusetts eight, Rhode Island and Providence Plantations one, Connecticut five, New York six, New Jersey four, Pennsylvania eight, Delaware one, Maryland six, Virginia ten, North Carolina five, South Carolina five, and Georgia three.

§ 4. When vacancies happen in the representation from any state, the executive authority thereof shall issue writs of election to fill such vacancies.

§ 5. The House of Representatives shall choose their speaker and other officers, and shall have the sole power of impeachment.

SECTION 3.

§ 1. The Senate of the United States shall be composed of two senators from each state, chosen by the legislature thereof, for six years, and each senator shall have one vote.

§ 2. Immediately after they shall be assembled in consequence of the first election they shall be divided as equally as may be into three classes. The seats of the senators of the first class shall be vacated at the expiration of the second year; of the second class, at the expiration of the fourth year, and of the third class, at the expiration of the sixth year, so that one-third may be chosen every second year, and if vacancies happen by resignation or otherwise during the recess of the legislature of any state, the executive thereof may make temporary appointments until the next meeting of the legislature, which shall then fill such vacancies.

§ 3. No person shall be a senator who shall not have attained to the age of thirty years, and been nine years a citizen of the United States, and who shall not, when elected, be an inhabitant of that state for which he shall be chosen.

§ 4. The Vice-President of the United States shall be President of the Senate, but shall have no vote, unless they be equally divided.

§ 5. The Senate shall choose their other officers, and also a President pro tempore in the absence of the Vice-President, or when he shall exercise the office of President of the United States.

§ 6. The Senate shall have the sole power to try all impeachments. When sitting for that purpose they shall be on oath or affirmation. When the President of the United States is tried the Chief Justice shall preside; and no person shall be convicted without the concurrence of two-thirds of the members present.

§ 7. Judgment in cases of impeachment shall not extend further than to removal from office and disqualification to hold and enjoy any office of honor, trust or profit under the United States; but the party convicted shall, nevertheless, be liable and subject to indictment, trial, judgment, and punishment, according to law.

SECTION 4.

§ 1. The times, places, and manner of holding elections for senators and representatives shall be prescribed in each state by the legislature thereof; but the Congress may at any time by law make or alter such regulations, except as to the places of choosing senators.

§ 2. The Congress shall assemble at least once in every year, and such meeting shall be on the first Monday in December, unless they shall by law appoint a different day.

SECTION 5.

§ 1. Each house shall be the judge of the elections, returns, and qualifications of its own members, and a majority of each shall constitute a quorum to do business; but a smaller number may adjourn from day to day, and may be authorized to compel the attendance of absent members, in such manner, and under such penalties as each house may provide.

§ 2. Each house may determine the rules of its proceedings, punish its members for disorderly behavior, and with the concurrence of two-thirds expel a member.

§ 3. Each house shall keep a journal of its proceedings, and from time to time publish the same, excepting such parts as may in their judgment require secrecy, and the yeas and nays of the members of either house on any question shall, at the desire of one-fifth of those present, be entered on the journal.

§ 4. Neither house during the session of Congress shall, without the consent of the other, adjourn for more than three days, nor to any other place than that in which the two houses shall be sitting.

SECTION 6.

§ 1. The senators and representatives shall receive a compensation for their services, to be ascertained by law and paid out of the Treasury of the United States. They shall in all cases except treason, felony, and breach of the peace, be privileged from arrest during their attendance at the session of their respective houses, and in going to and returning from the same; and for any speech or debate in either house they shall not be questioned in any other place.

§ 2. No senator or representative shall, during the time for which he was elected, be appointed to any civil office under the authority of the United States, which shall have been created, or the emoluments whereof shall have been increased during such time; and no person holding any office under the United States shall be a member of either house during his continuance in office.

SECTION 7.

§ 1. All bills for raising revenue shall originate in the House of Representatives; but the Senate may propose or concur with amendments as on other bills.

§ 2. Every bill which shall have passed the House of Representatives and the Senate shall, before it become a law, be presented to the President of the United States. If he approve he shall sign it, but if not he shall return it, with his objections, to that house in which it shall have originated, who shall enter the objections at large on their journal and proceed to reconsider it. If after such reconsideration two-thirds of that house shall agree to pass the bill, it shall be sent, together with the objections, to the other house, by which it shall likewise be reconsidered, and if approved by two-thirds of that house it shall become a law. But in all such cases the votes of both houses shall be determined by yeas and nays, and the names of the persons voting for and against the bill shall be entered on the journal of each house, respectively. If any bill shall not be returned by the President within ten days (Sundays excepted) after it shall have been presented to him, the same shall be a law, in like manner as if he had signed it, unless the Congress by their adjournment prevent its return, in which case it shall not be a law.

§ 3. Every order, resolution, or vote to which the concurrence of the Senate and House of Representatives may be necessary (except on a question of adjournment) shall be presented to the President of the United States; and before the same shall take effect shall be approved by him, or, being disapproved by him, shall be repassed by two-thirds of the Senate and House of Representatives, according to the rules and limitations prescribed in the case of a bill.

SECTION 8.

§ 1. The Congress shall have power to lay and collect taxes, duties, imposts, and excises, to pay the debts and provide for the common defense and general welfare of the United States; but all duties, imposts, and excises shall be uniform throughout the United States;

§ 2. To borrow money on the credit of the United States;

§ 3. To regulate commerce with foreign nations, and among the several states, and with the Indian tribes;

§ 4. To establish an uniform rule of naturalization, and uniform laws on the subject of bankruptcies throughout the United States;

§ 5. To coin money, regulate the value thereof, and of foreign coin, and fix the standard of weights and measures;

§ 6. To provide for the punishment of counterfeiting the securities and current coin of the United States;

§ 7. To establish postoffices and postroads;

§ 8. To promote the progress of science and useful arts by securing for limited times to authors and inventors the exclusive right to their respective writings and discoveries;

§ 9. To constitute tribunals inferior to the Supreme Court;

§ 10. To define and punish piracies and felonies committed on the high seas and offenses against the law of nations;

§ 11. To declare war, grant letters of marque and reprisal, and make rules concerning captures on land and water;

§ 12. To raise and support armies, but no appropriation of money to that use shall be for a longer term than two years;

§ 13. To provide and maintain a navy;

§ 14. To make rules for the government and regulation of the land and naval forces;

§ 15. To provide for calling forth the militia to execute the laws of the Union, suppress insurrections, and repel invasions;

§ 16. To provide for organizing, arming, and disciplining the militia, and for governing such part of them as may be employed in the service of the United States, reserving to the states respectively the appointment of the officers, and the authority of training the militia according to the discipline prescribed by Congress;

§ 17. To exercise exclusive legislation in all cases whatsoever over such district (not exceeding ten miles square) as may, by cession of particular states and the acceptance of Congress, become the seat of the Government of the United States, and to exercise like authority over all places purchased by the consent of the legislature of the state in which the same shall be, for the erection of forts, magazines, arsenals, dockyards, and other needful buildings; and

§ 18. To make all laws which shall be necessary and proper for carrying into execution the foregoing powers, and all other powers vested by this Constitution in the Government of the United States, or in any department or officer thereof.

Section 9.

§ 1. The migration or importation of such persons as any of the states now existing shall think proper to admit shall not be prohibited by the Congress prior to the year one thousand eight hundred and eight, but a tax or duty may be imposed on such importation, not exceeding ten dollars for each person.

§ 2. The privilege of the writ of habeas corpus shall not be suspended, unless when in cases of rebellion or invasion the public safety may require it.

§ 3. No bill of attainder or ex post facto law shall be passed.

§ 4. No capitation or other direct tax shall be laid, unless in proportion to the census or enumeration hereinbefore directed to be taken.

§ 5. No tax or duty shall be laid on articles exported from any state.

§ 6. No preference shall be given by any regulation of commerce or revenue to the ports of one state over those of another; nor shall vessels bound to or from one state be obliged to enter, clear, or pay duties in another.

§ 7. No money shall be drawn from the Treasury, but in consequence of appropriations made by law, and a regular statement and account of the receipts and expenditures of all public money shall be published from time to time.

§ 8. No title of nobility shall be granted by the United States; and no person holding any office of profit or trust under them shall, without the consent of the Congress, accept of any present, emolument, office, or title of any kind whatever from any king, prince or foreign state.

Section 10.

§ 1. No state shall enter into any treaty, alliance, or confederation, grant letters of marque and reprisal, coin money, emit bills of credit, make anything but gold and silver coin a tender in payment of debts, pass any bill of attainder, ex post facto law, or law impairing the obligation of contracts, or grant any title of nobility.

§ 2. No state shall, without the consent of Congress, lay any imposts or duties on imports or exports, except what may be absolutely necessary for executing its inspection laws; and the net produce of all duties and imposts laid by any state on imports or exports shall be for the use of the Treasury of the United States; and all such laws shall be subject to the revision and control of the Congress.

§ 3. No state shall, without the consent of Congress, lay any duty of tonnage, keep troops or ships of war in time of peace, enter into any agreement or compact with another state or with a foreign power, or engage in war, unless actually invaded or in such imminent danger as will not admit of delay.

ARTICLE II.

Section 1.

§ 1. The executive power shall be vested in a President of the United States of America. He shall hold his office during the term of four years, and, together with the Vice-President, chosen for the same term, be elected as follows:

§ 2. Each state shall appoint, in such manner as the legislature thereof may direct, a number of electors, equal to the whole number of senators and representatives to which the state may be entitled in the Congress; but no senator or representative, or person holding an office of trust or profit under the United States, shall be appointed an elector.

§ 3. The electors shall meet in their respective states and vote by ballot for two persons, of whom one at least shall not be an inhabitant of the same state with themselves. And they shall make a list of all the persons voted for, and of the number of votes for each, which list they shall sign and certify, and transmit sealed to the seat of government of the United States, directed to the President of the Senate. The President of the Senate shall, in the presence of the Senate and House of Representatives, open all the certificates, and the votes shall then be counted. The person having the greatest number of votes shall be the President, if such number be a majority of the whole number of electors appointed; and if there be more than one who have such majority, and have an equal number of votes, then the House of Representatives shall immediately choose by ballot one of them for President; and if no person have a majority, then from the five highest on the list the said House shall in like manner choose the President. But in choosing the President the votes shall be taken by states, the representation from each state having one vote. A quorum for this purpose shall consist of a member or members from two-thirds of the States, and a majority of all the states shall be necessary to a choice. In every case, after the choice of the President, the person having the greatest number of votes of the electors shall be the Vice-President. But if there should remain two or more who have equal votes, the Senate shall choose from them by ballot the Vice-President. [This paragraph superseded by Amendment XII.]

§ 4. The Congress may determine the time of choosing the electors and the day on which they shall give their votes, which day shall be the same throughout the United States.

§ 5. No person except a natural-born citizen, or a citizen of the United States at the time of the adoption of this Constitution, shall be eligible to the office of President; neither shall any person be eligible to that office who shall not have attained to the age of thirty-five years, and been fourteen years a resident within the United States.

§ 6. In case of the removal of the President from office, or of his death, resignation, or inability to discharge the powers and duties of the said office, the same shall devolve on the Vice-President, and the Congress may by law provide for the case of removal, death, resignation, or inability, both of the President and Vice-President, declaring what officer shall then act as President, and such officer shall act accordingly until the disability be removed or a President shall be elected.

§ 7. The President shall, at stated times, receive for his services a compensation, which shall neither be increased nor diminished during the period for which he may have been elected, and he shall not receive within that period any other emolument from the United States or any of them.

§ 8. Before he enter on the execution of his office he shall take the following oath or affirmation:

"I do solemnly swear (or affirm) that I will faithfully execute the office of President of the United States, and will to the best of my ability preserve, protect, and defend the Constitution of the United States."

SECTION 2.

§ 1. The President shall be Commander-in-Chief of the Army and Navy of the United States, and of the militia of the several states when called into the actual service of the United States. He may require the opinion in writing of the principal officer in each of the executive departments upon any subject relating to the duties of their respective offices, and he shall have power to grant reprieves and pardons for offenses against the United States, except in cases of impeachment.

§ 2. He shall have power, by and with the advice and consent of the Senate, to make treaties, provided two-thirds of the senators present concur; and he shall nominate, and, by and with the advice and consent of the Senate, shall appoint ambassadors, other public ministers and consuls, judges of the Supreme Court, and all other officers of the United States, whose appointments are not herein otherwise provided for, and which shall be established by law; but the Congress may by law vest the appointment of such inferior officers as they think proper in the President alone, in the courts of law, or in the heads of departments.

§ 3. The President shall have power to fill up all vacancies that may happen during the recess of the Senate by granting commissions which shall expire at the end of their next session.

SECTION 3.

He shall from time to time give to the Congress information of the state of the Union, and recommend to their consideration such measures as he shall judge necessary and expedient. He may, on extraordinary occasions, convene both houses, or either of them, and in case of disagreement between them with respect to the time of adjournment, he may adjourn them to such time as he shall think proper; he shall receive ambassadors and other public ministers; he shall take care that the laws be faithfully executed, and shall commission all the officers of the United States.

SECTION 4.

The President, Vice-President, and all civil officers of the United States shall be removed from office on impeachment for and conviction of treason, bribery, or other high crimes and misdemeanors.

ARTICLE III.

SECTION 1.

The judicial power of the United States shall be vested in one Supreme Court, and in such inferior courts as the Congress may from time to time ordain and establish. The judges, both of the supreme and inferior courts, shall hold their offices during good behavior, and shall, at stated times, receive for their services a compensation which shall not be diminished during their continuance in office.

SECTION 2.

§ 1. The judicial power shall extend to all cases, in law and equity, arising under this Constitution, the laws of the United States, and treaties made, or which shall be made, under their authority; to all cases affecting ambassadors, other public min-

isters, and consuls; to all cases of admiralty and maritime jurisdiction; to controversies to which the United States shall be a party;
to controversies between two or more states; between a state and
citizens of another state; between citizens of different states; between citizens of the same state claiming lands under grants of
different states, and between a state, or the citizens thereof, and
foreign states, citizens, or subjects.

§ 2. In all cases affecting ambassadors, other public ministers
and consuls, and those in which a state shall be a party, the Supreme Court shall have original jurisdiction. In all the other cases
before mentioned the Supreme Court shall have appellate jurisdiction, both as to law and fact, with such exceptions and under
such regulations as the Congress shall make.

§ 3. The trial of all crimes, except in cases of impeachment,
shall be by jury; and such trial shall be held in the state where
the said crimes shall have been committed; but when not committed
within any state, the trial shall be at such place or places as the
Congress may by law have directed.

Section 3.

§ 1. Treason against the United States shall consist only in levying war against them, or in adhering to their enemies, giving them
aid and comfort. No person shall be convicted of treason unless
on the testimony of two witnesses to the same overt act, or on con-
fession in open court.

§ 2. The Congress shall have power to declare the punishment
of treason, but no attainder of treason shall work corruption of
blood or forfeiture except during the life of the person attainted.

ARTICLE IV.

Section 1.

Full faith and credit shall be given in each state to the public
acts, records, and judicial proceedings of every other state. And
the Congress may by general laws prescribe the manner in which
such acts, records, and proceedings shall be proved, and the effect
thereof.

Section 2.

§ 1. The citizens of each state shall be entitled to all privileges
and immunities of citizens in the several states.

§ 2. A person charged in any state with treason, felony, or other
crime, who shall flee from justice and be found in another state,
shall, on demand of the executive authority of the state from which

he fled, be delivered up, to be removed to the state having jurisdiction of the crime.

§ 3. No person held to service or labor in one state, under the
laws thereof, escaping into another, shall, in consequence of any
law or regulation therein, be discharged from such service or labor, but shall be delivered up on claim of the party to whom such
service or labor may be due.

SECTION 3.

§ 1. New states may be admitted by the Congress into this
Union; but no new states shall be formed or erected within the
jurisdiction of any other state; nor any state be formed by the
junction of two or more states or parts of states, without the consent of the legislatures of the states concerned, as well as of the
Congress.

§ 2. The Congress shall have power to dispose of and make
all needful rules and regulations respecting the territory or other
property belonging to the United States; and nothing in this Constitution shall be so constructed as to prejudice any claims of the
United States or of any particular state.

SECTION 4.

The United States shall guarantee to every state in this Union
a republican form of government, and shall protect each of them
against invasion, and on application of the legislature, or of the
executive (when the legislature cannot be convened), against domestic
violence.

ARTICLE V.

The Congress, whenever two-thirds of both houses shall deem
it necessary, shall propose amendments to this Constitution, or,
on the application of the legislature of two-thirds of the several
states, shall call a convention for proposing amendments, which in
either case shall be valid to all intents and purposes as part of
this Constitution, when ratified by the legislatures of three-fourths
of the several states, or by conventions in three-fourths thereof,
as the one or the other mode of ratification may be proposed by
the Congress, provided that no amendments which may be made
prior to the year one thousand eight hundred and eight shall in
any manner affect the first and fourth clauses in the ninth section of the first article; and that no state, without its consent,
shall be deprived of its equal suffrage in the Senate.

ARTICLE VI.

§ 1. All debts contracted and engagements entered into before the adoption of this Constitution shall be as valid against the United States under this Constitution as under the Confederation.

§ 2. This Constitution, and the laws of the United States which shall be made in pursuance thereof, and all treaties made, or which shall be made, under the authority of the United States, shall be the supreme law of the land; and the judges in every state shall be bound thereby, anything in the constitution or laws of any state to the contrary notwithstanding.

§ 3. The senators and representatives before mentioned, and the members of the several state legislatures, and all executive and judicial officers, both of the United States and of the several states, shall be bound by oath or affirmation to support this Constitution; but no religious test shall ever be required as a qualification to any office or public trust under the United States.

ARTICLE VII.

The ratification of the conventions of nine states shall be sufficient for the establishment of this Constitution between the states so ratifying the same (1).

Done in convention by the unanimous consent of the states present, the seventeenth day of September, in the year of our Lord, one thousand seven hundred and eighty-seven, and of the independence of the United States of America the twelfth. In witness whereof, we have hereunto subscribed our names.

George Washington, President and Deputy from Virginia.

New Hampshire—John Langdon, Nicholas Gilman.

Massachusetts—Nathaniel Gorham, Rufus King.

Connecticut—William Samuel Johnson, Roger Sherman.

New York—Alexander Hamilton.

New Jersey—William Livingston, David Brearly, William Patterson, Jonathan Dayton.

---

(1) The Constitution became operative March 4, 1789. Owings v. Speed, 5 Wheat. 420.

The States ratified the Constitution in the following order:

Delaware	December 7, 1787	South Carolina	May 23, 1788
Pennsylvania	December 12, 1787	New Hampshire	June 21, 1788
New Jersey	December 18, 1787	Virginia	June 25, 1788
Georgia	January 2, 1788	New York	July 26, 1788
Connecticut	January 9, 1788	North Carolina	November 21, 1789
Massachusetts	February 6, 1788	Rhode Island	May 29, 1790
Maryland	April 28, 1788		

Pennsylvania—Benjamin Franklin, Thomas Mifflin, Robert Morris, George Clymer, Thomas Fitz Simons, Jared Ingersoll, James Wilson, Gouverneur Morris.

Delaware—George Read, Gunning Bedford, Jr., John Dickinson, Richard Bassett, Jacob Broom.

Maryland—James McHenry, Daniel of St. Thomas Jenifer, Daniel Carroll.

Virginia—John Blair, James Madison, Jr.

North Carolina—William Blount, Richard Dobbs Spaight, Hugh Williamson.

South Carolina—John Rutledge, Charles Cotesworth Pinckney, Charles Pinckney, Pierce Butler.

Georgia—William Few, Abraham Baldwin.

Attest: William Jackson, Secretary.

AMENDMENTS.

ARTICLE I.

Congress shall make no law respecting an establishment of religion, or prohibiting the free exercise thereof; or abridging the freedom of speech or of the press; or the right of the people peaceably to assemble, and to petition the government for a redress of grievances.

ARTICLE II.

A well-regulated militia being necessary to the security of a free state, the right of the people to keep and bear arms shall not be infringed.

ARTICLE III.

No soldier shall, in time of peace, be quartered in any house without the consent of the owner, nor in time of war, but in a manner to be prescribed by law.

ARTICLE IV.

The right of the people to be secure in their persons, houses, papers, and effects, against unreasonable searches and seizures shall not be violated, and no warrants shall issue but upon probable cause, supported by oath or affirmation, and particularly describing the place to be searched, and the person or things to be seized.

ARTICLE V.

No person shall be held to answer for a capital or otherwise infamous crime, unless on a presentment or indictment of a grand jury, except in cases arising in the land or naval forces, or in the militia, when in actual service in time of war or public danger; nor shall any person be subject for the same offense to be twice put in jeopardy of life or limb; nor shall be compelled in any criminal case to be a witness against himself, nor be deprived of life, liberty, or property, without due process of law; nor shall private property be taken for public use without just compensation.

ARTICLE VI.

In all criminal prosecutions the accused shall enjoy the right to a speedy and public trial, by an impartial jury of the state and district wherein the crime shall have been committed, which district shall have been previously ascertained by law, and to be informed of the nature and cause of the accusation; to be confronted with the witnesses against him; to have compulsory process for obtaining witnesses in his favor, and to have the assistance of counsel for his defense.

ARTICLE VII.

In suits at common law, where the value in controversy shall exceed twenty dollars, the right of trial by jury shall be preserved, and no fact tried by a jury shall be otherwise re-examined in any court of the United States, than according to the rules of the common law.

ARTICLE VIII.

Excessive bail shall not be required, nor excessive fines imposed, nor cruel and unusual punishments inflicted.

ARTICLE IX.

The enumeration in the Constitution of certain rights shall not be construed to deny or disparage others retained by the people.

ARTICLE X.

The powers not delegated to the United States by the Constitution, nor prohibited by it to the states, are reserved to the states respectively or to the people (2).

ARTICLE XI.

The judicial power of the United States shall not be construed to extend to any suit in law or equity, commenced or prosecuted against

---

(2) Amendments I to X were in force Nov. 3, 1791.

one of the United States by citizens of another state, or by citizens or subjects of any foreign state(3).

ARTICLE XII.

The electors shall meet in their respective states and vote by ballot for President and Vice-President, one of whom, at least, shall not be an inhabitant of the same state with themselves; they shall name in their ballot the person voted for as President, and in distinct ballots the person voted for as Vice-President, and they shall make distinct lists of all persons voted for as President and of all persons voted for as Vice-President, and of the number of votes for each; which lists they shall sign and certify, and transmit sealed to the seat of the government of the United States, directed to the President of the Senate. The President of the Senate shall, in the presence of the Senate and House of Representatives, open all the certificates and the votes shall then be counted. The person having the greatest number of votes for President shall be the President, if such number be a majority of the whole number of electors appointed; and if no person have such majority, then from the persons having the highest numbers, not exceeding three on the list of those voted for as President, the House of Representatives shall choose immediately, by ballot, the President. But in choosing the President the votes shall be taken by states, the representation from each state having one vote; a quorum for this purpose shall consist of a member or members 'from two-thirds of the states, and a majority of all the states shall be necessary to a choice. And if the House of Representatives shall not choose a President whenever the right of choice shall devolve upon them, before the fourth day of March next following, then the Vice-President shall act as President, as in the case of the death or other constitutional disability of the President.

The person having the greatest number of votes as Vice-President shall be the Vice-President, if such number be a majority of the whole number of electors appointed; and if no person have a majority, then from the two highest numbers on the list the Senate shall choose the Vice-President; a quorum for the purpose shall consist of two-thirds of the whole number of Senators, and a majority of the whole number shall be necessary to a choice. But no person constitutionally ineligible to the office of President shall be eligible to that of Vice-President of the United States (4).

---

(3) In force Jan. 8, 1798.
(4) In force Sept. 25, 1804.

ARTICLE XIII.

SECTION 1. Neither slavery nor involuntary servitude, except as a punishment for crime whereof the party shall have been duly convicted, shall exist within the United States or any place subject to their jurisdiction.

SECTION 2. Congress shall have power to enforce this article by appropriate legislation (5).

ARTICLE XIV.

SECTION 1. All persons born or naturalized in the United States, and subject to the jurisdiction thereof, are citizens of the United States and of the state wherein they reside. No state shall make or enforce any law which shall abridge the privileges or immunities of citizens of the United States; nor shall any state deprive any person of life, liberty, or property, without due process of law; nor deny to any person within its jurisdiction the equal protection of the laws.

SECTION 2. Representatives shall be apportioned among the several states according to their respective numbers, counting the whole number of persons in each state, excluding Indians not taxed. But when the right to vote at any election for the choice of electors for President and Vice-President of the United States, Representatives in Congress, the executive and judicial officers of a state, or the members of the legislature thereof, is denied to any of the male inhabitants of such state, being twenty-one years of age, and citizens of the United States, or in any way abridged, except for participation in rebellion, or other crime, the basis of representation therein shall be reduced in the proportion which the number of such male citizens shall bear to the whole number of male citizens twenty-one years of age in such state.

SECTION 3. No person shall be a Senator or Representative in Congress, or elector of President and Vice-President, or hold any office, civil or military, under the United States or under any state, who, having previously taken an oath as a member of Congress, or as an officer of the United States, or as a member of any state legislature, or as an executive or judicial officer of any state, to support the Constitution of the United States, shall have engaged in insurrection or rebellion against the same, or given aid or comfort to the enemies thereof. But Congress may, by a vote of two-thirds of each house, remove such disability.

---

(5) In force Dec. 18, 1865.

SECTION 4. The validity of the public debt of the United States, authorized by law, including debts incurred for payment of pensions and bounties for services in suppressing insurrection or rebellion, shall not be questioned. But neither the United States nor any state shall assume or pay any debt or obligation incurred in aid of insurrection or rebellion against the United States, or any claim for the loss or emancipation of any slave; but all such debts, obligations, and claims shall be held illegal and void.

SECTION 5. The Congress shall have power to enforce, by appropriate legislation, the provisions of this article (6).

ARTICLE XV.

SECTION 1. The right of citizens of the United States to vote shall not be denied or abridged by the United States or by any state on account of race, color, or previous condition of servitude.

SECTION 2. The Congress shall have power to enforce this article by appropriate legislation (7).

ARTICLE XVI.

The Congress shall have power to lay and collect taxes on incomes from whatever source derived, without apportionment among the several states, and without regard to any census or enumeration (8).

ARTICLE XVII.

The Senate of the United States shall be composed of two senators from each state, elected by the people thereof, for six years; and each senator shall have one vote. The electors in each state shall have the qualifications requisite for electors of the most numerous branch of the state legislature.

When vacancies happen in the representation of any state in the Senate, the executive authority of such state shall issue writs of election to fill such vacancies provided that the legislature of any state may empower the executive thereof to make temporary appointments until the people fill the vacancies by election as the legislature may direct (9).

ARTICLE XVIII.

§ 1. After one year from the ratification of this article, the manufacture, sale, or transportation of intoxicating liquors within, the importation thereof into, or the exportation thereof from, the United States and all territory subject to the jurisdiction thereof for beverage purposes is hereby prohibited.

§ 2. The Congress and the several states shall have concurrent power to enforce this article by appropriate legislation.

§ 3. This article shall be inoperative unless it shall have been ratified as an amendment to the Constitution, by the legislatures of the several states, as provided in the Constitution, within seven years from the date of the submission hereof to the states by the Congress. (10).

Note: For footnotes see page 392b.

ARTICLE XIX.

§ 1. The right of the citizens of the United States to vote shall not be denied or abridged by the United States or by any state on account of sex.

§ 2. Congress shall have power by appropriate legislation to enforce the provisions of this article. (11)

ARTICLE XX.

SECTION 1. The terms of the President and Vice-President shall end at noon on the twentieth day of January, and terms of senators and representatives at noon on the third day of January, of the years in which such terms would have ended if this article had not been ratified; and the terms of their successors shall then begin.

SECTION 2. The Congress shall assemble at least once in every year, and such meeting shall begin at noon on the third day of January, unless they shall, by law, appoint a different day.

SECTION 3. If at the time fixed for the beginning of the term of the President, the President-Elect shall have died, the Vice-President-Elect shall become President. If a President shall not have been chosen before the time fixed for the beginning of his term, or if the President-Elect shall have failed to qualify, then the Vice-President-Elect shall act as President until a President shall have qualified; and the Congress may by law provide for the case wherein neither a President-Elect nor a Vice-President-Elect shall have qualified, declaring who shall then act as President, or the manner in which one who is to act shall be selected, and such person shall act accordingly until a President or Vice-President shall have qualified.

SECTION 4. The Congress may by law provide for the case of the death of any of the persons from whom the House of Representatives may choose a President whenever the right of choice shall have devolved upon them, and for the case of the death of any of the persons from whom the Senate may choose a Vice-President whenever the right of choice shall have devolved upon them.

SECTION 5. Sections 1 and 2 shall take effect on the fifteenth day of October following the ratification of this article.

SECTION 6. This article shall be inoperative unless it shall have been ratified as an amendment to the Constitution by the legislatures of three-fourths of the several states within seven years from the date of its submission (12).

ARTICLE XXI

SECTION 1. The eighteenth article of amendment to the Constitution of the United States is hereby repealed.

SECTION 2. The transportation or importation into any state, territory, or possession of the United States for delivery or use therein of intoxicating liquors, in violation of the laws thereof, is hereby prohibited.

Section 3. This article shall be inoperative unless it shall have been ratified as an amendment to the Constitution by conventions in the several states, as provided in the Constitution, within seven years from the date of the submission hereof to the states by the Congress (13).

ARTICLE XXII

Section 1. No person shall be elected to the office of the President more than twice, and no person who has held the office of President, or acted as President, for more than two years of a term to which some other person was elected President shall be elected to the office of the President more than once. But this article shall not apply to any person holding the office of President when this Article was proposed by the Congress, and shall not prevent any person who may be holding the office of President, or acting as President, during the term within which this article becomes operative from holding the office of President or acting as President during the remainder of such term.

Section 2. This article shall be inoperative unless it shall have been ratified as an amendment to the Constitution by the legislatures of three-fourths of the several States within seven years from the date of its submission to the States by the Congress (14).

ARTICLE XXIII

Section 1. The District constituting the seat of Government of the United States shall appoint in such manner as the Congress may direct:
A number of electors of President and Vice President equal to the whole number of Senators and Representatives in Congress to which the District would be entitled if it were a State, but in no event more than the least populous State; they shall be in addition to those appointed by the States, but they shall be considered, for the purposes of election of President and Vice President, to be electors appointed by a State; and they shall meet in the District and perform such duties as provided by the twelfth article of amendment.

Section 2. The Congress shall have power to enforce this article by appropriate legislation. (15).

---

(6) In force July 28, 1868.
(7) In force Mar. 30, 1870.
(8) In force Feb. 25, 1913.
(9) In force, May 31, 1913.
(10) Ratified Jan. 16, 1919; effective Jan. 16, 1920.
(11) In force Aug. 26, 1920.
(12) Ratified Feb. 6, 1933; in effect Oct. 15, 1933.
(13) Ratified and in effect Dec. 5, 1933.
(14) Ratified by the 35th and 36th States, Utah and Nebraska, on February 26, 1951, the required number for ratification being 36. Ratification proclaimed and the amendment certified to be a part of the Constitution of the United States by the Administrator of General Services on March 1, 1951.
(15) The Twenty-third Amendment was proposed by the Eighty-sixth Congress on June 16, 1960, and was declared by the Administrator of General Services on April 3, 1961, to have been ratified.

APPENDIX B

QUESTIONS — CONSTITUTIONAL LAW.

§ 2. Is it legally possible to have a constitution unless it is in writing?

§ 5. What are the various functions of the constitution of the American States?

§ 8. What state has the oldest constitution?

§ 10. Did the Constitution of the United States become effective as soon as passed by the constitutional convention?

§ 12. If a constitution contains no provision providing for its amendment how may it be amended?
may it be amended in other ways not specified?

§ 13. If a constitution provides one specific way of amendment,

§ 18. If a court should decide in favor of a corporation could the legislature or Congress by unanimous vote constitutionally set aside the judgment?
Could it constitutionally do so if the act was affirmed by the governor or President?

§ 20. Would a statute providing that where an act of the legislature had been vetoed by the governor it might nevertheless become a law if assented to by a majority of the Supreme Court judges be constitutional?

§ 21. Could a statute constitutionally deprive a court of its power to punish summarily a person who was guilty of contempt in the presence of the court?

§ 23. Would a statute giving the county court power to assess and collect the county taxes be constitutional?

§ 27. If the Constitution of the United States neither expressly nor by implication confers power upon Congress to pass certain kinds of statutes, but on the other hand neither expressly nor by implication denies it that power, may Congress pass such statutes?

§ 28. The constitution of the United States gives Congress the power to regulate commerce with foreign nations; there is nothing

393

in the constitution saying that states may not also do so. May a state pass a statute regulating commerce with a foreign nation?

§ 32. Have the English courts power to declare an act of Parliament unconstitutional?

§ 33. What are the historical reasons for the American doctrine of Constitutional Law that the courts may declare acts of the legislative branch unconstitutional?

§ 36. What are the objections to the arguments for the doctrine that the courts may declare an act of Congress unconstitutional?

§ 37. Has the court constitutional power to notify Congress that an act which is about to pass or has passed is unconstitutional?

§ 38. A legislature passed an act providing that women should not work over 9 hours a day. The members of the Supreme Court are of the opinion that such legislation is ill-advised, and that a woman may, without injury to herself, work more than 9 hours a day. Should the court therefore declare the act unconstitutional?

§ 41. A statute of the United States declared all the waters within 1,000 miles of the coast of Alaska to be American waters and forbade any foreigner to fish or seal there. May the court declare such an act unconstitutional for the reason that such waters clearly do not politically belong to the United States?

§ 42. Suppose the constitution of a state requires the governor to either approve or veto every act of the legislature submitted to him and the governor refuses to do either. May he be compelled by the court to do one or the other?

§ 43. Suppose a statute created an unnecessarily large number of officers and gave them unreasonably large salaries so that the whole scheme was obviously one to plunder the state. Could the act be declared unconstitutional for this reason?

§ 44. A statute forbade naturally competing railroads to agree as to rates. A suit was brought by a stockholder against his railroad to enjoin it from making an agreement as to rates with a competing road. The suit was brought to test the act and both the stockholder and the railroad wanted it declared unconstitutional. If this fact was brought to the attention of the court could it decline to hear the case?

What condition might it require before it would hear it?

§ 45. A statute was passed authorizing constables to attach property without warrants. A constable attached the property of Jones under this statute. It was later declared unconstitutional. Has Jones a right of action against the constable?

§ 46. Suppose the statute in the above case had also provided in another part for the arrest of persons upon warrants duly sworn out. Would the fact that the first part was declared unconstitutional necessarily render this latter part also bad?

§ 47. Are there any states in which the court may legally give its opinion on the constitutionality of statutes not in litigation?

§ § 62, 65. What is the difference in the nature of the legal rights created and the scope and purpose of the following constitutional provisions:—that regulating the qualifications of members of Congress; that providing that no state may coin money; that providing that no person shall be deprived of life, liberty, or property without due process of law; that providing that if the governor vetoes an act of the legislature he must give his reason for so doing?

§ 67. A state passes a statute doing away with jury trials where the amount involved is less than $30. Is such a statute in conflict with the seventh amendment to the Constitution of the United States?

§ 68. What are the more important provisions of the original Constitution of the United States that limit the powers of the state governments?

§ 72. A hotel keeper refused admission to a negro citizen of the United States solely for the reason that he was a negro. Was his action in violation of the fourteenth amendment?

Would it have made any difference if there had been an act of Congress forbidding keepers of hotels to exclude citizens of the United States solely on account of their color?

§ 73. Would it have made any difference in the above case if the statute had included the registrar of deeds and a negro citizen had been excluded from the offices of a registrar of deeds solely because he was a negro?

§ 74. Would a state statute requiring all barbers to be licensed be in violation of that part of the fourteenth amendment to the Constitution of the United States which forbids a state to abridge the privileges and immunities of the citizens of the United States?

Would a state statute that forbade a person to send out of the state any manufactured product not made wholly in the state be in violation of the above mentioned amendment?

§ 77. Is a Chinese child born in this country a citizen of the United States?

§ 79. Might it make any difference in the above case according as the child was born in New Mexico or the Philippines?

§ 81. Would the child of the British Ambassador, if born in Washington, be a citizen of the United States?

§ 82. Would a child born of French parents on a French warship while lying in New York harbor be a citizen of the United States?

§ 85. Is it possible for a person born of Indian parents to be a citizen of the United States?

§ 87. Is a corporation chartered in any of the states a citizen of the United States?

§ 88. Which of the following persons could be naturalized, assuming in each case that he could show the necessary length of residence in one of the United States: a Japanese, a Mexican, a Samoan, a Filipino?

§ 90. Would a child of American parents born in France be a citizen of the United States?

§ 92. Could Congress constitutionally provide when and how the members of the House of Representatives should be chosen in the different states?

Could a state constitutionally provide that its presidential electors should be appointed by the governor of the state?

§ § 93, 94. Could a state constitutionally limit the suffrage to persons having an income of $10,000 a year or more?

§ 95. Does a citizen of the United States have as such a right to vote?

§ 98. Would an act of Congress forbidding the sending of indecent matter through the mails be in violation of the provision that "Congress shall make no law abridging the freedom of speech or of the press?"

§ 100. Would a statute that forbade a person to own or carry firearms unless he had a license, be a violation of the constitutional provision that "the right of the people to bear arms shall not be infringed?"

§ 102. A sailor who deserted his vessel was arrested and brought back under a statute covering the case. Was this a violation of the thirteenth amendment against involuntary servitude except as a punishment for crime?

§ 103. Would the same principle apply to the case of a person who agreed to work on a farm for six months and left before that time and was forcibly brought back under a statute and compelled to work?

§ 105. Would a statute forbidding religious meetings in the crowded streets of a city be in violation of the clause that "Congress shall make no laws respecting an establishment of religion or prohibit the free exercise thereof?''

§ 106. What are the historical origins of the provisions of the Constitution protecting the rights of a person accused of crime?

§ 107. What is a bill of attainder?

§ 108. Is a statute that gives a right of appeal in cases where it did not formerly exist *ex post facto* as to cases already tried?

§ 109. Would a statute that allowed a three-fourths verdict in criminal cases be *ex post facto* as to crimes already committed?

§ 110. Would a statute that changed the punishment of a wife-beater from imprisonment to whipping be *ex post facto* as to offenses committed before it was passed?

§ 111. Would a statute that increased the number of challenges on the part of both the accused and the state be *ex post facto* as to previous offenses?

§ 113. A state passed a statute requiring all chauffeurs to be licensed and provided that no person who had ever been convicted of a criminal offense could obtain a license. Is such a statute un-constitutional?

§ 114. Alexander Jones was accused of murder and denied that he was the man wanted. On his trial he was compelled to turn up his shirt sleeve and show the name ''Alexander Jones'' tattooed on his arm. Was this a violation of any constitutional right?

§ 115. A corporation known as the United Flour Company was indicted for criminally receiving rebates in violation of a United States statute. The president was called as a witness and compelled to admit that the company had received such rebates. Was this a violation of the constitutional privilege against self-incrimination and if so whose right had been violated?

§ 117. Suppose the testimony given in the last case had been of a kind that rendered the president of the company personally liable to criminal indictment, would the protection of the constitution of the United States forbid an indictment against him in a state court based upon the evidence given in the first case?

§ 118. Suppose that a United States statute provided that where any person brought an action to recover goods alleged to be in the possession of another person, the house of the latter might at any time be searched by an officer without a warrant and the property so claimed recovered. Would such a statute be a violation of the constitutional provision that ''the right of the people to be secure in their........houses........shall not be violated''?

§ 119. If the language of the statute authorizing the action is clear, may a letter in the mails be opened upon order of the Postmaster General for the purpose of obtaining evidence against persons suspected of crimes?

§ 121. May Congress by appropriate legislation provide that a verdict of three-fourths of a jury shall be sufficient?

§ 123. A defendant was indicted in a federal court for a mis demeanor. He asked for and was refused a trial by jury. Is this a violation of the constitutional provision that "in all criminal prosecutions the accused shall enjoy the right to a........trial........by a jury?"

§ 125. Suppose in the above case that the punishment for the misdemeanor was a fine of not more than $10, would the fact that the defendant was tried without having been indicted by a grand jury be a violation of his constitutional rights?

§ 128. A statute provided that any saloonkeeper who should keep his saloon open beyond the legal closing hour should be punished by a fine of not less than $5.00 nor more than $10.00 for each hour the saloon was so kept open. Smith, a saloonkeeper, for two months kept his saloon open five hours a night later than the regular closing time. He was indicted under the above statute and it being proved that he had illegally kept open a total of 300 hours, the court fined him $3,000. He appealed on the ground that this was a violation of the constitutional provision against cruel and unusual punishments. Is his contention sound?

§ 132. A state statute provided that if courts were so busy that they were behind in their work they might refer cases where the amount in dispute was less than $100 to any disinterested lawyer, who should give proper notice to the parties and then proceed to try the case without a jury. Is such a statute in violation of the fourteenth amendment providing for "due process of law?"

§ 134. A statute authorized the boards of health of cities and towns to summarily seize and destroy any decayed vegetables or meat that should be offered for sale. Was this statute unconstitutional?

§ 137. A United States statute provided that if any Mongolian laborer without a passport should be found in the United States he should be ordered deported by the Commissioner of Immigration. A Chinese laborer found in the United States without a passport, on being ordered by the Commissioner of Immigration to be deported, swore out a writ of habeas corpus on the ground that the statute violated that part of the Constitution which provides that "no person should be deprived of ....liberty without due process of law." Is his contention sound?

§ 138. Would it make any difference if the Chinaman had been born in the United States and was therefore a citizen thereof?

§ 143. The law of a state provided that no woman should be eligible to sit on a jury. A woman was being tried for some crime and claimed that the statute in effect was in violation of that part of the fourteenth amendment that forbids states to deny to persons the equal protection of the laws. Is the claim sound?

§ 146. Would a state statute be constitutional that provided that no resident of the state should make any contract or engage in business with a person not a resident of the state?

§ 148. A state statute provided that all motormen must undergo a state examination and receive a state license before they could act as motormen in cities of more than 25,000 inhabitants. Is this law open to the objection of class legislation because it does not apply to chauffeurs and locomotive engineers; or because it does not apply to cities of less than 25,000?

§ 149. A state increased the requirements as to amount of reserve, protection of policy holders, etc., in the insurance business and provided that all insurance companies not conforming thereto should not do business in the state. Is this statute unconstitutional as to insurance companies already doing business in the state?

§ 153. John Doe owned a house in a respectable though not wealthy part of Chicago. The legislature passed an act authorizing city councils to set off parts of their respective cities as quarters in which prostitutes should be confined. The council of Chicago set off that part of the city in which Doe lived as a section for prostitutes. As a result his property was greatly depreciated in value. He claims that the statute is unconstitutional as being a deprivation of property without due process of law. Is his contention sound?

§ 156. Would a statute be constitutional that required all boot blacks to go before an examining board to take out a license?

§§ 159, 160. Which of the following statutes would be held unconstitutional today: a statute forbidding the giving of trading stamps: one forbidding the discharge of an employee because he belonged to a labor union; one forbidding the collection of debts by threatening to get the debtor's employer to discharge him if he did not pay?

§ 161. Why would a statute fixing the rates at which sellers of automobiles should sell their machines be held unconstitutional while a statute fixing the rates at which railroad companies should carry passengers and freight might be held constitutional?

§ 163. Would a statute forbidding the growers of private forests to cut them in such a way as to waste the lumber be constitutional?

§ 165. Could a state constitutionally require street railway companies to equip their cars with fenders at their own expense?

§ 167. In 1902 John Brown took up a homestead on state lands. In 1905 he received his deed from the state; and six months later conveyed the land to James White. At that time a state law required that all persons selling homesteaded lands within one year after they got the title thereto should acknowledge the deed before the judge of the county court. Brown did not so acknowledge so that the title to the property still remained in him. In 1907 the state passed a statute validating all conveyances of homesteaded land made since 1900. Under this statute White laid claim to the land. Brown claimed that the statute was unconstitutional (1) because it was *ex post facto;* (2) because it deprived him of his property without due process of law. Is either contention sound?

§ 175. The T. H. & U. R. R., an Illinois corporation, running from Chicago, Ill., through Iowa, and Nebraska to Denver, Colo., had rolling stock, rails, etc., worth $3,000,000. Its terminal in Chicago was worth $3,000,000, and in Denver $100,000. Its other stations, etc., were worth $400,000 divided equally between the four states. Its total corporate assets, tangible and intangible, were $56,500,000. The amount of business done in the four states was Illinois, 4-12; Iowa, 3-12; Nebraska, 3-12; Colorado, 2-12. Upon what amount may the railroad be taxed in Iowa?

§ 179. Suppose that 100 shares of the above railroad are owned by Peter Abbott, a resident of New York. May he be taxed on those shares in New York?

Suppose the shares are kept in a safety deposit vault in Philadelphia, may he be taxed on them by the state of Pennsylvania? May he be taxed on them by the state of Illinois?

§ § 181-85. John Smith was a citizen and resident of New York. He died leaving the following property:

1. 500 acres of land in New York.

2. 1000 acres of land in Montana.

3. A claim for $10,000 against William Conway, a citizen of Illinois.

4. 100 shares of stock in a Maine corporation, the stock certificate being kept in Boston, Mass.

5. 10 bonds of a New Jersey corporation payable to bearer and kept in New York.

Assuming that each state wishes to collect all possible inheritance taxes, what states can tax with respect to the above properties?

§ 186. Could Congress constitutionally impose a tax to raise money to establish a central bank under government supervision?

§ 192. During a fire which burnt most of a city, five citizens voluntarily advanced a large amount of money to the authorities to buy food, clothing, etc., for the fire sufferers. May the state properly appropriate money to recompense the citizens making this contribution?

§ 196. May a city raise money by a tax levied on all real property in the city and then use the money to build public golf links in one extreme corner of the municipality where it was practically inaccessible to most of the inhabitants?

§§ 199, 200. A city ordered a certain street to be asphalted and provided that the cost of asphalting should be borne by the abutters in proportion to their frontage on the street. One of the abutters objected to the assessment on the ground that his lot was not used by him; a second objected on the ground that his house faced on another street and his sole driveway was from that other side; a third objected on the ground that his land was a high knoll, rocky, and impossible of access from the street asphalted; a fourth objected on the ground that no provision was made for a proportionate assessment upon neighboring abutters on intersecting streets who were also benefitted. Which if any of the above objections are sound?

§ 205. Would a graduated tax of 1% on real estate worth less than $75 an acre to 20% on real estate worth more than $100,000 an acre be constitutional?

§ 209. May the state take by eminent domain the house and land of a private citizen for the purpose of converting it into a home for disabled firemen?

§ 211. May the state of New York condemn the power plants and other factories using Niagara Falls in order to preserve the natural beauty of the falls?

§ 213. A state made a contract with John Dale giving him the exclusive right for 5 years to supply coal to the state institutions at $3.00 a ton. The constitution of the state forbade the state to pass any law impairing the obligation of a contract. Is there any way in which the state may terminate the contract with Dale?

§ 215. Abbott owned a piece of waste land; he conveyed to Smith the right to dump ashes on the land for ten years. Three years later the H. & N. R. R. Co. condemned the land for a station site. The company paid Abbott for his interest in the property. Smith claimed that he was also entitled to be recompensed for his right. Is his claim sound?

§ 216. Immediately below Abbott's lot in the above mentioned case was a lot belonging to Brown. The railroad company began to fill in the Abbott lot. Brown's lot was so much lower that the filling material kept working down onto his lot and finally encroached on it for a width of about twenty feet. Brown claimed that this amounted to a taking of his property. The railroad claimed it did not because Brown could have kept off the gravel by a wall. Which is right?

§ 217. Suppose Brown had a house on this lot and the clanging of the engine bells, and the whistle and the noise of the trains so seriously disturbed the quiet of the neighborhood that his tenants left and he could not rent his house. Would this amount to a taking of property by the railroad?

§ 219. Jones lived on First street and Smith on Maple avenue which crossed First street at right angles. A street railway company obtained a franchise to raise the grade of First street and did so. Opposite Jones' house the grade was raised about 15 feet, thus putting Jones' lot in a much poorer position. To keep Maple avenue on the same grade, the city raised it; and at a point opposite Smith's house it was 15 feet above the old level. Has either Jones or Smith a right of action for deprivation of property rights and if so, what are the rights of which they are deprived?

§ 220. Suppose the grades of First street and Maple avenue in the last case had not been touched but street car lines had been put on each. Would Jones or Smith have had a cause of action?

§ 222. A farmer had two tracts of land, one on either side of the highway. The tract to the west of the road was farm land and his house and barn were there. The tract to the east was 50 acres of woodland. A railroad condemned a strip one hundred feet wide through the woodland near the highway. The value of the land actually taken was $100; the railroad put in a road to the rest of the woodland that bettered it to the extent of $25. The noise and nuisance of the passage of the trains near the lot on the west side damaged it $200. How much may be recovered from the railroad?

§ 225. Suppose the railroad in the last case had begun to grade their right of way through the woodland before they had secured the title thereto. What remedy would the owner have had?

Would he be entitled under the Constitution, in the event of condemnation proceedings, to have the value of the land determined by the verdict of a jury?

§ 227. A state supreme court decided that by the law of the state, interest up to 10% was not illegal under the usury statute. On the strength of that decision, Smith loaned Jones money at 10% interest. Later Smith sued Jones on the contract. The supreme court said that the old decision was wrong and that the state law properly interpreted forbade over 7% interest. Smith claimed that the decision was unconstitutional because it violated the obligation of his contract made on the strength of the old decision. Is his contention right?

§ 228. Herbert Smith and Alice Hall were married in 1880. At that time the law of the state allowed divorce only for adultery and desertion. In 1890 the law was changed by allowing divorce for incompatibility of temperament and Herbert attempted to get a divorce from Alice on that ground. She contended that so far as the statute related to marriage contracts made before 1890 it was unconstutional as impairing the obligation of a contract. Is she right?

§ 230. Could the state constitutionally revoke the charter of a street railway company which contained no clause authorizing the state so to revoke?

§ 231. Could a state constitutionally pass a bankruptcy act in 1890 providing that an insolvent debtor could surrender all his property to a trustee for his creditors and thereby discharge the debts and make the statute cover a debt contracted in 1887?

§ 233. The city of Salt Springs issued $1,000,000 of bonds to build a sewer system. At that time the law of the state provided that all real and personal property in the city could be taxed and that the tax rate might be as high as 5% of the assessed valuation. Just before the bonds matured, the law was changed allowing taxation only on personal property and limiting it to 1-2% of the assessed valuation. Is this law constitutional as to the bondholders?

§ 234. Suppose in an attempt to evade the payment of the bonds in the last case, the city of Salt Springs had been abolished by the legislature and its territory annexed to three adjacent cities. What relief, if any, would the bondholders have had?

§ 235. Suppose in the last mentioned bond case, at the time the bonds were issued an action to enforce them could be brought at any time within seven years after they matured, but that when the bonds matured the time had been cut to five years, would this change be unconstitutional?

§ 236. May special privileges given to a corporation in its charter, such as fixing the rate of taxation, freedom from supervision, etc., be afterward revoked by the legislature?

§ 239. The Bayside corporation had a clause in its charter that it should never be taxed at over 1% of its assessed valuation. The Riverview corporation had a clause in its charter exempting it from all taxation. A special act of the legislature authorized the two corporations to convey all their ''property, franchises and rights'' to a new corporation, the Bayview Co. They did so. The general rate of taxation in the state is 2%. At what rate may the property of the Bayview Co. be taxed?

§ 241. The charter of the P. L. & T. R. R. Co. provided that the kinds of passengers it should carry should not be subject to control by the state. Later during an epidemic of smallpox the state forbade all railroads to carry smallpox patients or corpses on their trains. Was this statute operative as to the P. L. & T. R. R.?

§ 243. Koch, the owner of a distillery in Kansas, made a contract with Hill whereby Hill agreed to act, and Koch to hire him, as selling agent for Koch for five years in the state. The following year Kansas passed a law forbidding the sale of liquor in the state. Hill contended that the law was unconstitutional as impairing his contract with Koch. Is his contention sound?

Would the result be the same if the state had, subsequent to the contract, provided that all contracts for more than two years employment should be void unless attested and this contract was not attested?

§ 246. Jones, a citizen of Illinois, while in New York executed his promissory note to Peters, a citizen of New York. The note was payable in New York. Jones returned to Illinois before the note was due, and went through bankruptcy under the Illinois bankruptcy law which was in force when he made the note and obtained his discharge in bankruptcy. Would this discharge bar Peters' claim on the note?

Would it make any difference if the note had been made and was payable in Illinois?

§ 248. Hill gave his note to Lynch for "$10,000 with interest" but the rate was not specified. The legal rate was at that time 6%. Subsequently the legislature increased the rate to 8% and made it applicable to all then existing notes. Is the law void as to Hill as impairing the obligation of the contract?

§ 252. Which of the following acts (1) may be done by the states only if Congress has not acted (2) even though Congress has acted (3) not done by the states even though Congress has not acted?

(1) Provide for the coinage of money.

(2) Make treaties with foreign powers.

(3) Provide for the naturalization of foreigners.

(4) Regulate the speed at which interstate trains may run in towns.

(6) Provide for discharges in bankruptcy.

(7) Provide for quarantining against infectious diseases.

§ 255. May Congress pass a statute forbidding the sale or storing of gunpowder in large cities?

§ 257. Under what clause of the constitution did Congress have the right to acquire the Philippines?

Suppose the President and Senate execute a treaty with Nicaragua declaring it to be United States territory, could it be shown in an action at law involving this question that in fact it was not United States territory?

§ 261. Into what classes may the territory over which the United States government may exercise authority be divided?

§ 262. Could a person be constitutionally convicted of a crime by less than a unanimous jury in the territory of Alaska?

Could federal judges be appointed for less than life in that territory?

§ 264. Could Congress in the Philippines:

(1) Establish a state religion and prohibit any other?

(2) Provide for trials by a jury of less than 12 men?

(3) Levy import duties different from those prevailing in the United States?

(4) Provide for punishment of crimes by burning at the stake?

§ 265. If the United States should go to war with Mexico and temporarily occupy part of its territory, which of the acts mentioned in the last question could be constitutionally provided for by Congress?

§ 276. Suppose that the United States government levied an excise tax upon liquor of a certain description and the only liquor of that kind in the country was made for the purpose of exportation, would this be unconstitutional as a tax on exports?

§ 277. Could the state of Texas constitutionally provide for a tax of ten cents a head on all cattle driven in from Mexico in order to provide a fund to pay for the examination of such cattle to see that they were not diseased?

§ 280. Could Congress, under the power to regulate interstate commerce, forbid the employment of women in factories where articles were manufactured for interstate trade?

§ 281. A manufacturer in Chicago hired a local expressman to take a load of machinery to a Chicago freight station to be carried to St. Louis. Was the expressman engaged in interstate commerce?

§ 282. Were the employees in the manufacturer's factory in the last case who brought the goods from the different parts of the factory to the shipping room engaged in interstate commerce?

§ 282. Suppose the goods above mentioned had been put on the train and started for St. Louis, and had then been stopped by the consignor and the car side-tracked. Would the car while so side-tracked be engaged in interstate commerce?

§ 286. May a state impose a tax of one cent a message upon all telegraph messages sent in the state?

§ 290. May a state impose a tax per pole upon all telegraph and telephone poles placed on public highways?

§ 293. How far may a state regulate freight and passenger rates?

§ 295. May a state require that interstate trains be heated to a certain fixed temperature while in the state?

§ § 297, 298. To what extent may a state forbid the importation and sale of intoxicating liquor?

§ 300. Would an act of Congress providing for the condemnation and nationalization of all the existing railroad and telegraph lines be constitutional?

§ 301. How far may Congress permit a state to determine for itself what articles of interstate commerce it will allow to be brought in the state?

§ 302. A power company built a dam on the Wisconsin river, making a long lake above the dam: the Wisconsin river flows into the Mississippi and is navigable below the dam. Would a steamer navigating above the dam be within the maritime jurisdiction of the United States?

§ 303. Would it make any difference if in the last case there was a canal around the dam?

§ 307. Could a state constitutionally issue bonds whose coupons were payable to bearer and receivable at their face value for all state taxes?

§ 309. Could a state constitutionally pass a law making void contracts that called for payment in gold?

§ 315. Would a Federal income tax that increased as the incomes taxed grew larger be in violation of the provision that all taxes "shall be uniform?"

§ 321. Could Congress constitutionally provide as a part of its postal system for the carrying of all articles weighing not over 2,000 pounds?

§ § 326, 327. Suppose that the United States made a treaty with Great Britain by which it was provided (1) that the eastern half of Maine should be regarded as British territory, (2) that citizens of Great Britain might acquire land in any of the United States, and that the state of Maine had statutes (1) that defined the boundaries of the state (2) that forbade foreigners to acquire land. Would either of these be affected by the treaty?

§ 330. Could Congress in time of war constitutionally declare confiscated all property found within the territory of the enemy even though the property belonged to citizens of the United States?

§ 332. Can the President in time of war constitutionally suspend the writ of habeas corpus in a part of the country where the regular courts are still open?

§ 337. A state bankruptcy statute provided that the property of an insolvent debtor should be used first in the payment of the claims of local creditors and only the balance, if any, should be devoted to the payment of creditors from other states. Is the statute constitutional?

§ 339. Suppose the statute last mentioned also provided that if a non-resident creditor wished to present his claim he must file a bond to pay costs in case the claim was rejected, no such requirement being made as to local creditors. Would such a provision be constitutional?

§ 343. The states of New York and Connecticut having a dispute as to their boundaries made an agreement as to where they should be fixed. By this agreement the land of Jones, who had always claimed to be a resident of Connecticut was allotted to New York. He claimed that New York had no jurisdiction over him because Congress had not consented to the agreement and the Constitution provides that "no state shall, without consent of Congress . . . enter into any agreement with another state." Is his contention sound?

§ 347. May a state levy an income tax which would cover the salary of a Federal officer?

§ 348. May it collect an inheritance tax upon the property of a deceased Federal officer?

§ 351. Into what two classes may the judicial powers of the Federal Constitution be divided?

§ 354. How are the various Federal courts at present organized?

§ 357. If a lawsuit between two citizens of the same state involves several questions, only one of which is a Federal question, how much of the case will be decided by the Federal court?

§ 358. Suppose the case has already been decided in the state Supreme court and it is then removed to the Federal court, what questions may be reviewed by the latter court?

§ § 365, 366, 367. In what cases will the Federal courts follow the decisions of the state courts as to what the local law is and in what cases will they refuse so to do?

§ 378. A state passed a law requiring its insurance commissioners to exclude from the state certain insurance companies that had not complied with the state statute as to rates of premiums. The insurance companies alleged that the state rates were unconstitutional and asked a Federal court to enjoin the insurance commissioners from taking steps to exclude them from the state. Should the injunction be refused on the ground that it is a suit against the state and so forbidden by the constitution?